The Enligh

The Enlightened Eater

A guide to well-being
through nutrition
by Marion Kane and
Rosie Schwartz

Methuen Toronto New York London Sydney Auckland

**Canadian Cataloguing in
Publication Data**

Kane, Marion
    The enlightened eater

Bibliography: p.
Includes index.
ISBN 0-458-80780-X

1. Diet. 2. Nutrition.
3. Cookery. I. Schwartz, Rosie.
II. Title.

TX355.K36 1987 641.1
C87-093078-8

Design: Ivan Holmes
Cover and illustrations: Falcom
    Design and Communications

Printed and bound in Canada

1 2 3 4   87   91 90 89 88

Contents

To good little eaters everywhere.

Marion Kane

To my husband, Earl, for his invaluable help in preparing the manuscript, and to my daughters, Alyssa and Farrah, for their patience and understanding during the chaos.

Rosie Schwartz

Acknowledgments

Heartfelt thanks and eternal gratitude to Janet Cornish, who presented us with twenty-five dishes a week for six weeks at recipe-testing/tasting time and only once served the garlic-laden eggplant caviar after the poached pears!

Too Many Choices

I first met Rosie Schwartz over a doctor's scale and a pair of callipers.

It was the winter of '84, and I was entering my second year as food editor of the Toronto *Sun*. Perhaps it was the demands of the job—constant tasting, testing, and, let's face it, plain old enjoyment of food—that had contributed to my gradually increasing girth. Perhaps the fact that I was inching my way toward forty—a time when the body starts refusing to take abuse—was another factor. Whatever the reasons, I, who am only a tad taller than five feet, was weighing in at an unprecedented 136 pounds—and felt every Rubenesque ounce of it.

Enter Rosie Schwartz, consulting dietitian, expert in nutrition, and soon-to-be girth-watching guiding light to me and a multitude of *Sun* readers. Rosie agreed that my plan to embark on a "public diet" as an optimistic begining to 1985 was a good one. As chief advisor in this plan of action, she came to meet me in the *Sun* newsroom.

It was here and then that it all began. It was also here and then that what started out as a public diet grew into something neither I nor my readers had surely anticipated. Not only did Rosie's plans for me not include a list of menus with amounts of food and accompanying calories, as I had expected, but they also included the equally unexpected—a whole new approach to eating.

After we established that a reasonable goal for my intended weight loss was 18 pounds, the next step in Rosie's weight-shedding plan was to map out my eating pattern. This meant that I had to keep detailed food records, writing down every mouthful of food that passed my lips for an entire week.

A glimpse at these records at week's end was my first surprise of many to come. Who would have thought that my Tuesday deadline dinner of an all-beef burger with salad, eaten at the local diner, was chock-full of hidden fats? Who would have realized that several lunches of Chinese stir-fries, downed at my favourite Chinatown locale, were loaded with salt? What a surprise to find that on a couple of days my main source of calcium was the puny amount contributed by the milk in my morning coffee! And I'll admit to being shocked when the seemingly innocent habits of sharing a bottle of wine with my spouse at dinner and consuming nothing but coffee until midday stared back at me in black and white!

But Rosie was not perturbed. Nor was she judgmental. She merely pointed out the nutritional consequences of this week-long tally and advised me to indulge in some menu revision. I would have to make certain adaptations to my diet to reduce my intake to about 1,200 calories a day, while ensuring that I did not go hungry and ate plenty of the right foods at the right times.

The next six months were never dull. There were setbacks—times when I could not lose weight for a couple of weeks at a time. There were sudden drops in weight that I couldn't understand. There was overwhelming hunger. There were days when I craved everything from chocolate truffles to cucumber with yogurt and fresh coriander.

But above all, those six months were a period of enlightenment. I learned, with Rosie's guidance and much to my surprise, that good nutrition and weight control are actually one and the same. I, who had started every day of my adult life with three cups of coffee, came to realize that a big breakfast of cheese, bread, and cereal topped with fruit and yogurt was an energy-packed accompaniment to said beverage that I soon began to crave. In addition, eating this kind of breakfast put me in touch with my body's need for food throughout the day. And lo and behold! I found that the ravenous hunger that used to beset me at my evening meal was gone, and I was eating dinner like a well-nourished and soon-to-be streamlined pauper!

And so the nutritional jigsaw gradually fell into place, piece by piece and week by week. As I learned from Rosie what was happening to my mind and body, so I relayed the information to my readers. And my readers lapped it up. They wanted to know more.

There were questions about many of the issues that have become confusing in an age when we are barraged with so much information on the hot topic of nutrition. Is fibre really as important as we hear it is, and what are the best ways to get enough? What kinds of fat are bad for you? How much calcium does a person need? What foods should children eat for best nutrition? What is lactose intolerance, and can it be overcome?

Over the next six months, as all of us gained in knowledge, my excess weight slowly slipped away—to the final tune of 17 pounds. In keeping with Rosie's game plan, when I lost, I averaged a 2-pound-a-week weight loss.

As for the setbacks, they were turned into learning experiences. One week I ate several meals that were loaded with soy sauce. Up went my weight: all that extra salt was retaining water in my body. I learned from this to go easy on salty food, including bottled waters that are high in sodium. Another week it was the attack of hidden fats lurking in a restaurant brunch buffet's dressings for its dazzling array of salads. This taught me that whenever I ate salads, I should look out for oily dressings, drizzle them on gently, and order as well as serve them on the side. There was the week I tried eating only cereal with milk and fruit at breakfast and found myself raiding the cafeteria at work at mid-morning. Rosie pointed to the need for extra protein on my breakfast menu, a need I easily filled by adding a piece of my favourite low-fat brick cheese.

And last but by no means least, I and my readers, with Rosie's help, discovered how to sort through the plethora of information, both correct and downright false, that inundates the public on the subject of weight loss. Every week, it seems, we hear about a new "magic" diet. Someone at a party swears that she has lost ten pounds in two weeks by eating nothing but fruit for breakfast and combining only certain foods at lunch and dinner. A celebrity on a TV talk show gushes about his instant formula for shedding pounds, which is two days of fasting followed by eating only three kinds of vegetables plus eggs! No wonder, I suppose, when more than 50 percent of North America's adult population is overweight, and many more mistakenly think they are, that fad diets have become the scam of the decade.

But there is hope.

Along with a fruitless search for the magic eating plan that will ensure slimness for all and sundry, there is a growing awareness of nutrition. Big food companies are responding to the public's concern about fat, fibre, calcium, and chemical additives. When a major fast-food chain decides to bow to public pressure and put lettuce and tomato on its hamburgers, it may seem like a minor move. However, even this is a stepping stone along the path to a more nutritious way of eating, one in which all of us can have our say.

Eat, enjoy, and above all, listen to your body. It, along with this book, will be your best advisor. So please read on!

Marion Kane

Throughout my years in practice, I have noted certain fundamental concerns common to the vast array of people seeking nutritional counselling. From housewife to executive, from children to seniors, good nutrition goes hand in hand with well-being. And this is what we address in *The Enlightened Eater:* nutrition for the life cycle—from infancy to the golden years. We include such topics as nutrition for singles, vegetarianism, caffeine, alcohol, and the role that exercise plays in nutrition. We also explode many of the common myths and fallacies that affect our daily eating habits. *Eating right* rather than *not eating* is our focus for successful weight loss and weight control.

Many people assume that if a dish is nutritious, it cannot be a gastronomic delight. But this is just not true. Throughout the book we include a large number of recipes created to be not only nutritionally sound but also irresistably delectable. Accompanying these recipes are nutrient values per individual serving. When recipes make variable servings, the nutrient values apply to the smaller serving. For example, if a recipe serves twelve to fifteen muffins, the nutrient values apply to one muffin out of a batch of fifteen.

The appendixes are tables of nutrient contents of various foods. These will be helpful to those of you who want more specific nutritional information about your food. For example, if you want to increase the amount of fibre in your diet, you can skim down the fibre column in Appendix A to find a high-fibre food that you like to eat. Another use of the nutrient tables can be to determine one day's intake of a particular vitamin, mineral, or other nutrient.

The information in *The Enlightened Eater* will provide you with a sound basis with which to assess the barrage of nutritional information and misinformation that we are constantly presented with. We hope you will find the book to be an invaluable guide to healthy and satisfying eating.

Rosie Schwartz

Too Many Choices

1   Getting into Groups

Our bodies need more than 50 nutrients, plus water, every day to achieve optimal health. These nutrients are carbohydrate, fat, protein, vitamins, minerals, fibre, and water. Optimal health means that all our bodies' functions, which run the gamut from building and maintaining cells to regulating bodily processes and supplying energy, are working efficiently.

As for the amounts in which these nutrients should be consumed, studies have come up with recommended levels of intake to maintain the health of an already healthy individual. In Canada these recommendations are called *Recommended Nutrient Intakes* (RNI). In the United States they have the title *Recommended Dietary Allowances* (RDA). However, figures showing these recommended intakes are of little help unless nutrient requirements are translated into actual foods. In Canada the *Canada Food Guide* was developed to do just this. In the United States the practical guide to recommended nutrients is called *The Basic Four*. Both frameworks group together those foods that have similar nutrients. Because these nutrients are similar, not identical, it is important to remember that a great variety of foods must be eaten to achieve top-notch nutrient balance.

No one food group can provide all the necessary nutrients. Nor are there any redundant food groups. A person who misses out on one food group on a regular basis is likely to suffer from nutritional deficiencies. Someone who is forced to do so because of allergies, for example, must make special adjustments to his or her diet.

The key is balance. And a balanced meal pattern for the average person means eating foods from all the food groups. Because the science of nutrition is currently attracting more and more attention, research into it is growing. And more connections between various nutrients and health are being discovered. One must therefore keep in mind that nutritional recommendations are not written in stone and may be revised as more information is assessed.

When you are choosing from the four basic food groups (protein, breads and cereals, fruits and vegetables, and dairy products), it is important to keep other factors in mind too—in particular, how much fat and fibre go hand in hand with other nutrients. After all, there's a big nutritional difference between a baked potato consumed with its fibre-laden skin and a plate of oily french fries!

The Enlightened Eater's Food Guide on pages 4 and 5 adds an extra dimension to the food group framework because it shows the four food groups *and* breaks down foods in each group by their nutritional quality. The "Cream of the Crop" are the best overall food choices because they take into account fat, fibre, sugar, and salt. "Go for It" includes good choices that do not, however, get a top-notch rating. "Proceed with Caution" includes foods that are lower on the nutritional scale or foods that may be loaded with nutrition but have drawbacks. Examples are eggs and liver, which contain high levels of cholesterol along with valuable protein, vitamins, and minerals. "Food Group Flunkies" may or may not contain nutrients, but their drawbacks outweigh their virtues. Such foods should not be eaten on a regular basis.

Two things are crucial to remember: first, when it comes to eating well, variety truly is the spice of life; and second, an individual's stage in the life cycle can affect the amounts of food eaten from each food group. For example, a growing adolescent or menopausal woman needs to dip more heavily into the dairy food group than a 25-year-old man.

Energy-Yielding Nutrients
The nutrients required by our bodies can be divided into two main categories: those that yield energy (calories) and those that do not. Nutrients that yield energy are carbohydrate, protein, and fat. Alcohol is the only substance that contains calories but no nutrients.

A calorie is the amount of energy or heat required to raise one litre of water one degree. When foods are burned up by the body, they give off energy or heat, which can be measured in calories. Protein and carbohydrate both contain four calories per gram. Fat harbours nine calories per gram and alcohol seven. A balanced diet should be made up of carbohydrate, 55 percent of total calories; protein, 15 percent of total calories; and fat, 30 percent of total calories.

Carbohydrate   Carbohydrate consists of either simple sugars or starch that is broken down by the body to yield energy.

Natural sugars are sugars that exist naturally in food. For example, lactose is the sugar in milk. Fructose is the sugar in fruits and vegetables, and sucrose is the sugar found in refined table sugar. Sugars, which can be identified by their *ose* ending, also include dextrose, maltose, and glucose, among others.

Refined sugars contribute calories without any redeeming nutrients and are often referred to as "empty calorie" foods. Our society's excessive sugar consumption goes hand in hand with eating too much fat and not enough nutrient-rich foods. Hence a large number of people are overweight.

A spoonful of sugar may make the medicine go down, and it often comes from obvious sources. But sugar does not always come on spoons, and it is particularly prevalent in many processed foods. Refined sugars sometimes appear on package labels simply as sugar (white or brown), but they can also show up in a number of disguises: as honey, glucose, fructose, corn syrup, dextrose, and liquid invert sugar. Because ingredients are listed in descending order of quantity, the closer sugar is to the beginning of the list, the higher the sugar content of the food.

Long chains of simple sugars are called *complex carbohydrates*. In humans complex carbohydrates are stored as glycogen. In plants they are stored as starch. When starch is broken down by the body, it becomes simple sugars that end up in the blood as blood sugar, or *glucose*. Glucose is essential to fuel our brain and muscles. If we consume too much carbohydrate, the excess glucose is removed from the bloodstream and stored in small amounts in the liver and muscles as glycogen. Once these glycogen stores are filled, excess carbohydrate is turned into fat and stored for future energy.

Protein   Protein is essential to build and repair body tissues, and this is its primary function. It can also provide energy in the absence of adequate carbohydrate. However, this is not the best use of protein because many of its benefits are not taken advantage of.

Fat   Fat can be used for energy when carbohydrate is not available. However, it produces more than twice as much energy (calories) as carbohydrate and can have other negative nutritional effects too.

On the positive side, fat contains linoleic acid—our

THE ENLIGHTENED EATER'S FOOD GUIDE

	MILK AND MILK PRODUCTS	BREADS AND CEREALS
Recommended servings are per day. Adapted from Health and Welfare Canada, "Canada's Food Guide" (Ottawa: Supply and Services Canada, 1983).	**Children up to 11 years:** 2–3 servings **Adolescents: 3–4 servings** **Pregnant, nursing, and post-menopausal women:** **3–4 servings** **Adults: 2 servings**	3–5 servings
Cream of the Crop	1 cup/250 mL skim milk 4 tbsp./20 mL skim-milk powder $\frac{3}{4}$ cup/175 mL skim-milk yogurt $1\frac{1}{2}$ oz./45 g skim-milk cheese $\frac{1}{2}$ cup/125 mL evaporated skim milk	1 slice whole-grain bread $\frac{1}{2}$ cup/125 mL whole-grain cereal Snack foods like air-popped, unsalted popcorn, $1\frac{1}{2}$ cups/375 mL
Go for It	1 cup/250 mL 2% milk $\frac{3}{4}$ cup/175 mL 2% yogurt $1\frac{1}{2}$ oz./45 g part-skim cheese (less than 15% B.F.) Fruit-flavoured skim-milk yogurt $\frac{1}{2}$ cup/125 mL evaporated 2% milk	Refined, enriched breads and cereals Whole-grain baked goods like muffins Homemade granolas
Proceed with Caution	1 cup/250 mL whole milk $\frac{3}{4}$ cup/175 mL whole-milk yogurt $1\frac{1}{2}$ oz./45 g whole-milk cheese Fruit-flavoured yogurt Low-fat chocolate milk	Enriched, sugared cereals Buttered popcorn Commercial granolas High-fat crackers
Food Group Flunkies	Whipping cream Cream cheese Sour cream Ice cream Sweetened condensed milk Butter High-fat processed cheese spreads	Commercial granola bars Cakes, pies, pastries Croissants Doughnuts High-fat snack foods like commercial tortilla chips, cheese puffs, etc.

MEAT, FISH, POULTRY, AND ALTERNATES 2 regular or 3 smaller servings	FRUITS AND VEGETABLES 4–5 servings Choose at least 2 vegetables. Include yellow, green, and green, leafy vegetables as well as cruciferous ones.
2–3 oz./60–85 g lean fish, fresh, frozen, or canned in water and unsalted $\frac{1}{2}$ cup/125 mL cottage cheese 1 cup/250 mL dried legumes (peas, beans)	Fresh fruits and vegetables, properly stored, $\frac{1}{2}$ cup/125 mL or 1 medium Frozen vegetables, no sauce Canned vegetables, no salt added
2–3 oz./60–85 g lean meat, chicken, turkey, fatty fish, or shellfish, fresh, frozen, or canned in oil and salt, rinsed Canned fish in oil and salt, rinsed 2 oz./60 g skim-milk cheese	$\frac{1}{2}$ cup/125 mL unsweetened fruit juice $\frac{1}{2}$ cup/125 mL canned fruit in its juice Canned vegetables, salt added
$\frac{1}{2}$ cup/125 mL nuts or seeds 4 tbsp./20 mL peanut butter 2 eggs 2 oz./60 g liver 2 oz./60 g duck or goose 2 oz./60 g untrimmed meat or lean processed meat 2 oz./60 g battered or fried fish or chicken 2 oz./60 g whole-milk cheese 2 oz./60 g pickled or smoked meat	$\frac{1}{2}$ cup/125 mL sweetened fruit juice $\frac{1}{2}$ cup/125 mL canned fruit in sugar syrup Frozen vegetables in sauce
Hot dogs Salty, high-fat processed meats Side bacon or bacon bits, regular or simulated	Fruit drinks Gelatin desserts Fruit pies Potato chips, regular french fries, onion rings Fruit-flavoured yogurt

one essential fatty acid because it cannot be manufactured by our bodies. Fat also aids in the absorption of fat-soluble vitamins and acts as insulation as well as a sort of cushion for the body.

Why Vitamins Keep Us Vital

Vitamins are organic (living) compounds that the body needs, in small amounts, to promote growth and maintain life. Minerals, which the body also needs in small amounts, are inorganic (non-living) and are thus classified separately from vitamins.

The key to any discussion of vitamins is the phrase *in small amounts*, because this is how they exist in food. Vitamins consumed in larger amounts, such as in the treatment of illness, are another matter; they should be considered drugs or therapeutic agents rather than food. Vitamins should be consumed not indiscriminately, but with the same caution as medication.

On the other hand, *regular, consistent intake* of both vitamins and minerals is very important. Although a lack of either may not cause a deficiency immediately (it could take a long time, sometimes years, to manifest itself), a deficiency could remain at a subclinical, barely discernible level and be detrimental to a person's health. Regular, day-to-day intake of vitamins and minerals is crucial; small lapses can easily add up.

There are two main categories of vitamins: water-soluble and fat-soluble.

Water-Soluble Vitamins

Because they are soluble in water, these vitamins can easily be lost by leaching into cooking water during food preparation. (This is discussed in detail in Chapter 5.) Water-soluble vitamins consist of the B vitamins and vitamin C.

Thiamin
(Vitamin B1)

Sources of thiamin are whole-grain and enriched cereals, meats like pork, beef, and lamb, nuts, and legumes.

Thiamin helps the body use carbohydrates as energy. It also promotes normal appetite and contributes to the functioning of the body's nervous system. The greater the carbohydrate intake, the greater the need for thiamin. The same is true for alcohol: the more it is consumed, the greater the recommended requirement for thiamin.

Riboflavin

The best source of riboflavin is milk and its by-products. Other sources include green vegetables, fish, eggs, liver, meat, and enriched breads and cereals. Riboflavin is sensitive to light, so storing milk in a clear container results in some loss of this nutrient.

Riboflavin is needed to convert protein, fat, and carbohydrate into energy. It also does wonders for the skin, eyes, and nervous system.

Niacin

Niacin comes from liver, meat, fish, poultry, peanuts, and enriched cereals. It helps the body get energy from carbohydrate, protein, and fat. It also helps keep the nervous system and digestive tract healthy.

Pyridoxine
(Vitamin B6)

Liver, beef, lamb, pork, salmon, whole-grain cereals, lima beans, cabbage, potatoes, spinach, and grapes are prime sources of pyridoxine.

Pyridoxine is necessary for the metabolism of protein and helps the nervous system function normally. The verdict is not yet in on whether vitamin B6 is an effective treatment for Pre-Menstrual Syndrome (PMS), but the side effects of taking too much have been documented. Even 50 mg a day over a long period of time can cause sensory nerve changes that decrease a person's sensitivity to hot and cold. Once that person stops taking the vitamin, however, these symptoms disappear. Women who take oral contraceptives should eat plenty of pyridoxine-rich foods, because it is thought that the pill increases one's need for this vitamin.

Pantothenic Acid

Almost all foods contain pantothenic acid, but especially good sources are whole-grain cereals and organ meats. Pantothenic acid is required for the metabolism of protein, fat, and carbohydrate. It also plays an important role in the manufacture of hemoglobin, steroid hormones, cholesterol, and fatty acids.

Biotin

Among the foods high in biotin are egg yolks, milk, and organ meats. Nuts, cereals, and legumes are other sources. Biotin is necessary for the release of energy from carbohydrates as well as for the metabolism of fat and protein.

Folacin
(Folic Acid)

Folacin comes from dark green, leafy vegetables like spinach and also from liver and kidneys. As with the other B vitamins, this vitamin can easily be lost during food preparation.

Folacin is important in the manufacture of compounds used to make genes. It is also needed to keep the red blood cells healthy and to prevent macrocytic anemia. It is easy for pregnant women to become deficient in this nutrient.

Vitamin B12	Liver and kidneys are especially rich in vitamin B12. It is also found in meat, fish, eggs, milk, and milk products. The only natural sources of B12 are animal ones. Some foods, such as soy milk, are fortified with it.

Vitamin B12 is of prime importance in the synthesis of hemoglobin and maintenance of healthy red blood cells. A lack can result in pernicious anemia. It is also important for the nervous and digestive systems. |
| Ascorbic Acid (Vitamin C) | Good sources of vitamin C are fruit and vegetables such as citrus fruits, broccoli, cabbage, tomatoes, peppers, cantaloupe, and strawberries.

Vitamin C is important for the manufacture of collagen, which acts as a cementing agent, binding cells together. It also helps to heal wounds, absorb iron, and maintain healthy teeth and gums. Vitamin C–rich foods may play a role in preventing certain cancers.

Vitamin C has been touted as a cure-all for a number of ailments, in particular the common cold. Doses advocated in such cases are sometimes more than 100 times the recommended amount. Studies have not conclusively proved the benefits of such megadoses of vitamin C. What is more, when consumed in excess, it is excreted in the urine and can cause kidney stones in predisposed individuals as well as nausea and diarrhea. Rebound scurvy can also occur. This is a type of vitamin C deficiency caused by a return to lower doses after excessive consumption. Rebound scurvy can also afflict infants born to mothers who took high doses of vitamin C during pregnancy. |

Fat-Soluble Vitamins
These vitamins are soluble in fat and, when consumed in excess, are stored in the body. Because of this, an excess can be toxic.

Vitamin A	Good sources of vitamin A are liver, kidneys, eggs, milk, yellow and dark green, leafy vegetables, and fruit.

One of the main benefits of vitamin A is taught by the old adage that carrots help you see in the dark. Because this vitamin aids in the formation of "visual purple" (rhodopsin), it is necessary for good night vision. It is also important for keeping the skin and the body's inner linings healthy, helping the body resist infection, promoting growth, and maintaining teeth, hair, bones, and glands.

However, taking large doses of vitamin A supple- |

ments can be dangerous. The symptoms of vitamin A toxicity include fatigue, headaches, loss of hair and nails, vomiting, skin changes, and enlargement of the liver.

Vitamin D   The main source of vitamin D is milk that has been fortified with it. Vitamin D does not occur naturally in plant foods but is found in certain fish such as salmon. It also exists in limited amounts in eggs and meat.

Vitamin D is produced by the body when sunlight irradiates a compound called 7-dehydrocholesterol, which is present in the skin. (This is one example of how the body needs a certain amount of cholesterol.) Vitamin D requirements can be met by food alone, by sunlight alone, or by a combination of the two.

Vitamin D is important for the body's absorption of calcium and phosphorus, two minerals needed to keep bones and teeth healthy. It also helps regulate certain substances in the blood.

Because this vitamin is fat-soluble, excess amounts are stored in the body. Toxic doses can cause loss of appetite, vomiting, and weight loss. They can also cause high levels of calcium in the blood, which can in turn produce calcium deposits in such tissues as the lungs and kidneys. Overdoses of vitamin D over long periods of time can even result in death. Foods are therefore fortified with care. Individuals must also be careful when taking vitamin D supplements such as fish liver oils. However, a person whose diet is low in calcium, who does not drink milk, and who has little exposure to sunlight should ensure that he or she has some dietary source of vitamin D.

Vitamin E   Vitamin E is found in polyunsaturated fats such as polyunsaturated oils and margarines, leafy, green vegetables, and some nuts and seeds like almonds and sunflower seeds. It is present to a lesser extent in whole grains, meat, and eggs. It is added to some foods as a preservative to prolong shelf life.

Contrary to popular belief, vitamin E has no magic powers that will do wonders for your sex life! One beneficial property it does possess, though, is that it takes up oxygen (is oxidized) before other compounds in the body. This is particularly beneficial for preventing the oxidization—the destruction—of vitamins A and C. The same process occurs with polyunsaturated fats, a fact that explains why vitamin E is used to prevent them from going rancid. This vitamin also helps keep the body's cell membranes intact, and research is currently being done to determine whether it can prevent cancer.

Toxic effects of too much vitamin E include fatigue, headaches, dizziness, and blurred vision accompanied by nausea.

Vitamin K   Vitamin K comes from soybean oil, liver, and dark green, leafy vegetables. It plays an important role in blood coagulation. Without it, blood cannot clot, and uncontrolled bleeding can result. A synthetic form of vitamin K, called *menadione*, can be dangerous if taken in a prenatal vitamin preparation, because it can cross the placenta of the pregnant woman and, if doses are large enough, cause anemia in the infant.

A Matter of Minerals
Minerals are inorganic compounds found in all foods, whether of animal or plant origin. They come from the earth and are passed on through living things by foods and water.

Minerals exist in varying amounts from soil to soil. If certain minerals have become depleted in the soil of a particular area, crops grown in it will be deficient in those minerals. As well as minerals that act as nutrients, there are those—arsenic, lead, and mercury—that should be avoided because of their toxicity.

Minerals fall into two categories depending on the amounts stored in our bodies. *Macronutrient minerals* found in larger amounts are calcium, phosphorus, sodium, chlorine, potassium, magnesium, and sulphur. *Micronutrient*, or *trace, minerals*, although stored in extremely small amounts, are just as vital to good health. These are iron, fluorine, iodine, selenium molybdenum, chromium, cobalt, copper, zinc, selenium, and manganese.

Calcium   Calcium has lately been the subject of much discussion in nutrition circles. It is stored by the body to be used as needed and is required for several functions. It is necessary for digestion and aids in blood clotting. Current research is also investigating a lack of calcium in the diet as a possible role in the development of hypertension. In addition, calcium is a crucial component in nerve-impulse transmission and muscle contraction, the latter of which is particularly important for the normal contraction and relaxation of the heart muscle. If necessary, the body will dip into its calcium storage spots, namely bones and teeth, to enable the heart to function normally.

One buzzword we hear these days is the disease caused by the lack of calcium—*osteoporosis*. The bones of a tiny infant are softer than the bones of an adult. As the child matures, calcium, along with other minerals like phosphorus, is deposited in the bone tissue and builds strong, hard bones. As the body needs calcium for other purposes, it takes it from the bones. This process is called *calcium exchange*. If our diet is rich in calcium, this mineral is constantly replaced, and so the process continues. However, if our diet is lacking in calcium, osteoporosis can result.

Osteoporosis causes the bones to become brittle and porous. This means that they can easily break or fracture. A person who has osteoporosis often has a "dowager's hump," or curvature of the spine, and problems with his or her teeth caused by a deterioration in the jawbones. An afflicted person becomes so fragile that he or she can fracture a bone from merely a sneeze or a hug. Particularly unfortunate is the fact that once osteoporosis has developed, the bones cannot be strengthened. Although treatments are being studied that could stop the disease from progressing, the only way we can currently deal with it is by prevention.

Osteoporosis strikes one in four women in varying degrees but can also affect men. Other factors associated with it are heredity, fair skin, lack of sex hormones in women, lack of weight-bearing exercise, and diet. Although we cannot control our skin colour, we can regulate the amount of exercise we do and what we eat. Inadequate calcium is a known cause of osteoporosis; caffeine, cigarette smoke, and alcohol are considered possible causes. Pre- and post-menopausal women are thought to need 1,200 to 1,500 mg of calcium a day, compared to the 800-mg daily requirement of average adult women.

Calcium is as crucial for the development and maintenance of strong teeth as it is for those of bones, but there is less calcium exchange between teeth and the rest of the body than is the case with bones. It is therefore vital that children consume enough calcium when their teeth are forming; otherwise, their teeth will become soft, with all the problems that ensue. Conversely, children who get plenty of calcium have a good chance of developing strong, healthy teeth that are resistant to decay.

CALCIUM CONTENT OF VARIOUS FOODS

Food	Amount	Calcium Content (mg) (approximate)
Milk, low fat or whole	1 cup/250 mL	300
Skim milk powder, dry	$\frac{1}{4}$ cup/50 mL	375
Yogurt, plain	$\frac{3}{4}$ cup/175 mL	350
Yogurt, fruit-flavoured	$\frac{3}{4}$ cup/175 mL	300
Cheese, hard, natural	$1\frac{1}{2}$ oz./45 g	300
Cheese, processed	1 1-oz./30-g slice	175
Cottage cheese	1 cup/250 mL	155
Ice cream	$\frac{1}{2}$ cup/125 mL	90
Sardines, canned	$3\frac{1}{2}$ oz./100 g	305
Salmon, canned with bones	3 oz./90 g	250
Tofu, made with calcium	$\frac{1}{2}$ cup/125 mL	150
Beans (kidney, lima, chickpeas), cooked	1 cup/250 mL	90
Soybeans, cooked	1 cup/250 mL	115
Almonds	2 tbsp./25 mL	50
Broccoli	$\frac{1}{2}$ cup/125 mL	75
Greens, mustard and beet	$\frac{1}{2}$ cup/125 mL	75
Rhubarb, cooked	$\frac{1}{2}$ cup/125 mL	175
Orange	1 medium	50

Absorption is another important factor to consider when discussing calcium. Both vitamin D- and lactose-containing foods such as milk enhance calcium absorption. So does lactose-hydrolyzed milk; thus, people with lactose intolerance need not miss out. It used to be thought that if the body's intake of phosphorus was higher than that of calcium, calcium absorption would be reduced, but recent studies have proved this invalid. However, an adequate phosphorus intake ensures good calcium absorption.

On the other hand, a severe excess of protein in the diet can hinder calcium absorption. So can such compounds as phytic and oxalic acid, which bind some of the calcium in food, making it unavailable for absorption. Phytic acid is found mainly in cereals but also in some other foods including nuts; oxalic acid occurs mainly in vegetables like spinach, beets, and rhubarb. These foods are all high in fibre, and because we are being encouraged to boost our fibre intake, it is particularly important that our diets are also rich in calcium.

Smoking also appears to have a negative influence on the body's calcium balance, as does a lack of exercise. People who are inactive or bedridden have a negative calcium balance, which means that their bodies are taking calcium from their bones for other needs. Research is currently investigating the effects of regular, weight-bearing exercise on the body's use of calcium. Aluminum-containing antacids taken for gastric discomfort can also negatively affect calcium absorption, something that is especially important for the elderly to consider, for they are often on long-term antacid therapy.

This discussion points to a pretty positive picture of one food as the ideal source of calcium—namely, milk.

Milk contains vitamin D, lactose, and phosphorus without the binding effects of the phytic and oxalic acids in plant foods. This makes milk the best choice for people who tolerate it. Other sources of calcium, however, such as sardines and salmon with their bones (conveniently precooked in the can), should not be ignored, because they can contribute appreciable amounts of calcium as well as variety to the diet.

With all the concern over what a lack of calcium in the diet can do, many people are turning to supplements. This is not advisable without consulting a physician about possible side effects, such as the formation of kidney stones.

Phosphorus	Sources of phosphorus are plentiful: dairy products, meats, fish, eggs, and peanuts.

Phosphorus — Sources of phosphorus are plentiful: dairy products, meats, fish, eggs, and peanuts.

The body uses phosphorus in the form of *phosphate*, which is required for the formation of teeth and bones. Like calcium, phosphorus also plays a role in energy release, protein synthesis, and fat transport, as well as being a component in the body's manufacture of genes. We also need phosphorus to ensure calcium absorption.

Protein foods yield a high amount of phosphates. Carbonated drinks contain considerable amounts of phosphates, but they are a kind that do not help with calcium absorption.

Iron — Iron is necessary for the production of hemoglobin—that part of the red blood cells that carries oxygen throughout the body. When the body lacks iron, there is not enough oxygen in the blood. This causes fatigue and explains why being tired is one symptom of an iron deficiency. Iron is also important for other bodily functions, such as the transformation of provitamin A to vitamin A.

Food sources of iron fall into two groups: heme and non-heme. Heme iron comes from meat; non-heme iron comes from non-meat sources. The body absorbs heme iron more easily than non-heme iron, which, it has been found, is more easily absorbed when consumed with vitamin C. This means that eating an orange with your iron-enriched cereal at breakfast will boost your body's absorption of iron.

People likely to suffer from an iron deficiency include teenagers, menstruating women (particularly teenagers), pregnant women, preschool children, and some athletes (see Chapter 9).

Sodium — Sodium winds up in our food via two routes. It can occur naturally or be added during processing or preparation of food. Milk and cheeses are natural sources of sodium, while salted snack foods or condiments acquire it during processing.

Sodium has several functions in the body. It maintains the *acid-base balance* (the balance of acid and alkaline), sends nerve impulses, and aids muscle contraction. It also helps maintain the balance of fluids inside and outside the body's cells. Sodium is found mainly in the outside fluids of cells and functions with potassium, which is found mainly in the cells' inside fluids. Sodium is a necessary part of our diet, but not often in the excessive amounts consumed by many North Americans.

IRON CONTENT OF VARIOUS FOODS

Food	Amount	Iron Content (mg)
Pork liver	3 oz./85 g	26
Beef kidney	3 oz./85 g	12
Beef liver	3 oz./85 g	8
Cream of wheat, enriched, cooked	$\frac{1}{2}$ cup/125 mL	8
Prune juice	$\frac{1}{2}$ cup/125 mL	5
Cereals, whole-grain, enriched	$\frac{3}{4}$ cup/175 mL	4
Beef, ham, pork, veal	3 oz./85 g	3
Blackstrap molasses	1 tbsp./15 mL	3
Legumes, cooked	$\frac{1}{2}$ cup/125 mL	2–3
Spinach	$\frac{1}{2}$ cup/125 mL	2
Sunflower seeds	$\frac{1}{4}$ cup/50 mL	2
Almonds	$\frac{1}{4}$ cup/50 mL	2
Wheat germ	1 tbsp./15 mL	2
Apricots	3	1
Bran muffin	1	1
Rice, brown or white	1 cup/250 mL	1
Broccoli	1 stalk	1
Chicken, turkey	3 oz./85 g	1
Egg	1 large	1
Dates, raisins, prunes	$\frac{1}{4}$ cup/50 mL	1
Tomato juice	$\frac{1}{2}$ cup/125 mL	1

SODIUM CONTENT OF VARIOUS FOODS

Food	Amount	Sodium Content (mg)
Beef, cooked	$3\frac{1}{2}$ oz./100 g	80
Corned beef	$3\frac{1}{2}$ oz./100 g	1,740
Frankfurter, beef	1	461
Chicken, roasted	$3\frac{1}{2}$ oz./100 g	85
Chicken, canned	$3\frac{1}{2}$ oz./100 g	500
Salmon, fresh, cooked	$3\frac{1}{2}$ oz./100 g	116
Salmon, canned	$3\frac{1}{2}$ oz./100 g	522
Fish, batter-dipped, frozen	$3\frac{1}{2}$ oz./100 g	411
Pork and beans in tomato sauce	$\frac{1}{2}$ cup/125 mL	450
Broccoli, frozen	$\frac{1}{2}$ cup/125 mL	14
Broccoli, frozen with cheese sauce	$\frac{1}{2}$ cup/125 mL	479
Cottage cheese, creamed	$\frac{1}{2}$ cup/125 mL	425
Cheddar cheese	1 oz./85 g	176
Cheddar cheese, processed	1 oz./85 g	406
Milk	1 cup/250 mL	120
Chicken noodle soup, dehydrated, reconstituted	1 cup/250 mL	1,280
Chicken noodle soup, canned	1 cup/250 mL	1,100

Puffed wheat	1 cup/250 mL	1
Corn flake–type cereal	1 cup/250 mL	300
Popcorn, unsalted	1 cup/250 mL	Less than 1
Potato chips, plain	1 oz./30 g	213
Potato chips, BBQ flavour	1 oz./30 g	317
Ketchup	1 tbsp./15 mL	156
Mustard	1 tbsp./15 mL	188
Soy sauce	1 tbsp./15 mL	1,030
Steak sauce	1 tbsp./15 mL	149
Teriyaki sauce, bottled	1 tbsp./15 mL	700
Pickle, kosher	1	581
Pickle relish	1 oz./30 g	375
Olives, green	2 medium	312
Soda, diet	12 oz./375 g	76
Mineral water (Perrier)	8 oz./250 g	5

The body rids itself of excess sodium through the kidneys and perspiration. People who perspire heavily during strenuous work or exercise could have a greater-than-average need for sodium. Research is continually in progress to discover the long-term effects of high sodium intake and the relationship between it and diseases like hypertension. Prolonged ingestion of high amounts of sodium seems to impair the body's ability to regulate its sodium balance and can result in hypertension in predisposed people. Again, moderation seems to be the order of the day.

Potassium
Bananas and oranges are well known as good sources of potassium. It is also present in varying quantities in dried fruit, kiwi fruit, tomatoes, potatoes, and some other fruits and vegetables.

Potassium works with sodium to maintain the body's balance of fluids. Too high a sodium intake can upset the balance and result in a need for more potassium. Diuretics, severe diarrhea, and vomiting can cause potassium loss. Potassium is also necessary to maintain the acid-base balance in the body, transmit nerve impulses, and release energy from carbohydrate, protein, and fat.

Chloride
Table salt, actually sodium chloride, provides more than enough chloride for the body. Meat, milk, and eggs are other good chloride sources. Along with sodium, chloride maintains the body's acid-base balance. It is an important part of hydrochloric acid, found in the stomach, which is needed for the early stages of digestion.

Fluoride
Fluoridated water is our main source of fluoride and is monitored to keep amounts safe. A person who relies heavily on bottled water as an alternative to tap water should therefore consider some kind of supplement. This mineral can also be found in sardines with their bones.

Fluoride helps build strong bones and teeth. A lack of it not only causes weak teeth but can also contribute to osteoporosis. Too much causes mottled teeth.

Magnesium
Magnesium is found in whole-grain breads and cereals, green, leafy vegetables, nuts, beans, and milk. It is needed to release energy from carbohydrate, synthesize protein, stimulate nerve and muscle action, and retain calcium in tooth enamel. Its status is not affected, however, by increasing calcium in the diet, as claimed by some food faddists. There is therefore no reason to take magnesium supplements simply because you are taking calcium supplements.

Manganese
Manganese occurs in nuts and whole-grain cereals and is required for normal bone development. Toxic amounts of this mineral can result in reduced iron absorption and anemia.

Iodine
Sources of iodine are saltwater fish, shellfish, and iodized salt. Iodine is a crucial component of the hormone

thyroxin, which regulates the thyroid gland. This gland plays an important role in controlling the body's basal metabolic rate. A lack of adequate iodine results in goitre (enlargement of the thyroid). Strangely enough, too much iodine can have a similar effect.

Iodine exists only at low levels in most foods, so it is added to table salt to compensate for this.

Selenium
Selenium is obtained from cereals and fish and acts as an anti-oxidant much like vitamin E. Vitamin E seems to protect selenium by binding with oxygen before the selenium and oxygen can combine. Too large a dose of selenium supplements can be toxic, causing hair loss as well as changes in teeth and nails.

Research is going on into the possible role of selenium in cancer prevention. It is thought that a low selenium intake might be linked to cancers of the esophagus, stomach, and rectum. Because of the dangers of ingesting too much selenium, more human studies are needed to determine safe levels of supplementation. The wisest way to obtain this mineral is be eating foods rich in it.

Zinc
Meat, eggs, liver, and shellfish are good sources of zinc. It is also contained in whole grains and milk. Zinc is important for its role in the body's metabolism of protein and carbohydrate and for insulin production. Dwarfism has been documented as one possible result of a zinc deficiency.

2 Long on Fibre, Short on Fat

If anything is for sure in this entire, often confusing debate about nutrition, it is that the North American diet is long on fat and short on fibre. And what seems increasingly clear is that there is a link between this and the continent's two major diseases—heart disease and cancer.

The Canadian Cancer Society has stated that 35 percent of all cancers can be linked to diet, and the main culprit seems to be fat. In addition, dietary fats, and a substance called *cholesterol* in particular, are major contributors to heart disease.

Jack Sprat Was on the Right Track

The evidence is steadily growing to connect a diet high in fats with certain cancers. At the top of the list are cancers of the colon and rectum, followed by cancers of the breast, endometrium, and the ovaries in women, and prostate cancer in men. Some foods actually contain *carcinogens* (cancer-causing agents), while others harbour substances that promote their production. There is a great deal of research currently under way and much debate about which foods can cause cancer. Some of these will be discussed in Chapter 3.

Affairs of the Heart

On the North American continent, where the burger with fries still reigns supreme and where we have one of the highest standards of living in the world, we can lay claim to another less welcome record—one of the highest rates of heart disease, a bigger cause of death than all the others combined. And high blood cholesterol, kissing cousin to dietary fat, is now known to be a major cause.

What is the cholesterol–heart disease connection?

Atherosclerosis, also known as hardening of the arteries, is a major form of heart disease. It is caused by a buildup of cholesterol deposits—a process that can begin during childhood—on the artery walls. These arteries eventually lose their elasticity and become narrow, sometimes even blocked.

In spite of ongoing research, the exact cause of atherosclerosis is not known, but heart disease has been linked to seven major factors: heredity, lack of exercise, diabetes, obesity, high blood pressure, smoking, and high levels of cholesterol in the blood. Several of these are related to diet and are therefore within our control. And when the National Institute of Health in the United States recommends, as it did in 1985, that we North Americans lower our cholesterol levels, it's time to sit up and take a good look at what's on our plates.

The North America–wide Lipid Research Clinics conducted a ten-year study on the prevention of heart disease, the results of which were published in 1984. Although it was already known that high blood cholesterol was a factor in the development of heart disease, no definite connection had been made between lowering blood cholesterol and preventing heart disease. The Lipid Research Clinics study concluded that a 1 percent reduction in cholesterol resulted in a 2 percent lower risk of coronary disease; this gives a 10 to 20 percent cholesterol–heart disease prevention ratio.

Criticisms of this study point to the use of drugs in conjunction with a cholesterol-reduced diet and to the fact that people used in the study, who had high cholesterol levels, were not typical. It would be extremely difficult, however, to conduct a long-term study such as this without using drugs (those with high cholesterol would be at risk), and the principles advocated in the study are in keeping with other disease-prevention strategies.

Cholesterol—The Good and the Bad of It

Cholesterol is a waxy, fat-like substance that occurs naturally in the blood of all animals, including humans. It is required, but only in the right amounts, to help produce hormones, make the brain function properly, and maintain the body's nerve structure. Problems begin when cholesterol occurs in excess—and this means that the North American diet that's heavy on burgers and fries but light on fresh fruit and veg could well do with a cholesterol-reducing overhaul!

Too high a cholesterol level is often hereditary. But eating too many cholesterol-rich foods such as eggs, organ meats, and foods high in animal fat is certainly not good for anyone. In addition, saturated fats, like those contained in butter, can work a little cholesterol trickery by increasing the body's cholesterol production, sometimes to an unhealthy degree.

CHOLESTEROL CONTENT OF VARIOUS FOODS

Food	Amount	Cholesterol Content (mg)
Egg	1 large	274
Liver, beef	3 oz./85 g	375
Kidneys, beef	3 oz./85 g	325
Sweetbreads, beef	3 oz./85 g	400
Brains	3 oz./85 g	1,785
Beef, lean	3 oz./85 g	77
Lamb, lean	3 oz./85 g	85
Pork, lean	3 oz./85 g	77
Veal, lean	3 oz./85 g	75
Poultry, skin removed	3 oz./85 g	75
Fish, lean	3 oz./85 g	45
Fish, fatty	3 oz./85 g	45
Clams	8 large	48
Crab	3 oz./85 g	70
Lobster	3 oz./85 g	70
Oysters	3 oz./85 g	50
Scallops	3 oz./85 g	50
Shrimp	10 large	90
Butter	1 tbsp./15 mL	36
Lard	1 tbsp./15 mL	15
Bacon, crisp	3 slices	15

Milk, whole	1 cup/250 mL	33
Milk, 2%	1 cup/250 mL	18
Milk, skim	1 cup/250 mL	4
Cheese, whole milk	1 oz./30 g	25–35
Cheese, part skim	1 oz./30 g	15
Cottage cheese, creamed	1 cup/250 mL	30
Cottage cheese, 2%	1 cup/250 mL	19
Ice cream	1 cup/250 mL	60

Because of the medical risks of high blood cholesterol, it is advisable for everyone to have their blood cholesterol level checked by a physician by means of a simple blood test. Individuals with an unhealthily high cholesterol count can then determine what dietary changes to make.

A lesser-known fact about cholesterol compounds is that there are two kinds—the bad and the good.

Most of us have heard plenty about the bad kind, known as LDL (*low-density lipoprotein*) or VLDL (*very low-density lipoprotein*) cholesterol. (And when we use the word *cholesterol* by itself, this is the kind we mean.) But many of us have never heard of the good kind of cholesterol, called HDL (*high-density lipoprotein*). HDL has the amazing property, so it seems, of removing cholesterol from the artery walls. The higher a person's HDL, therefore, the better. While regular exercise can increase one's HDL, smoking and stress both reduce it. Diet, body weight, and heredity, on the other hand, are the main factors controlling LDL.

The bottom line is that we must find ways to eat, cook, and organize our lives that promote the production of HDL cholesterol and diminish our levels of LDL cholesterol.

The fat in foods and the fat in our bodies is made up of substances called *triglycerides*. Trigylcerides are the form in which our bodies store fat to be used for extra energy or to insulate our bodies and protect our vital organs.

Triglycerides, which circulate throughout the body in the bloodstream, seem to act somewhat like cholesterol when they occur in excess. Although the jury is still out on this, it is wise to keep triglycerides at what is considered normal levels. A diet low in fat (in particular the saturated kind) and simple sugars and high in complex carbohydrates is recommended to achieve this. High alcohol consumption and excess body weight seem to increase tryglyceride levels in people prone to this condition—yet another reason to follow the healthy principles of eating that are outlined in this book!

Some Important Facts about Fat

Fat makes up about 40 percent of the North American diet. This is in contrast to the 30 percent recommended by the Canadian Cancer Society and the American Heart Association. Of this 30 percent, it is recommended that about 10 percent should be saturated fats, 10 percent mono-unsaturated, and 10 percent polyunsaturated.

How does this affect our food intake and its calories?

If a person consumes 2,000 calories a day, 40 percent of which is fat, he or she is eating 89 grams of fat (fat supplies nine calories per gram). To reduce fat intake to the desirable 30 percent, a person should consume only 67 grams of fat a day, reducing consumption by 22 grams. This can be achieved by cutting out six teaspoons of fat.

Here are some examples of how this can be done. Switching from whole to skim milk reduces fat by eight grams a glass. Measuring out salad dressing instead of pouring it on with gay abandon can save four to eight grams. And slicing one or two ounces from a helping of meat can slice off a generous three to eight grams.

All Fats Are Not Created Equal

There are three basic kinds of fats—saturated, polyunsaturated, and mono-unsaturated. All the fats we eat are made up of a combination of all three and are classified according to which one predominates. One tablespoon of sunflower oil, for example, which contains 8.9 grams of polyunsaturated fat, 1.5 grams of saturated fat, and 2.9 grams of mono-unsaturated fat, falls into the polyunsaturated group. Here is how these three fat types differ.

Saturated Fats	These are the fats that raise cholesterol in the body, and it is these fats that most of us eat in excess. Usually solid when at room temperature, saturated fats are mainly found in foods of animal origin such as whole-milk dairy products, cream, butter, and the fat on meat and poultry. Two vegetable fats, palm oil and coconut oil, used widely in commercial baking and in non-dairy whiteners, also fall into this group of fats.
Polyunsaturated Fats	These fats, which have the wonderful effect of lowering cholesterol, are found mainly in vegetable oils—oils that do not harden at room or refrigerated temperatures. Unfortunately, these fats are sadly lacking in most people's diets. The effects of too many polyunsaturated fats are not yet known, although it is agreed that we should not consume more than 10 percent of calories as polyunsaturated fats. Another benefit of these fats is that they contain linoleic acid, an essential fatty acid that, unlike other fatty acids, cannot be produced by the body from fat, protein, or carbohydrate. Safflower, sunflower, soybean, and corn oils all contain polyunsaturated fats; so do margarines made from these oils. These fats can also be found in some nuts and seeds such as sunflower and sesame seeds.
Mono-Unsaturated Fats	Found in oils such as olive and peanut oils as well as in certain nuts, these are usually liquid at room temperature but turn solid when refrigerated. Because of the low level of heart disease in Mediterranean countries, where olive oil is a diet staple, it is thought that mono-unsaturated fats may be a contributing factor. But so far, although continuing research may prove otherwise, these fats do not seem to have the cholesterol-lowering abilities of their polyunsaturated cohorts.

Some Tips on Fat
A little knowledge and a good dose of discrimination when choosing what you eat can go a long way toward cutting down on unwanted fats. Understanding labels on foods can also help demystify some fat facts and fallacies. For example, if the label on a package of cheese states that there are 93 calories and seven grams of fat per slice, we can deduce that, because fat contains nine calories per gram, this cheese has a total of 63 fat calories. This leaves a measly 30 calories for its good nutrients!

There has been considerable controversy over the fatty virtues and vices of butter versus margarine.

Because butter is considered a saturated fat, it contains all the nutritional hazards of other saturated fats. For people with good cholesterol levels, however, who do not consume much saturated fat from other sources, a moderate amount of butter, often preferred for its taste, is all right.

As for margarines, they are not all they seem. When a polyunsaturated fat is hardened, it becomes saturated. This means that most of the fat in hard margarine winds up being saturated even though it did not start out that way. Soft margarines with a two-to-one ratio of polyunsaturated to saturated fat listed on the label (for example, 55 percent polyunsaturated to 25 percent saturated, or 40 percent polyunsaturated to 18 percent saturated) are best bets.

The process of hydrogenation changes liquid fats into solids. These fats then behave like saturated fats and may raise cholesterol accordingly. Reading labels on such foods as margarine, shortening, and peanut butter is the best way to determine if hydrogenation has occurred. The less hydrogenated the better, as in the case of soft, polyunsaturated margarines.

The following chart shows how to reduce your fat intake.

Low-Fat-Cooking Tips
Here are some nifty ways to reduce the amount of fat you use in cooking. You'll be surprised at how little fat you actually need for taste results that are still tops.

- Use lean meat. Trim off any excess fat before cooking.

- When buying meat, look for lean cuts. The fat content of meat is low only if meat is lean (well trimmed). Examples of lean cuts are beef—flank, round, chuck, sirloin, T-bone, and rib-eye; lamb—loin, roast, and chops; pork—leg, tenderloin, ham, and Canadian (back) bacon; and all cuts of veal.

- Remove the skin from poultry before cooking, but be careful not to overcook it, or it will become dry.

- Bake, roast, steam, or broil instead of frying to reduce the fat content.

- When roasting or baking meat, place it on a wire rack in

WAYS TO TRIM THE FAT

High-Fat Choices	Lower-Fat Alternatives	Fat Savings (tsp.)
Granola, 1 oz./30 g	100% Bran, $\frac{1}{3}$ cup/75 mL	1
Croissant	Whole-grain roll	2
Processed meat, 2 oz./60 g	Sliced chicken, 2 oz./60 g	2
Salad dressing, liberally poured	Salad dressing, measured	2–3
French fries, 10 pieces	Baked potato, 1 large	1
Beef, 6-oz./175-g serving, untrimmed	Beef, 3-oz./85-g serving, lean only	3
Milk, whole, 8 oz./250 mL	Milk, skim, 8 oz./250 g	2
Potato chips, 10 pieces	Popcorn, air-popped, 1 cup/250 mL	2
	Total	15–16

a baking pan to let the fat drain off. Use wine or stock for basting.

- When making stews or casseroles, refrigerate them after cooking to let the fat harden on top. It is then much easier to remove than when the food is hot and the fat is floating on the liquid.

- When making stock, sauce, or gravy, follow the preceding method to remove fat from the surface.

- Use non-stick pans to sauté foods. Use a thin coating of oil by applying it with a brush or piece of waxed paper. Add stocks when sautéeing or stir-frying to stop foods from sticking to the pan.

- If the flavour of the oil is important in a particular recipe, use a good-quality oil such as virgin olive or nut oil and augment it with corn, safflower, soybean, or sunflower oil, which are polyunsaturated.

- The oil called for in a recipe (except in baking) can usually be substantially reduced without negative results. Experiment with using less.

- When baking, look for recipes that are low in fat.

- If you are deep-frying foods, make sure the oil is as hot as possible without burning before adding the food. Food absorbs less oil this way.

Fabulous Fibre: Fact or Fiction?

The fibre furor dates back to the 1970s, when British physician Dr. Denis Burkitt discovered that people in countries where the diet was high in fibre had less intestinal cancer, diverticular disease of the bowel, hiatus hernia, appendicitis, varicose veins, and heart disease than we who exist to a great extent on refined foods.

And recent reports from bodies such as the Canadian Cancer Society and the National Cancer Institute in the United States have taken up the call, urging North Americans to increase their fibre intake. In fact, a survey on dietary fibre by the Expert Advisory Committee on Dietary Fibre (Health and Welfare Canada), published in 1985, suggested that we double the amount of fibre we consume to 20 or 30 grams a day.

What is fibre, and why is it so good for us? Fibre is the material in plant foods that is resistant to digestion by humans. Here are the ways it can contribute to the prevention of certain diseases.

Heart Disease
Fibre can combine with bile salts, which are made partially from cholesterol, and prevent them from being absorbed. When this happens, the body takes cholesterol from the blood to manufacture more bile salts. The result is lower blood cholesterol, which helps prevent heart disease.

Diverticular Disease
Diverticula are small bulges on the wall of the bowel caused by increased pressure and weakness of the bowel muscle. Fibre increases the bulk of bowel material while softening its texture, thereby reducing pressure on the bowel walls. Increased fibre in the diet therefore reduces stress on the bowel walls and prevents outpockets from appearing there.

Large-Bowel Cancer
Fibre helps speed the path of waste materials through the gut. This means that waste products come into contact with the gut wall for a shorter time, thereby reducing the risk of irritation, infection, and the growth of potential cancer-causing substances.

Obesity
Foods that are high in fibre take longer to chew and are

bulkier once they are ingested. They therefore cause a greater feeling of fullness than their refined counterparts and give us a feeling of satisfaction without a huge quantity of calories.

Fibre Comes in Two Forms
There are two kinds of fibre—soluble and insoluble. There are foods that contain one or the other and a third group that contains both.

Soluble Fibres

Soluble in water, these are gummy fibres found in pectins, gums, and mucilages—that is, in foods such as legumes (dried beans like kidney beans and lentils) and grains such as oats (specifically oat bran) and rye.

When these foods are eaten, the soluble fibres swell and form a gel-like structure that traps nutrients like sugars and starch, which then take longer to be absorbed into the blood. This effect is beneficial for everyone, because blood sugar and thereby energy levels are stabilized, but it is particularly beneficial for diabetics.

Another benefit of soluble fibres is that they bind with bile salts. Bile salts come from cholesterol, so the higher the soluble fibre in the diet (especially from oat bran), the lower the cholesterol.

Insoluble Fibres

These consist mainly of a substance called *cellulose* and are insoluble in water. They include fibres such as wheat bran and other cereal fibres, which help promote regularity of the bowels by holding water in the stool. This makes the stool bulkier, enabling it to pass out of the body more easily. Because these fibres work in conjunction with water, a person who increases the amount of these fibres in his or her diet must also drink more water, or constipation will be the unpleasant result.

The Soluble-
Insoluble
Combination

Some foods contain a mixture of both types of fibre. Most notable of these are fruits and vegetables.

Tips on Fibre
- Increase your fibre intake gradually, or you will have abdominal discomfort. In other words, if you eat eight bran muffins in one day, your bloated stomach is going to be a real pain!

- As with all changes in eating habits, begin gradually and adapt the changes to your taste in foods. Eating a whole slew of unfamiliar foods at once may result in a temporary change, but chances are you'll be back eating the same old foods in no time. So if you hate hot cereal but love the flavour of rye bread, you're well advised to get soluble fibre in your favourite sandwich instead of trying to force down some rib-hugging gruel at breakfast time!

- Eat fresh fruits and vegetables rather than their juices to enjoy all their fibre potential.

- Eat whole-grain breads such as rye, whole wheat, bran, and oatmeal rather than white.

- Add nuts and seeds (in small amounts because of their high fat content) to salads and keep them handy along with dried fruit as healthy snacks.

- Use bran (either the oat or wheat variety) as a filler for hamburgers and meat loaf, a topping in casseroles, and a substitute for breadcrumbs when cooking.

- Try to eat fibres from both the soluble and insoluble groups throughout the day. For example, have oatmeal at breakfast, fruit as a morning snack, and a bran muffin in the afternoon.

Some Warnings about Fibre

Eating too much fibre in too short a time, introducing fibre too suddenly into one's diet, and not drinking enough water (about eight glasses a day is a good idea) can result in gas and therefore bad stomach pains.

People on low-calorie diets should beware of fibre supplements designed to decrease a dieter's appetite. Someone who is dieting might already be lacking important minerals such as calcium and iron, and a fibre supplement might further decrease the absorption of the few minerals that the dieter is consuming. In keeping with the general rule, it is best to get fibre from food rather than from supplements—we don't know the dangers of consuming too much fibre.

There has also been some concern among health professionals about "non-native" fibres—fibres not inherent in one food but added to it from another. They worry that these fibres might act differently when consumed in a foreign food. For example, does the pea fibre act the same way when it is added to a "high fibre" bread as it does when it is eaten in a pea?

"Novel" fibres such as the wood fibre found in some breads are also unknown quantities. More research and detailed labelling are needed in these areas.

SOURCES OF DIETARY FIBRE

	Food	Amount	Calories per Serving
Very High Source of Dietary Fibre: Greater than 7 Grams per Serving	All-Bran	$\frac{1}{3}$ cup/75 mL	71
	Bran Buds	$\frac{1}{3}$ cup/75 mL	73
	100% Bran	$\frac{1}{2}$ cup/125 mL	76
	Baked beans in tomato sauce	$\frac{1}{2}$ cup/125 mL	155
	Kidney beans	$\frac{1}{2}$ cup/125 mL	110
High Source of Dietary Fibre: 4.5–6.9 Grams per Serving	Bran Chex	$\frac{2}{3}$ cup/150 mL	91
	Corn Bran	$\frac{2}{3}$ cup/150 mL	98
	Dried peas	$\frac{1}{2}$ cup/125 mL	115
	Lima beans	$\frac{1}{2}$ cup/125 mL	64
	Navy beans	$\frac{1}{2}$ cup/125 mL	112
Moderate Source of Dietary Fibre: 2.0–4.4 Grams per Serving	40% bran cereal	$\frac{3}{4}$ cup/175 mL	93
	Cracklin' Bran	$\frac{1}{3}$ cup/75 mL	108
	Raisin Bran	$\frac{3}{4}$ cup/175 mL	115
	Shredded Wheat	$\frac{2}{3}$ cup/150 mL	102
	Total	1 cup/250 mL	100
	Wheat Chex	$\frac{2}{3}$ cup/150 mL	104
	Wheaties	1 cup/250 mL	99
	Wheat germ	$\frac{1}{4}$ cup/50 mL	108
	Bran muffin	1	120

Food	Amount	Calories per Serving
Crisp crackers, rye	2 crackers	50
Whole-wheat bread	2 slices	120
Lentils	$\frac{1}{2}$ cup/125 mL	95
Broccoli	$\frac{1}{2}$ cup/125 mL	20
Brussels sprouts	$\frac{1}{2}$ cup/125 mL	30
Carrots	$\frac{1}{2}$ cup/125 mL	24
Corn	$\frac{1}{2}$ cup/125 mL	88
Peas	$\frac{1}{2}$ cup/125 mL	60
Potato with skin	1 medium	90
Spinach	$\frac{1}{2}$ cup/125 mL	20
Apple	1 medium	80
Banana	1 medium	105
Blueberries	$\frac{1}{2}$ cup/125 mL	40
Cantaloupe	$\frac{1}{2}$ small	80
Orange	1	60
Pear	$\frac{1}{2}$	50
Prunes	2	40
Raisins	3 tbsp./15 mL	80
Raspberries	$\frac{1}{2}$ cup/125 mL	35
Strawberries	1 cup/250 mL	45

Therefore, by making small changes in your diet, you can increase your fibre intake. Here are some sample menus:

	Normal	High Fibre
Breakfast	Orange juice	Fresh orange
	Refined cereal	100% Bran
	Milk	Milk
	Egg	Egg
	White toast	Whole-wheat toast
	Beverage	Beverage
Lunch	Cream soup	Pea soup
	Sandwich on white	Sandwich on whole wheat
	Fruit-flavoured yogurt	Fresh fruit and plain yogurt
	Water	Water
Snack	Doughnut	Bran muffin
	Milk	Milk
Dinner	Baked chicken with premixed crumb coating	Baked chicken with wheat germ and almond coating
	French fries	Baked potato with skin
	Iceberg lettuce salad	Spinach salad
	Broccoli, stems peeled	Broccoli, unpeeled
	Apple pie	Apple crisp with bran topping

3 The Power of Protein

Protein is the main nutrient from which our bodies grow and regenerate. Amino acids, which make up proteins, are to proteins what bricks are to a wall. Although more than 20 amino acids are known to exist in the human body, only eight are considered essential, that is, required for growth, repair, and maintenance of tissues. These essential amino acids cannot be synthesized by the body; they must come from what we eat.

Proteins that contain all these essential amino acids in proportions and amounts most useful to the body have *high biological value*. In general, animal proteins such as meat, poultry, eggs, milk, and cheese supply plentiful amounts of essential amino acids and are therefore considered excellent dietary sources of protein.

Proteins of plant origin (except soybeans) lack or are low in one or more essential amino acids. However, nuts, seeds, dried peas and beans, lentils, and grains yield high-quality, complete protein in combination with each other and some other foods.

Prorating Proteins

Foods that contain protein do not always contain complete protein; some contain varying amounts of incomplete protein. Complete, high-quality proteins are found in meat, fish, poultry, eggs, milk in all its forms, and cheese—cottage, hard, and processed. Another source is soybeans—dry, curds, milk, and tofu. Nuts and legumes (dried peas and beans, chick peas, lentils, and so on) yield partially incomplete proteins. And grains (wheat, oats, rye, rice, etc.), and breads and cereals made from them, supply incomplete proteins.

Completing the Protein Picture

These days a growing sector of the population is deciding to become vegetarian. However, many people are blissfully unaware of the adjustments they should be making to their new-found eating style, especially in the protein department. Telling meat to move over to make way for vegetables simply isn't good enough. A teenage convert to vegetarianism, for example, who eats the same meals as the rest of the family without the meat—namely, the

COMPLEMENTARY PROTEINS

Milk products	+	Grains	=	Complete protein
Legumes	+	Grains	=	Complete protein
Nuts or seeds	+	Grains	=	Complete protein
Milk products	+	Legumes	=	Complete protein
Nuts or seeds	+	Legumes	=	Complete protein
Nuts or seeds	+	Milk products	=	Complete protein

protein food—is heading for trouble in the shape of an unbalanced diet.

There are, however, solutions to the problem of how to satisy the needs of carnivores and vegetarians who eat at the same table. The following protein information is also useful for anyone contemplating a meatless diet. The secret lies in complementary proteins.

When proteins are called *complementary*, it means that a combination of two or more of them supply all the amino acids our bodies need. Complementary proteins can be formed in two ways: by combining plant and animal protein—for example, by eating pasta with cheese—and by eating, at the same meal, two or more plant proteins that together provide the necessary amino acids. Timing is important here. The same result is not achieved if complementary proteins are eaten at widely spaced intervals during the day. For example, peanut butter spread on whole-wheat bread produces full protein value, but if the bread and peanut butter are eaten at separate meals, there is no such effect.

Eggs, milk, cheese, wheat germ, and brewer's yeast are all handy foods that can be included in a meal of incomplete proteins as complements to increase protein value. Sprinkling wheat germ on your breakfast oatmeal or grating some cheddar or Monterey Jack cheese over a bowl of vegetarian chili are two ways to maximize incomplete proteins in combination.

Protein Keeps Good Company
High-protein foods are a good source of several important vitamins and minerals.

Iron	Many high-protein foods are high in iron. Iron comes in good amounts from meats (especially organ meats), egg yolk, dried peas and beans, lentils, nuts, and seeds. The heme iron that comes from meat is absorbed more easily by our bodies than non-heme iron, which comes from foods like egg yolk, cereals, and beans. Vitamin C helps the body absorb non-heme iron, so a fresh orange eaten along with a boiled egg is a terrific way to get the most out of that egg.
Other Minerals	High-protein foods also supply zinc, copper, phosphorus, and magnesium.
Vitamins	Significant amounts of thiamin, riboflavin, and niacin come from high-protein foods. Dried peas, beans, and lentils are important sources of folacin. Organ meats are good ways to ingest vitamin A. Vitamin B12 is found only in foods of animal origin and may be lacking in the diet of strict vegetarians (vegans) if they do not take a B12 supplement of some kind. This is discussed at greater length in Chapter 10.

Timing Is of the Essence

When eating protein, the crucial factor—and where most people go wrong—is timing.

Protein is thought to be crucial for keeping us mentally alert, and trying to function without eating any protein is like attempting to drive a car without gas. The best time to fuel our bodies with protein is when we're most in need of it—at the beginning of the day. We should then restock with smaller amounts of protein at intervals throughout the day. Eating a large meal after a hard day's work, as many people do, is not the best way to treat our minds or our bodies.

Why is timing so important when eating protein? Protein foods take longer to digest than other foods, such as carbohydrate, so they help keep our blood sugar levels and, consequently, our energy levels stable. Fewer dips in blood sugar cause fewer dips in energy levels, all of which produces sounder bodies and minds.

Traditional eating habits have not been helpful in all this. A large evening meal based on protein—a sizable main meat course—counteracts the ideal protein-eating pattern. The best way to pace your protein is to eat most of it at breakfast and lunch, tapering off your intake toward the end of the day. For example, the person who eats a green salad, slice of bread, and an apple for lunch will crave a snack a couple of hours later. However, adding a few ounces of tuna or chicken to the same lunch prevents that person's blood sugar from dropping rapidly and eliminates that craving.

As with all things, however, too much of a good thing can also be a problem. Excess protein is not broken down by the body and is stored as fat. Also, a person who eats too much protein (as some high-protein weight-loss diets recommend) could upset his or her calcium balance.

Mainly Because of the Red Meat

Nobody with a knowledge of nutrition is going to shed a tear over the demise of the ten-ounce steak that many North Americans used to consider their rightful meat portion. More and more people are realizing that a chicken breast marinated in herbs and lemon juice, then grilled and topped with a mustard sauce can be just as satisfying as a huge slab of sirloin done on the barbecue.

There are, however, some dangers in the growing trend toward eating less red meat—a trend based mainly on a sound fear of consuming too many saturated fats. Many people who give up red meat because of its high fat content unwittingly replace it with equally fat-laden foods. Opting for the fried fish fillet instead of a burger at a fast-food chain or choosing fish in puff pastry instead of the filet mignon in a restaurant are cases in point.

What is more, giving up red meat means giving up important nutrients like iron, and they must be replaced in the rest of the diet—a fact that many who renounce red meat are not aware of. Our mothers were right when they told us to eat our liver. Liver is high in iron, but also in cholesterol, so it should be eaten in moderation. A person who gives up red meat should eat foods high in iron, such as legumes and enriched cereals, to fill that gap.

The best way to solve the legitimate concern of consuming the excess of saturated fats contained in red meat without losing out on its benefits is to eat it in smaller portions. A little red meat goes a long way, and a four-ounce steak eaten with plenty of vegetables and some carbohydrate is a good source of protein and makes a satisfying meal.

Red meat takes longer to digest than white meat or fish because of its higher fat content, so it takes longer to satisfy the eater. It is therefore difficult to know when you've eaten the right amount, and if you keep eating until you're full, you will probably have eaten too much. So make a conscious effort to reduce your portions of red meat. It will help if you supplement red meat with plenty of other foods to make up a healthy, square meal.

Cooking smaller portions of red meat into stir-fries along with a bevy of tender-crisp vegetables, and serving a small amount of meat sauce with a generous helping of pasta, are a couple of painless, healthy ways to cut down on red meat.

Taste in food is a powerful factor in deciding what we eat. North Americans have been conditioned to think that a prime roast of beef, the perfect juicy burger that bulges out of its bun, and a succulent T-bone steak are the epitome of culinary delight. A change of eating habits doesn't come overnight. To make matters more difficult, fat—the culprit in all this—*does* add flavour. So if we want to eliminate or at least reduce fat and still have good taste, we must find new ways to season and enhance our food.

Poultry Isn't for the Birds

Poultry is an extremely healthy protein alternative to red meat. Chicken, for example, is wonderfully versatile. Not only is it superb roasted with a few herbs and perhaps a little soy sauce, but it can also be cooked cacciatore one night, done Szechuan the next, or poached in a little white wine and lemon juice with artichokes the following dinnertime.

Turkey is another good choice of poultry, but avoid fatty birds such as duck, goose, and stewing hens. It is also best to remove the skin from poultry before cooking, because it is high in fat and cholesterol.

Fish—A Food for the Eighties

Fish is an excellent, low-fat, nutritious alternative to red meat as a source of protein. And these days fish is just beginning to overcome the bad reputation it has long had. One reason for this is our bad memories of how fish used to taste once it arrived at inland destinations without today's advanced methods of shipping and preserving freshness. Another reason is a fear of coming across bones. Still others are that most people overcook fish and have a fear of cooking it at all.

Finding a reputable fishmonger who sells fresh fish is the first step toward enjoying eating fish at home. Choosing a fresh fish yourself means finding one that does not have a strong smell, has bright eyes if the head is still attached, and has a firm texture—enough that you feel resistance when you press the flesh with a finger. And fish fillets are a simple solution to a fear of bones. You can buy packaged fillets fresh or frozen or ask your fishmonger to fillet fresh fish for you.

The next step is finding good ways to cook fish. This part is much easier than you might think. Fish is wonderfully versatile and takes only minutes to cook—perfect for today's fast-paced lifestyle.

If you don't have the time or inclination to cook fish, canned salmon and tuna are tasty alternatives. When buying these, choose the water-packed versions rather than those packed in oil. They save a lot of calories and fat. There are now also several brands of fish canned without salt—another wise choice.

Some people are rightly concerned about the effects of polluted waters where fish have been caught. One way to avoid this problem is to eat fish from a variety of places. If you are concerned about a specific fish, check with local government officials.

Recent studies point to a particularly important benefit of eating fish. One such study conducted in Holland showed that the respondents who included a lot of fish in their diets suffered much less from heart disease than those who did not eat much fish. The particular substance in fish thought to stave off heart disease is polyunsaturated fatty acid, called *omega-3 fatty acid*.

A good guide for judging the omega-3 fatty-acid levels in fish is its total fat content. Good sources of omega-3 are fish with more than 5 percent fat. Some saltwater examples are mackerel, salmon, sea herring, sablefish, anchovies, mullet, canned sardines, and smelts. Freshwater fish high in fat are lake trout, rainbow trout, and catfish. Fish with medium oil content are halibut, sea trout, rockfish, ocean perch, red snapper, and swordfish. Canned white albacore—the Rolls Royce of tuna fish—has a medium fat content. Other kinds of tuna have the fatty acids removed in processing. Shellfish is low in fat but higher in omega-3 fatty acid than other low-fat fish.

Many health-food stores advocate taking fish-oil supplements as an alternative to eating fish itself, but there is reason for concern about their effect on blood clotting. Taking large, regular doses of these supplements lengthens bleeding time and could cause wound-healing problems. Cod liver oil is lower in omega-3 fatty acid than the other fish oils, but so much of it would be needed for any benefit to occur that a person would simultaneously take in toxic amounts of vitamins A and D.

Some Meats Are out to Lunch

As if we needed yet another thing to worry about when it comes to eating meat! But there is good cause for concern about luncheon meats—meats that have been highly salted, smoked, and/or nitrite-cured. The worry surrounds *nitrates* and *nitrites*—compounds that are found naturally in some foods but are added to others such as bacon and many cold cuts. Nitrate is changed to nitrite in the body and can act with other substances called amines or amides to produce nitroso compounds called nitrosamines or nitrosamides. Many nitroso compounds are carcinogenic and are believed to increase the risk of stomach and other cancers.

Foods that naturally contain nitrates and nitrites also contain vitamin C, which, it is thought, blocks the conversion of nitrites to nitroso compounds. The concern is mainly over those foods to which nitrates and nitrites have been added. This leads to another controversy.

Sodium nitrate and sodium nitrite are added to cured meats for the wholesome purpose of preventing botulism poisoning. If they were not used, there might be an increase in botulism, which is fatal. Here is another case of the devil and the deep blue sea. For this reason, nitrates and nitrites are still added to meat, but in the smallest amounts possible to still be effective.

Another reason to go easy on luncheon meats is their high salt content. Stomach irritation can result from too much salt and may ultimately cause stomach cancer.

Luncheon meats are quick and easy, but they do have hazards, as we have discussed. To avoid relying on them, try the following. When cooking chicken or other lean meat, cook extra and wrap small portions of the leftovers in plastic, label with their name and date, and freeze. This gives you handy packages of unsalted, uncured, lean meat for making sandwiches. If you're too busy to do this, buy a rotisserie chicken or plain cooked turkey breast at the local deli rather than relying on salami and luncheon meats.

Let's Eat More Legumes

If there is one food group that is underrated in North America, it is legumes. Legumes are the seeds that grow inside the pods of leguminous plants. Most legumes fall into the categories of dried peas, beans, and lentils. Legumes have fabulous properties. They are a superb, inexpensive source of protein. They are packed with soluble fibres. They are loaded with B vitamins. Raw, they keep indefinitely without preservatives. Once cooked, they can easily be frozen.

It is therefore hard to understand why legumes have such a bad image on this continent and why the average person eats them so rarely. Perhaps it's because they are considered a staple in other, poorer parts of the world. Perhaps it's because they produce gas after they have been eaten!

It's important to know the protein value of legumes in order to maximize their nutritional benefits. Except for soybeans, which supply complete protein when eaten alone, legumes contain complementary proteins and must be eaten with other foods to bring out their full nutritional potential.

A Litany of Legumes' Virtues

Legumes are the only protein foods that contain a substantial amount of fibre—another reason to include them in your diet. They contain soluble fibres, which slow down the rate of absorption of carbohydrate. This in turn keeps you feeling satisfied longer and prevents you from overeating. Because of their fibre content, legumes also help lower cholesterol.

Legumes are a good source of B vitamins, but only when they are cooked properly. B vitamins are light-sensitive, so to avoid vitamin loss, store legumes in a dark place or in the fridge in airtight jars. They keep indefinitely this way too.

B vitamins are also water-soluble. To avoid pouring them down the drain along with the liquid you've soaked or cooked the legumes in, don't soak legumes; instead, boil them for two minutes, then let them sit for an hour and cook as normal. This method of cooking also gets rid of lectins. Lectins are the toxins in beans and other legumes that cause stomachache. Boiling is the only way to destroy them. When cooking beans, bring them to a brief boil, then simmer them slowly for as long as required.

If this sounds like a lot of time and effort just to cook up some beans, you might find it more tempting to just run out and buy a can of them. In addition to paying a higher price, you get more salt this way—something you can likely do without. Cooking up a big batch of beans for salads, soups, or chili is worth the work if you freeze it to have on hand and reheat quickly.

Legumes have one last virtue—they're amazingly versatile. They absorb the flavour of the liquid they're cooked in and are thus terrific in spice-laden chili, thick soups loaded with herbs, or main-dish salads tossed with well-seasoned dressings.

Here are the most common and versatile legumes that you can include in your cooking repertoire.

Black Beans
: Also known as turtle beans, these are small, black-skinned, and oval in shape. They are a staple of South American cuisine and are excellent in soup or cooked with rice.

Black-Eyed Peas
: A tradition in the southern United States, these are a Cajun specialty when cooked with rice or just served alone with spicy seasoning.

Chick Peas
: Also called garbanzo beans, these are round, beige beans commonly used in Spanish, Italian, and Middle Eastern cooking. They are terrific tossed in a vinaigrette with some chopped red onion or sweet red pepper, a tasty, protein-filled addition to any salad, and superb blended with lemon juice and herbs in hummus (see page 71). They take two to three hours to cook, so it is a good idea to make a large batch at a time and freeze some.

Flageolets
: These are the authentic French beans to use in cassoulet. They are pricey, small, white, kidney-shaped beans that are tasty cooked in a herb-flavoured stock or served with roast poultry or lamb.

Kidney Beans
: Large and kidney-shaped, these come in both red and white. The red variety is more common and is best known as the crucial ingredient in chili con carne.

Lentils
: Small and flat, these are either brown or red. The red ones turn soft and mushy when cooked, so they are best used in purées and soups. Brown lentils, which hold their shape, are ideal as a cold salad mixed with vinaigrette and some chopped onion.

Mung Beans
: The green ones are the most common of these small, round beans. They can be eaten raw as sprouts and often wind up in Oriental noodles, sometimes called cellophane or glass noodles, or pasta made from mung-bean flour.

Pinto Beans
: These are pink with black dots and smaller than kidney

beans, with which they are more or less interchangeable.

Soybeans   These are small, oval, beige-coloured beans that are the only legumes containing complete protein, so they are extremely nutritious and versatile. They are easiest to use in cooking once they are processed into tofu, or bean curd, which can be made into a fabulous dip (see page 209), mayonnaise (page 208), and a divine cheesecake (pages 212 to 213).

Split Peas   Small and flattened on one side, these take less time to cook than most legumes. The green version is the basis for pea soup when simmered together with a ham bone and seasoning. The yellow ones can only be made into soup or curried, as in Indian dahl.

White Beans   These come in several types, most common of which are the pea and navy beans used to make baked beans. Either of these types can also be used in cassoulet, pur-ées, and many Italian dishes using beans.

Tofu—A Terrific Source of Protein

Tofu, often known as bean curd, is made from soybeans; it's the only variety of legume that is a complete protein. The beans are cooked to form a milky liquid and then processed in a manner similar to the way cottage cheese is made from cow's milk. Tofu is a boon to vegetarians because it is a meatless, complete protein that is not only low in fat and calories but also high in important minerals such as calcium, magnesium, phosphorus, and iron.

Soft and moist in texture and lacking a definite taste of its own, tofu is amazingly versatile when it is cooked properly. Anyone who has enjoyed it in a bowl of Szechuan hot and sour soup or deep-fried in a Japanese tempura knows what we mean. And tofu cheesecake and mayonnaise are dishes that have a delicate flavour and give you superb taste and texture without the cholesterol or calories!

Tofu is available in most Chinese groceries, health food stores, and some major supermarkets. When buying tofu, look for the varieties made with calcium rather than the synthetic rennet often added for extra firmness. It comes packaged in water and should be stored in the fridge. Change this water every couple of days. Tofu will keep this way for up to two weeks, but it is best when it is fresh. It also freezes well, although its texture then becomes more crumbly.

When you cook with tofu, drain it well before using it in any dish. If you are adding it to a stir-fry, soup, or baked dish like lasagna, when it should be as firm as possible, press the slabs between tea towels covered with a baking sheet or cutting board topped with a two- to five-pound weight such as a couple of cans of food. Leave for 30 minutes to two hours, depending on the desired firmness.

Nuts about Seeds

Seeds and nuts are valuable sources of incomplete proteins. So if you use them at meals, round them out with other foods to bring out their protein potential.

One problem with nuts and seeds is that they are high in fat, and although they make a terrific protein snack when eaten between meals, it is important not to eat too many. They are often highly salted—one more reason to go easy on the quantities you eat—so buy the unsalted variety if possible. Also avoid nuts and seeds that have been roasted with oils, because the oils are likely to be the saturated type, such as coconut. A good idea is to roast your own nuts and seeds by placing them on a baking sheet with a few herbs or spices if desired (this isn't really necessary, because roasting brings out wonderful flavour) and roasting for 20 to 30 minutes at 325°F (160°C). Package them in small quantities for a fast snack and to avoid eating too many at one time.

Peanut Butter Isn't Just for Kids

Peanuts are the only nut belonging to the legume group. Consumed with other proteins, peanut butter—as North American as apple pie but twice as healthy—is a terrific source of protein.

Natural peanut butter is healthier for you than the more processed kind. Its fat is less saturated than peanut butters made from hydrogenated vegetable oils. And the natural versions do not have added sugar—another plus. All peanut butter, however, is high in fat and should not be eaten in excess.

Another hazard of this yummy food is the danger of consuming mouldy nuts. If you grind your own peanut butter at a health food store, be careful not to include any mouldy or shrivelled nuts. Mould contains substances called aflatoxins, which are thought to be a health risk. Commercial brands of peanut butter are monitored for this and should not be cause for concern.

The Controversial Egg

There is considerable debate and confusion about the nutritional virtues and vices of eggs. Some people, worried about eggs' cholesterol content, omit them entirely from their diets; others have no concerns at all about eating them. Still others try to moderate their consumption of eggs, all the while disregarding the number they use in cooking.

Let's try to set the record straight. Although eggs are extremely high in cholesterol—270 mg per large egg—they also contain a number of valuable nutrients. Rich in protein (in the yolk), B vitamins, vitamin A, and iron, eggs are also too easy on the budget and versatile in cooking to be completely eliminated from our diets.

Because the current recommendation for cholesterol intake is about 300 mg per day, consuming one egg a day would eat up that ration without leaving room for other nutritious cholesterol-containing foods like meat, fish, and dairy products. If, however, your intake of cholesterol-containing foods is extremely low, you could eat eggs more frequently. Your guide to eating eggs should be your cholesterol count, which can easily be checked by a simple blood test.

If you have not been advised by a physician to cut down on eggs, the most prudent plan is to limit the number of egg yolks you eat to three a week. Egg whites, which do not contain cholesterol, need not be limited. One nifty way to stretch out your egg consumption is to add extra egg whites or milk to an omelette or other egg dish.

Calories 1
Protein *1 g
Fat *1 g
Carbohydrate *1 g

*Less than

Fish Stock

Makes about 4 cups/1 L.

Great to keep in the freezer to use in soups or fish sauces. You can get bones from the fishmonger for next to nothing. Use this recipe as a guideline for quantities, including whatever mild-flavoured veggies you have on hand.

1	tsp. corn, safflower, soybean, or sunflower oil	5 mL
1	small onion, chopped	
1	leek, chopped	
1	celery stalk, chopped	
1	carrot, chopped	
2	sprigs parsley	
1½	lb. bones of lean fish, cut into pieces	750 g
5	cups cold water	1.25 L

Heat the oil in a large, heavy saucepan and sauté the vegetables until soft. Add the parsley, fish bones, and water and bring to a boil. Reduce heat; simmer, uncovered, for 30–40 minutes, skimming off the scum at intervals. Strain and cool. Refrigerate or freeze until needed.

Calories *1
Protein *1 g
Fat *1 g
Carbohydrate *1 g

*Less than

Chicken Stock

Makes about 6 cups/1.5 L.

An absolute must to have on hand for healthy cooking. Save the bones from boned chicken to use in this, freezing them if necessary until you have a sizable batch.

4	lb. chicken bones	2 Kg
2	onions, peeled and quartered	
2	carrots, scrubbed and sliced	
2	celery stalks, sliced	
1	bouquet garni (see note)	
1	clove garlic, unpeeled	

Place all the ingredients in a large stockpot with enough cold water to cover. Bring to a boil, then reduce heat. Simmer, skimming off the scum at intervals, for about 2 hours or until reduced by one-third. Strain. For stronger flavour, reduce further. Refrigerate overnight. Remove the fat from the surface.

Note: To make the bouquet garni, wrap in cheesecloth a few stalks fresh parsley, 1 bay leaf, 1 sprig fresh or 1 pinch dried thyme, and 10 whole peppercorns. Tie with string to make a small bag.

Calories	3
Protein	*1 g
Fat	*1 g
Carbohydrate	*1 g

*Less than

Beef Stock

Makes about 6 cups/1.5 L.

Browning the bones in the oven is essential for a dark, rich stock. Have your butcher chop the bones for you.

4	lb. beef bones, cut into chunks	2 Kg
2	onions, peeled and quartered	
2	carrots, scrubbed and cut into chunks	
2	celery stalks, cut into chunks	
1	bouquet garni (see above)	
1	clove garlic, unpeeled	
1	tomato, seeded and chopped	

Roast the bones in a roasting pan at 450°F/230°C for about 30 minutes or until browned. Add the vegetables to the pan and roast until browned, about 30 minutes.

Drain the fat from the pan. Transfer the bones and vegetables to a large stockpot. Add the bouquet garni, garlic, tomato, and enough water to cover. Bring to a boil and reduce heat. Simmer, skimming the scum off the surface, for 3–4 hours or until the stock is reduced by one-third. Strain. For stronger flavour, reduce further. Refrigerate overnight. Remove the fat from the surface.

Roasted Red Pepper Sauce

Calories 16
Protein *1 g
Fat *1 g
Carbohydrate 4 g

*Less than

Makes about 1 cup/250 mL.

Once you've tried roasting peppers, you'll find yourself an addict. This sauce is enhanced by the slightly sweet, delicate flavour that results from the roasting. For a luxurious touch, add 2 tbsp./25 mL fromage blanc (see page 154), but if you are heating the sauce to serve it hot, remember not to boil it. Great with grilled, poached, or baked meat, poultry, or fish.

2	large red bell peppers	
$\frac{1}{4}$	tsp. Tabasco sauce	1 mL
$\frac{1}{2}$	tsp. white wine vinegar	2 mL
2	tbsp. dry white wine	25 mL
2	tbsp. chopped fresh basil	25 mL

Salt and pepper to taste

To roast the peppers, place them on a barbecue grill over medium heat or under the broiler and grill, turning at intervals, until blistered and slightly charred all over—about 10 minutes. Place the peppers in a brown paper bag; seal tightly. Leave for about 10 minutes, then peel off the skin with a sharp knife. Cut in half and remove seeds, working over a bowl to catch the juice.

Process the roasted peppers, their juice, the Tabasco, vinegar, and wine in a food processor or blender until smooth. Add the basil, salt, and pepper. To serve this sauce with pasta, cook it in a saucepan until heated through. It is also excellent served cold with cold chicken or fish or hot with grilled or baked chicken or fish.

Note: This sauce makes a terrific dip for vegetables by using $\frac{1}{4}$ cup/50 mL 2% plain yogurt instead of wine.

Calories	3
Protein	*1 g
Fat	*1 g
Carbohydrate	*1 g

*Less than

Carrot Sauce

Makes about 1 cup/250 mL or enough to serve as a sauce with chicken or fish for 4.

Great hot or cold as a sauce for grilled or poached chicken or fish. And a great way to get in some vitamin A.

4	medium carrots, thinly sliced	
2	tsp. lemon juice	10 mL
1	tbsp. orange juice	15 mL
½	tsp. grated orange peel	2 mL
½	cup 2% plain yogurt	125 mL
1	tbsp. finely chopped fresh coriander (also called Chinese parsley or cilantro)	15 mL

Salt and pepper to taste

Place the carrots in a saucepan with enough water to cover. Bring to a boil, then reduce heat and simmer, covered, for about 10 minutes or until tender. Drain, reserving 3 tbsp./45 mL of cooking liquid.

Process the cooked carrots, reserved cooking liquid, lemon juice, and orange juice in a food processor or blender until very smooth. Transfer to a bowl. Stir in the remaining ingredients and mix well. Cover and chill.

Poached Chicken Breasts

Calories 159
Protein 29 g
Fat 4 g
Carbohydrate 0 g

Poaching chicken breasts this way is unequalled. It makes the meat juicy and tender—perfect for eating hot or cold. It's a good idea to have a couple of these in the fridge or freezer to use in sandwiches, salads, or as a cold main dish with our red pepper or carrot sauce (see pages 48 and 49). Freeze the cooking liquid to add when making stock.

Single chicken breasts
Mixed herbs
Ground black pepper

Place the chicken breasts in a single layer in a large, heavy skillet. Add cold water to cover. Sprinkle on the herbs and pepper. Heat until the water just begins to boil. Reduce heat and simmer, covered, for 5 minutes. Remove from the heat. Turn the chicken over and let sit, covered, for another 5 minutes. Remove the lid and let sit 10 minutes longer. Take the chicken from the broth and remove the skin and bones. If you are eating the chicken cold, cool it and wrap in plastic wrap. Chill in the fridge.

Cold Chicken in Yogurt Sauce

Calories 164
Protein 29 g
Fat 4 g
Carbohydrate *1 g

*Less than

Serves 6.

The perfect main dish for patio dining on a summer's day, this is basic poached chicken, bathed in a divine sauce laced with toasted cumin, ground ginger, and fresh coriander.

6	single boned, skinned chicken breasts, poached (see page 50)	
$\frac{1}{2}$	tsp. cumin seeds, toasted	2 mL
2	cups 2% plain yogurt	500 mL
1	tbsp. chopped fresh coriander	15 mL
2	tbsp. chopped fresh parsley	25 mL
2	tbsp. lime juice	25 mL
$\frac{1}{4}$	tsp. ground ginger	1 mL
1	clove garlic, minced	
Large pinch cayenne pepper		
Salt and pepper to taste		

Chill the chicken breasts after poaching. To toast the cumin seeds, place them in a small, heavy skillet over low heat. Cook them, shaking the skillet occasionally, until fragrant—about 3 minutes. Transfer to a mortar and crush coarsely with the pestle. Use a coffee or other small grinder if you prefer.

Place the yogurt in a small bowl. Stir in the ground cumin and the remaining ingredients; mix well.

Place the chicken in a single layer in a shallow dish and pour the yogurt sauce over. Marinate overnight in the fridge or for 2–4 hours at room temperature, turning the chicken once or twice in the marinade. Serve with salad and crusty bread.

Calories 314
Protein 31 g
Fat 19 g
Carbohydrate 4 g

Chinese Chicken Salad

Serves 4.

The perfect salad to make ahead for summertime entertaining. Once again, the succulent, cold poached chicken breast is front and centre, this time set off by the crunch of bean sprouts and water chestnuts.

4	chicken breasts, poached (see page 50), skinned, boned, and cut into strips	
1	small zucchini, cut into matchstick strips	
1	large carrot, peeled and cut into matchstick strips	
1	sweet red pepper, cut into matchstick strips	
2	cups bean sprouts	500 mL
1	cup drained, sliced water chestnuts	250 mL

Dressing
1	clove garlic, minced	
1	tsp. minced fresh ginger root	5 mL
3	tbsp. sesame oil	45 mL
1	tbsp. low-sodium soy sauce	15 mL
1	tbsp. red wine or tarragon vinegar	15 mL

Pinch sugar
Pinch dry mustard
Freshly ground black pepper to taste
$\frac{1}{4}$ cup toasted sesame seeds for garnish 50 mL
$\frac{1}{4}$ cup chopped green onion for garnish 50 mL

Combine the chicken and vegetables in a large bowl. Whisk together the dressing ingredients in a small bowl until blended. Pour them over the salad and toss. Garnish with the sesame seeds and green onion. Serve in a lettuce-lined bowl if you wish as a main course.

Note: To toast sesame seeds, cook over low heat in a heavy skillet until golden brown.

Almond Herbed Chicken Roll-Ups

Calories 314
Protein 35 g
Fat 13 g
Carbohydrate 5 g

Serves 8.

A low-fat version of chicken Kiev, this is a big hit with children. It's crisp and juicy all at the same time.

8	single chicken breasts, boned and skinned	
1	tsp. dried thyme	5 mL
1	tsp. dried oregano	5 mL
1	tsp. dried basil	5 mL
Salt and pepper to taste		
2	tbsp. chopped fresh parsley	25 mL
2	tbsp. soft margarine	25 mL
1	cup whole-wheat breadcrumbs	250 mL
$\frac{1}{3}$	cup wheat germ	75 mL
$\frac{3}{4}$	cup chopped almonds	175 mL
2	eggs, beaten	

Pound the chicken breasts with a mallet between two sheets of plastic wrap until they are about $\frac{1}{4}$ inch/$\frac{1}{2}$ cm thick.

Combine the seasonings in a small bowl and sprinkle them evenly over the chicken. Divide the margarine into 8 portions; place each portion near the end of each flattened chicken breast. Roll the chicken up jelly roll style, tucking in the ends to form a package.

Combine the breadcrumbs, wheat germ, and almonds in a shallow dish. Place the eggs in a separate shallow dish. Dip each chicken roll in the crumb mixture, then in the egg mixture, and back in the crumb mixture, turning to coat well. Place on a lightly greased baking sheet.

Bake at 350°F/180°C for 30—40 minutes or until crisp and golden brown.

Calories 249
Protein 32 g
Fat 8 g
Carbohydrate 13 g

Tarragon Chicken

Serves 6.

One of the quickest and most delicious ways to cook chicken. Its incomparably rich-tasting sauce is made by reducing the vinegar and chicken stock.

4	medium onions, sliced	
$\frac{1}{4}$	cup water	50 mL
2	large tomatoes, peeled, seeded, and coarsely chopped (see page 86)	
2	cloves garlic, minced	
1	bay leaf	
1	tsp. dried or 2 tbsp. fresh tarragon	5 mL/25 mL
1	tbsp. corn, safflower, soybean, or sunflower oil	15 mL
6	single chicken breasts, skinned and boned	
1	cup red or white wine vinegar	250 mL
1	cup homemade chicken stock (see pages 46–47)	250 mL

Salt and pepper to taste

Place the onions and water in a large, heavy casserole. Bring to a boil, then reduce heat. Cover and simmer for 30 minutes, stirring occasionally and adding a little more water if necessary. Add the tomatoes, garlic, bay leaf, and tarragon. Cover and simmer 5 minutes longer.

Heat the oil in a large, heavy skillet. Add the chicken and brown on both sides. Transfer the chicken to the onion-tomato mixture in the casserole. Bring the mixture to a boil and reduce heat. Cover and simmer for 20 minutes or until the chicken is cooked.

Add the vinegar to the skillet in which the chicken was browned, stirring up the brown bits from the bottom of the pan with a spoon. Bring to a boil and cook over high heat until thick and syrupy—about 10 minutes. Add the stock and return to the boil. Cook over high heat until it is reduced to about $\frac{1}{4}$ cup/50 mL—about 10 minutes. Strain and add to the chicken mixture in the casserole. Remove the chicken and keep warm. Discard the bay leaf.

Purée the vegetable mixture in a food processor or blender until smooth. Return to the casserole with the chicken. Cook until heated through. Season to taste with salt and pepper. Serve with noodles, potatoes, or rice and steamed veggies.

Barbecued Breast on a Bun

Calories 161
Protein 29 g
Fat 5 g
Carbohydrate 1 g
(bun not included)

Serves 4.

A great substitute for the traditional burger. Be careful not to overcook, or the meat will be dry.

2	tbsp. corn, safflower, soybean, or sunflower oil	25 mL
2	tbsp. low-sodium soy sauce	25 mL
3	tbsp. red or white wine vinegar	45 mL
3	tbsp. dry red or white wine	45 mL
1	tsp. minced fresh ginger root	5 mL
1	clove garlic, minced	
Freshly ground pepper to taste		
4	single chicken breasts, skinned and boned	

Whisk together all the ingredients except the chicken in a small bowl. Place the chicken in a single layer in a shallow dish. Pour the marinade over. Let sit for 2–4 hours at room temperature or overnight in the fridge, turning once or twice.

Remove the chicken from the marinade. Barbecue over medium heat for 3–4 minutes per side or until just cooked through, basting with the marinade at intervals. Serve on toasted whole-wheat buns with lettuce, tomatoes, pickles, and other hamburger garnishes.

Lemon Artichoke Chicken

Calories 236
Protein 34 g
Fat 8 g
Carbohydrate 11 g

Serves 4.

Perfect for a quick family meal served on a bed of noodles with a green salad. Cut the chicken into chunks for a variation on this theme.

4	single chicken breasts, skinned and boned	
4	tsp. all-purpose flour	20 mL
1	tbsp. corn, safflower, soybean, or sunflower oil	15 mL
1	medium onion, finely chopped	
1	cup sliced mushrooms	250 mL
1	clove garlic, minced	
$\frac{1}{2}$	cup homemade chicken stock (see pages 46–47)	125 mL
2	tsp. lemon juice	10 mL
$\frac{1}{3}$	cup dry white wine	75 mL
1	bay leaf	
2	tbsp. finely chopped fresh parsley	25 mL
$\frac{1}{2}$	tsp. dried or 2 tbsp. chopped fresh basil	2 mL/25 mL
1	14-oz./398-mL can artichoke hearts packed in water, drained and halved	
Salt and pepper to taste		
$\frac{1}{2}$	lemon, thinly sliced, for garnish	

Dredge the chicken in flour. Heat the oil in a large, heavy saucepan or skillet. Add the onion, mushrooms, and garlic; sauté until soft. Add the chicken, stock, lemon juice, wine, and bay leaf. Bring to a boil, then reduce heat and simmer, uncovered, for 10 minutes. Stir in the parsley, basil, and artichokes. Turn the chicken breasts over in the sauce. Cover and simmer 10 minutes longer or until the chicken is cooked and the sauce is slightly thickened. Season with salt and pepper and garnish with lemon.

Calories 84
Protein 13 g
Fat 2 g
Carbohydrate *1 g

*Less than

Chicken Liver Pâté

Serves 8–10 as an appetizer.

This creamy pâté is so silky smooth, you'll wonder where this recipe's been all your life! As good in a sandwich smeared with plenty of grainy mustard as it is spread on a cracker as a party appetizer. And brimming with iron!

1	tsp. corn, safflower, soybean, or sun-flower oil	5 mL
1	small onion, chopped	
1	clove garlic, finely chopped	
1	lb. chicken livers, trimmed of fat and green sac	500 g
$\frac{1}{2}$	cup dry white wine	125 mL
$\frac{1}{2}$	tsp. dried thyme	2 mL
1	tbsp. brandy or dry sherry	15 mL
1	tbsp. drained green peppercorns packed in water	15 mL
$\frac{1}{4}$	tsp. ground allspice	1 mL
	Salt and freshly ground black pepper to taste	
2	tbsp. chopped fresh parsley for garnish	25 mL

Heat the oil in a large, heavy skillet. Add the onion and garlic; sauté until soft. Add the chicken livers and cook, stirring, over medium heat for 2–3 minutes or until lightly browned on the outside. Add the wine and thyme. Bring to a boil, then reduce heat and cook, covered, over low heat for 5–6 minutes or until the livers are just cooked through.

Transfer the liver mixture to a food processor. Add all the remaining ingredients except the parsley. Process until smooth. Spoon the pâté into an earthenware dish or attractive crock—it will be runny at this stage. Chill.

To serve, sprinkle with parsley and surround with toast triangles or crackers.

Chicken Livers au Vinaigre

Calories 55
Protein 8 g
Fat 2 g
Carbohydrate *1 g

*Less than

Serves 4.

A classic French way to cook chicken livers—surely one of the most succulent yet underrated parts of the bird that is worth eating for its taste as well as all the iron and B vitamins.

1	tbsp. corn, safflower, soybean, or sunflower oil	15 mL
1	lb. chicken livers, trimmed of fat and green sac	500 g
$\frac{1}{2}$	cup thinly sliced leeks or green onion	125 mL
$\frac{1}{4}$	cup red wine vinegar	50 mL
3	cloves garlic, minced	
$\frac{1}{2}$	cup homemade chicken stock (see pages 46–47)	125 mL
1	large ripe tomato, peeled, seeded, and chopped (see page 86)	
	Dash Tabasco sauce	
	Salt and pepper to taste	
2	tbsp. chopped fresh chives	25 mL

Heat the oil in a heavy skillet over high heat. Sauté the livers in a single layer for 1 minute, stirring constantly. Do not let them overlap. Cook in two batches if necessary. Transfer to a sieve and let drain over a bowl.

Add the leeks to the skillet, adding a little chicken stock if necessary. Sauté over medium-high heat until soft. Add the vinegar and garlic and bring to a boil. Boil the liquid until reduced to a syrupy consistency. Add the stock, tomato, and the liquid drained from the livers. Return to the boil. Add the Tabasco, salt, and pepper and reduce heat. Add the livers; warm gently without boiling. Sprinkle with chives and serve at once.

Calories 307
Protein 25 g
Fat 20 g
Carbohydrate 2 g

Grilled Pork Tenderloin

Serves 3.

Follow the recipe for barbecued breast on a bun, substituting for the chicken breasts a 12-oz./375-g pork tenderloin trimmed of all fat.

Before marinating the pork, butterfly it by slicing it almost in half lengthwise and spreading it out to make one flat piece of meat. Grill over medium heat on a barbecue or under the broiler, for about 5 minutes per side or until just cooked through, basting with the marinade at intervals. Delicious served with roasted red peppers (see page 48) and boiled new potatoes.

Calories 162
Protein 4 g
Fat 13 g
Carbohydrate 8 g

Cucumber Sauce

Makes 1 cup/250 mL.

Great as an accompaniment to barbecued, poached, or baked fish with or without the capers.

1	cup peeled, seeded, and shredded cucumber	250 mL
$\frac{1}{2}$	cup 2% plain yogurt	125 mL
2	tbsp. light mayonnaise	25 mL
2	tbsp. chopped fresh dill	25 mL
2	tsp. chopped capers (optional)	10 mL
Salt and pepper to taste		

Wrap the cucumber in a clean tea towel and squeeze out the excess water. Combine the yogurt and mayonnaise in a bowl and mix well. Stir in the cucumber and remaining ingredients. Chill. Serve with cooked fish.

Calories 197
Protein 28 g
Fat 8 g
Carbohydrate 3 g

Ceviche

Serves 6 as an appetizer.

A Mexican-influenced appetizer of raw, marinated fish that is nothing short of sublime! This will make a convert of any carnivore.

1	lb. firm-fleshed fish (cod, halibut, white-fish, scrod, etc.), cut into small chunks	500 g
$\frac{1}{4}$	cup lime juice	50 mL
1	large ripe tomato, peeled, seeded, and chopped (see page 86)	
$\frac{1}{2}$	cup chopped green onion	125 mL
1	small jalapeno pepper (canned or fresh), seeded and finely chopped	
1	clove garlic, minced	
	Salt and pepper to taste	
2	tbsp. chopped fresh parsley	25 mL
	Lettuce leaves	
	Fresh coriander leaves for garnish	

Place the fish in a shallow glass dish. Pour the lime juice over and marinate for 1 hour at room temperature or until the fish is opaque. Drain.

Combine the tomato, green onion, jalapeno pepper, garlic, salt, pepper, and parsley in a small bowl. Let the mixture sit in the fridge for 1 hour.

Transfer the fish and tomato mixture to another bowl and toss. Line an attractive bowl or platter with lettuce leaves and spoon the ceviche on top. Garnish with coriander leaves.

Basic Grilled Fish

Do as the fisherfolk do and cook fish the simplest way—over hot coals or an open fire. You can barbecue or broil any fish with superb results if you follow this basic method, which requires only a little oil for brushing on the fish.

- If the fish has been in the fridge, bring it to room temperature before grilling.

- Clean and descale the fish with a sharp knife. Do not remove the tail or head until the fish is cooked.

- Season the fish inside and out with a little salt, plenty of freshly ground black pepper, and herbs if you wish.

- Preheat the grill of a barbecue or broiler until very hot. Grill the fish over high heat so the skin sears; this way it will not break during cooking. Reduce the heat to medium. Cook the fish until it flakes with a fork—3 or 4 minutes per side for medium-sized fish. Do not overcook, or the fish will be dry.

- While the fish is cooking, brush it lightly at intervals with a little corn, safflower, soybean, or sunflower oil that has been mixed with fresh or dried herbs.

- Serve with a sauce such as cucumber sauce (see page 59) on the side.

Oriental Fish with Noodles

Calories 363
Protein 28 g
Fat 4 g
Carbohydrate 53 g

Serves 6.

This succulent, beautiful dish was inspired by one served at Arowhon Pines, a gorgeous lodge serving fine food in Ontario's Algonquin Park. Chinese noodles work best in this recipe, but fresh or dried linguini taste almost as good.

3	tbsp. low-sodium soy sauce	45 mL
$\frac{1}{4}$	cup water	50 mL
$\frac{1}{4}$	cup dry sherry	50 mL
2	tsp. minced fresh ginger root	10 mL
	Freshly ground black pepper to taste	
6	firm-fleshed fish fillets (about 4 oz./125 g each)	
1	lb. fresh or dried Chinese egg noodles	500 g
1	tbsp. corn, safflower, soybean, or sunflower oil	15 mL
1	clove garlic, minced	
3	small carrots, cut into thin julienne strips	
3	small zucchini, cut into thin julienne strips	
4	cups bean sprouts	1 L
3	green onions (green part only), cut into thin julienne strips, for garnish	

Whisk together the soy sauce, water, sherry, and 1 tsp./5 mL ginger root in a small bowl. Place the fish in a large, shallow dish. Pour the soy sauce marinade over and let sit for 15–20 minutes at room temperature. Remove the fish from the marinade and place in a single layer in a large ovenproof dish with a lid. Sprinkle with $\frac{1}{4}$ cup/50 mL of marinade. Cover and bake at 400°F/200°C for 8–10 minutes or until the fish flakes easily.

Meanwhile, drop the noodles into a large pot of boiling, salted water and cook for 1 minute or until al dente. Drain.

Heat the oil in a wok or large, heavy skillet. Add the remaining 1 tsp./5 mL ginger root, garlic, and carrots and stir-fry over high heat for 1–2 minutes or until the garlic is soft. Add the zucchini and stir-fry for 1 minute. Add the bean sprouts, cooked noodles, and remaining marinade. Stir-fry for 1 minute or until all the ingredients are heated through.

To serve, place each fish fillet on an individual plate on a bed of the vegetable-noodle mixture. Sprinkle with green onion.

<table>
<tr><td>Calories</td><td>236</td></tr>
<tr><td>Protein</td><td>27 g</td></tr>
<tr><td>Fat</td><td>9 g</td></tr>
<tr><td>Carbohydrate</td><td>12 g</td></tr>
</table>

Crisp Fish Sticks

Serves 4–6.

A nourishing, low-fat creation that will have the kids coming back for seconds. A tasty, healthy substitute for frozen fish sticks.

$\frac{1}{2}$	cup 2% plain yogurt	125 mL
1	tbsp. chopped fresh parsley	15 mL
Salt and pepper to taste		
$\frac{1}{2}$	cup wheat germ, toasted	125 mL
$\frac{1}{2}$	cup whole-wheat breadcrumbs	125 mL
2	cups grated low-fat cheese	500 mL
1	lb. firm-fleshed fish fillets (halibut, cod, haddock, bluefish, etc.), cut into 8 1-inch/2-cm sticks	500 g

Combine the yogurt, parsley, salt, and pepper in a shallow dish and mix well.

To toast the wheat germ, cook in a heavy skillet over low heat for 2–3 minutes or until golden brown, shaking the skillet constantly. Combine the toasted wheat germ, breadcrumbs, and cheese in a separate shallow dish.

Dip each fish stick into the yogurt, then into the wheat germ mixture, coating well. Place on a lightly greased baking sheet. Bake at 425°F/220°C for 5 minutes. Turn and bake 5 minutes longer or until the coating is crisp and the fish flakes easily.

Calories	108
Protein	20 g
Fat	1 g
Carbohydrate	5 g

Scallops in a Pouch

Serves 4–6.

The delicate taste of scallops is enhanced by the flavour of ginger, lemon, and garlic in this aromatic creation cooked in a foil pouch for maximum flavour and nutrients. Adapted from a recipe from B.C. Fisheries.

Aluminum foil
Corn, safflower, soybean, or sunflower oil for brushing
1   lb. scallops   500 g
1   medium carrot, peeled and cut into thin
     julienne strips
1   leek (white part only), cut into thin
     julienne strips
1   celery stalk, cut into thin julienne strips
1   clove garlic, minced
1   tsp. minced fresh ginger root   5 mL
Juice of $\frac{1}{2}$ lemon
Salt and pepper to taste

Lightly brush 1 large or 4 smaller squares of foil with the oil and place the scallops on them. Top with the vegetables, garlic, and ginger root. Sprinkle with the lemon juice, salt, and pepper. Fold the foil over and crimp the edges to seal well and form 1 large or 4 individual pouches. Place on a baking sheet.

Bake at 400°F/200°C for about 10 minutes or until the scallops are opaque. Place pouch(es) on 1 large or 4 individual plates and open at the table to let the aroma escape.

Super Seafood Kebabs

Calories 182
Protein 18 g
Fat 11 g
Carbohydrate 3 g

Serves 4–6.

The distinct flavour of orange peel combined with fresh ginger in this recipe, also from B.C. Fisheries, makes these grilled kebabs tops for taste as well as nutrition. A great way to include those omega-3 fatty acids in your diet.

$\frac{1}{2}$	cup orange juice	125 mL
3	tbsp. corn, safflower, soybean, or sun-flower oil	45 mL
$\frac{1}{4}$	cup low-sodium soy sauce	50 mL
$\frac{1}{4}$	cup wine vinegar	50 mL
1	clove garlic, minced	
1	tsp. minced fresh ginger root	5 mL
1	tbsp. grated orange peel	15 mL
	Freshly ground black pepper to taste	
4	oz. fresh salmon steak, cut into 1-inch/2-cm cubes	125 g
4	oz. fresh halibut steak, cut into 1-inch/2-cm cubes	125 g
4	oz. monkfish, cut into 1-inch/2-cm cubes	125 g
4	oz. large shrimp, peeled and deveined	125 g

Whisk together the first 8 ingredients in a small bowl. Place the fish and shrimp in a shallow glass dish. Pour the marinade over and let sit for 2 hours in the fridge, turning once or twice.

Drain the seafood, reserving the marinade for basting. Thread the salmon, halibut, monkfish, and shrimp alternately on bamboo skewers that have been soaked in water for 1 hour.

Barbecue the kebabs on a lightly oiled grill over medium heat for 8–10 minutes, turning once. Serve with rice and salad.

Calories 194
Protein 17 g
Fat 6 g
Carbohydrate 13 g

Bouillabaisse

Serves 12 as a main course.

A fish-filled concoction from the south of France that puts the day's catch to superb use, this recipe is designed to feed a crowd and can be adapted to incorporate almost any fresh fish. Great served with crusty bread and a crisp salad. Halve the recipe if you wish.

2	tbsp. olive oil	25 mL
1	cup finely chopped onion	250 mL
2	cups finely chopped leeks	500 mL
2	tbsp. minced garlic	25 mL
1	cup finely diced celery	250 mL
2	cups finely diced red pepper	500 mL
1	tsp. saffron	5 mL
$\frac{1}{2}$	tsp. crushed fennel seeds	2 mL
1	bay leaf	
$\frac{1}{2}$	tsp. dried thyme	2 mL
2	tbsp. tomato paste	25 mL
6	cups fish stock (see page 46)	1.5 L
1	cup dry white wine	250 mL
1	cup peeled, seeded, and chopped tomatoes (see page 86)	250 mL
1	lb. monkfish fillets, cut into chunks	500 g
1	lb. halibut fillets, cut into chunks	500 g
1	lb. swordfish fillets, cut into chunks	500 g
$\frac{1}{2}$	lb. large shrimp, peeled and deveined	250 g
18	littleneck clams	
2	lb. mussels, scrubbed and with beard removed	1 Kg
$\frac{1}{2}$	cup chopped fresh parsley	125 mL

Heat the oil in a large, heavy pot. Add the onion, leeks, and garlic and sauté until soft. Add the celery and red pepper. Cook for 1 minute, stirring. Add the saffron, fennel seeds, bay leaf, thyme, tomato paste, stock, and wine. Bring to a boil, reduce heat, and simmer for about 10 minutes. Add the tomatoes and fish. Simmer for 2–3 minutes. Add the shrimp, clams, and mussels. Return to the boil, then reduce heat. Cover and simmer for 3–4 minutes or until the clams and mussels open. To serve, remove and discard the bay leaf. Sprinkle with parsley.

Calories 209
Protein 13 g
Fat 8 g
Carbohydrate 22 g

Clam Chowder

Serves 4–6.

If you wish, substitute about $\frac{3}{4}$ lb./375 g fresh fish fillets cut into chunks for the canned clams.

2	tbsp. soft margarine	25 mL
1	small onion, finely chopped	
2	tbsp. finely chopped green pepper	25 mL
1	clove garlic, minced	
3	tbsp. all-purpose flour	45 mL
$3\frac{1}{2}$	cups 2% milk	875 mL
2	medium carrots, peeled and finely diced	
2	celery stalks, finely diced	
2	medium potatoes, peeled and finely diced	
2	medium tomatoes, peeled, seeded, and chopped (see page 86)	
2	5-oz./142-g cans baby clams, undrained	
2	tsp. dried chervil	10 mL

Salt and pepper to taste

Heat the margarine in a large, heavy saucepan. Sauté the onion, green pepper, and garlic until soft. Stir in the flour and cook, stirring, over low heat for 1 minute. Whisk in the milk and bring to a boil. Add the carrots, celery, and potatoes and simmer for 20 minutes or until the potatoes are soft. Add the tomatoes and simmer 10 minutes longer. Add the clams with their juice, chervil, salt, and pepper. Cook until they are heated through.

Calories 272
Protein 14 g
Fat 5 g
Carbohydrate 47 g

Lentil Soup

Serves 4.

Use red rather than brown lentils for this rib-hugging soup, which packs a terrific protein punch, is high in soluble fibre, and turns an attractive yellow when cooked.

1	tbsp. corn, safflower, soybean, or sunflower oil	15 mL
1	cup finely chopped onion	250 mL
1	large clove garlic, minced	
1	cup red lentils, rinsed	250 mL
4	cups homemade chicken or vegetable stock (see pages 46–47 and 126–27) or water	1 L
1	bay leaf	
$\frac{1}{2}$	tsp. dried thyme	2 mL
1	cup finely chopped carrots	250 mL
1	cup finely chopped celery	250 mL
1	cup peeled, seeded, and chopped tomatoes (see page 86)	250 mL
	Juice of 2 limes or lemons	
2	tsp. honey	10 mL
	Salt and pepper to taste	

Heat the oil in a large, heavy pot. Add the onion and garlic; sauté until soft. Add the lentils, stock, bay leaf, and thyme. Bring to a boil, reduce heat, and simmer, covered, for 1 hour or until the lentils are tender. Add the carrots and celery. Return to the boil, then reduce heat. Simmer for 30 minutes or until the vegetables are soft. Discard the bay leaf. Add the tomatoes, lime juice, honey, salt, and pepper. Cook until heated through.

Black Bean Soup

Calories 357
Protein 22 g
Fat 3 g
Carbohydrate 61 g

Serves 8–10.

Thick, rich, creamy, and loaded with soluble fibre, this soup makes a complete protein meal when eaten with whole-grain bread. Dried black beans, sometimes called turtle beans, are available in most health, Mexican, or South American food stores.

1	tbsp. corn, safflower, soybean, or sunflower oil	15 mL
1	medium onion, finely chopped	
2	leeks, finely chopped	
3	cloves garlic, minced	
2	celery stalks, finely chopped	
2	cups black beans, soaked for 2 hours in 8 cups/2 L water	500 mL
1	bay leaf	
1	tbsp. ground cumin	15 mL
2	tsp. dried oregano	10 mL
$\frac{1}{2}$	tsp. dried thyme	2 mL
	Pinch cayenne pepper or to taste	
$\frac{1}{4}$	cup dry sherry	50 mL
1	tbsp. lemon juice	15 mL
	Salt and pepper to taste	
$\frac{1}{2}$	cup 2% plain yogurt	125 mL
$\frac{1}{4}$	cup finely chopped fresh parsley for garnish	50 mL

Heat the oil in a large, heavy pot. Add the onion and leeks and sauté until soft. Add the garlic and celery; sauté for 1 minute over medium heat. Add the beans with their soaking liquid, bay leaf, cumin, oregano, thyme, and cayenne. Bring to a boil, reduce heat, and simmer, partially covered, for $1\frac{1}{2}$–2 hours or until the beans are soft.

Process the mixture in a food processor or blender in batches, if necessary, until smooth. Return to the pot, then stir in the sherry, lemon juice, salt, and pepper. Return to the boil.

To serve, ladle the soup into individual bowls, place a dollop of yogurt on top, and sprinkle with parsley.

Calories 120
Protein 6 g
Fat 2 g
Carbohydrate 20 g

Bean and Pasta Soup

Serves 6–8.

Popular in the Tuscany region of Italy, this soup is a great one to keep in the fridge or freezer for a quick winter meal. Because beans and pasta complement each other, this soup makes a complete protein meal that sticks magnificently to the ribs! You can substitute black-eyed peas or pinto, white pea, or navy beans for the kidney beans if you wish.

1	tsp. corn, safflower, soybean, or sunflower oil	5 mL
1	tsp. olive oil	5 mL
1	onion, finely chopped	
2	cloves garlic, minced	
1	stalk celery, finely chopped	
1	carrot, finely chopped	
1	cup peeled and seeded (see page 86) and puréed canned or fresh tomatoes	250 mL
3	tbsp. finely chopped parsley	45 mL
2	tsp. dried basil	10 mL
$\frac{1}{2}$	tsp. dried sage	2 mL
$\frac{1}{4}$	tsp. dried hot pepper flakes	1 mL
7	cups vegetable or chicken stock (see pages 126–27 and 46–47)	1.75 L
1	cup dried white or red kidney beans, soaked for at least 2 hours in 3 cups/750 mL water	250 mL
1	cup elbow macaroni or other small pasta	250 mL

Salt and pepper to taste

Heat the oils in a large pot. Add the onion and garlic and sauté until soft. Add the celery and carrot; sauté over medium heat for 1 minute. Stir in the tomatoes, parsley, basil, sage, and pepper flakes. Add the stock and beans with their soaking liquid. Bring to a boil, then reduce heat. Simmer, partially covered, for about 2 hours or until the beans are soft. Return the soup to the boil and add the macaroni. Cook until al dente and season with salt and pepper. Serve with grated Parmesan cheese on the side and plenty of crusty bread.

Calories 159
Protein 9 g
Fat 2 g
Carbohydrate 28 g
(per $\frac{1}{2}$ cup/125 mL)

Hummus

Makes about $2\frac{1}{2}$ cups/625 mL.

The tastiest thing ever to happen to the chick pea, this Middle Eastern dip or spread is best eaten with triangles of warm pita bread or raw veggies. This version is surprisingly easy to make as long as you are patient and let the chick peas simmer their way to softness. You can also make it in two stages by cooking the chick peas, freezing them, and making the hummus later. The complementary proteins of chick peas and tahini (sesame paste) make this a nutritious nibble for vegetarians and meat eaters alike.

1	cup dried chick peas, soaked for 2 hours in 4 cups/1 L water	250 mL
2	cloves garlic, minced	
5	tbsp. lemon juice	65 mL
	Pinch cayenne pepper or to taste	
$\frac{1}{4}$	tsp. ground cumin	1 mL
$\frac{1}{4}$	tsp. dried basil	1 mL
$\frac{1}{4}$	cup tahini or peanut butter	50 mL
	Salt and freshly ground black pepper to taste	
$\frac{1}{4}$	cup finely chopped fresh parsley for garnish	50 mL

Place the chick peas and their soaking liquid in a large, heavy saucepan. Bring to a boil, then reduce heat. Cover and simmer for 2 hours or until the peas are soft, adding more water if necessary.

Drain the chick peas, reserving their cooking liquid. Process in a food processor or blender with $\frac{3}{4}$ cup/175 mL of the cooking liquid and the remaining ingredients, except the parsley, until smooth and light in colour. Add more cooking liquid if necessary for desired consistency.

To serve hummus, sprinkle with parsley. To store in the fridge, cover the surface directly with plastic wrap to prevent discolouration.

Note: Substitute a 19-oz./540-mL can of chick peas for dried, cooked ones if you wish, adding enough liquid from the can plus extra water when blending to achieve the desired consistency. Those who do not like the flavour of tahini (sesame paste, available at Middle Eastern and health food stores) can omit it.

Calories 527
Protein 31 g
Fat 10 g
Carbohydrate 81 g

Chili con Carne

Serves 8.

Made with chunks of lean beef and dried rather than canned beans, this is great served piping hot with a good sprinkling of low-fat cheese, which melts into the chili and tastes magnificent. Use left-over chili to make a serve-yourself meal of tacos with toppings such as grated low-fat cheese, plain yogurt, shredded lettuce, chopped tomato, and snipped fresh coriander.

3	tbsp. corn, safflower, soybean, or sunflower oil	45 mL
1	lb. lean stewing beef, cut into tiny cubes	500 g
1	medium onion, chopped	
2	cloves garlic, minced	
1	tsp. dried hot red pepper flakes	5 mL
1	tsp. dried basil	5 mL
1	tsp. dried oregano	5 mL
1	tsp. ground cumin	5 mL
1	28-oz./796-mL can Italian plum tomatoes, undrained and chopped	
1	tbsp. tomato paste	15 mL
2	cups dried red kidney beans, soaked for at least 2 hours in water to cover	500 mL

Salt and pepper to taste

Heat 2 tbsp./25 mL of the oil in a large, heavy saucepan. Brown the meat on all sides, then transfer to a paper towel. Pour off the remaining oil in the saucepan. Add the remaining 1 tbsp./15 mL of oil. Add the onion and garlic; sauté until soft. Add the pepper flakes, basil, oregano, cumin, tomatoes, tomato paste, and the beans and their soaking liquid. Bring to a boil and reduce heat. Simmer for $2\frac{1}{2}$–3 hours or until the beans are soft. Season with salt and pepper. Serve sprinkled with grated cheese and with cornbread on the side. Use leftover chili in tacos or as a topping for baked potatoes.

4   Sticking up for Starch

If there is one food group with an undeservedly bad reputation, it is without a doubt breads and cereals. Who hasn't been told that eating too much bread or pasta will make us as rotund as a Russian rye or as voluptuous as a freshly steamed dumpling? In a nutshell, we've been led to believe that carbohydrates are fattening and not much else.

But the hard facts expose this bad image for what it is—another food myth. Carbohydrate contains four calories per gram, the same amount as protein. This is less than half the calorie count of fat, which racks up a whopping nine calories per gram. It is, in fact, the butter you smear on your bread and the cream sauce in which you lovingly douse those fettuccine, not the bread and pasta themselves, that are the *real* culprits when it comes to calories.

Sure enough, if you suddenly eliminate carbohydrates from your diet, as many fad diets recommend, you will experience a sudden drop in weight. But this is loss of water, not fat, and you will regain the weight the moment you return to eating cereal and bread, not to mention cakes and cookies!

Not only are carbohydrates *not* fattening when consumed in moderation (too many calories of any food result in fat deposition), they are just plain good for you when eaten in balance with the other food groups.

Caring about Carbohydrate
The main nutrient in the bread and cereal food group is carbohydrate, of which there are two main types: simple sugars and complex carbohydrates. Simple sugars are easy to spot because they usually taste sweet; they include glucose, fructose, lactose, and sucrose. Complex carbohydrates do not taste sweet and are made up of long chains of sugars. In plant foods complex carbohydrates are called *starch*. Breads and cereals are also a terrific source of nutrients—namely, thiamin, riboflavin, niacin, iron, trace minerals, and fibre.

This food group is the main source of dietary fibre—either or both of the soluble and insoluble varieties, depending on the grain from which the food is made.

Whole-wheat bread, for example, is high in insoluble fibre, while oat products contain mostly soluble fibre.

Choosing Your Daily Bread

When you are choosing bread on the basis of its fibre content, it is not a simple matter of one kind being healthier than another. In deciding among whole-wheat, oatmeal, and mixed-grain breads, you must take into consideration your own constitution as well as other sources of soluble and insoluble fibre in your diet.

For example, a person who suffers from constipation should increase his or her intake of insoluble fibre and would be wise to opt for bran or whole-wheat bread. A diabetic, however, might more often choose a bread such as rye that is high in soluble fibre, while someone with a high cholesterol count should eat oatmeal because of the cholesterol-reducing effects of oat bran. Mixed-grain bread covers most nutritional angles and makes a good all-round choice. So do breads that contain nuts and seeds, which offer added protein as well as added taste.

As usual, purchasing bread is another case of "Buyer beware," and reading the label is the best way to avoid nutritional pitfalls. A dark loaf often gets its colour from the addition of caramel colouring, cocoa, or molasses and may in fact be only 60 percent whole wheat. This kind of bread gives you more sugar and less fibre for your bread-buying buck.

Breads and cereals contain protein, but only of the incomplete type, and they must therefore be consumed with complementary foods. A healthy grating of Parmesan cheese, for example, on top of your plate of pasta primavera, or your pita filled with hummus (made from chick peas), complement the proteins. There are also pastas on the market that are fortified with protein, which comes from the addition of whey to the dough. This makes them a better source of protein than the regular types.

Whole-grain foods contain larger amounts of vitamins and minerals than refined foods do. Whole-grain products are higher in vitamin B6, pantothenic acid, and folate than refined cereals, as well as vitamin E and trace minerals such as zinc, copper, and manganese.

White flour has lost some of its nutrients through processing, but the word "Enriched" on the label means that most of these nutrients have been replaced. Canadian food regulations require that white flour be enriched with iron, thiamin, riboflavin, and niacin. The fibre, however, is the important nutrient not added back to white flour after the whole grain is processed.

Let's Get Serious about Cereals

With the fibre fad in full swing these days, the battle between big food companies for your cereal dollar is heating up. And as usual in such instances, the consumer is often caught in the middle, faced with too much choice and a deluge of confusing information.

The best policy when buying cereals is to read the labels carefully and do some quick calculations, keeping personal taste preferences in mind, to find the brands that contain the most nutrients and the least fat and sugar. One important word of warning: don't let the labels "Natural" or "No preservatives added" make your decision—they do not necessarily imply the best nutrients.

The first thing to look for is the cereal's sugar content. Ingredients are listed in descending order of quantity, so if sugar is the first ingredient listed, then the cereal contains more sugar than it does grains and is not the healthiest choice. Sometimes the added sugar listed in the ingredients section is low, but there may be other sugars listed in the nutrient information. This could be natural sugar from dried fruit, which is acceptable because it contains other nutrients.

A cereal with a high sugar content might seem acceptable because it is fortified with all kinds of vitamins and minerals. Not so. Eating such a cereal is really the same as eating a bowlful of table sugar followed by a vitamin supplement. In other words, we're not talking real food!

Then there is the whole confusing issue of granola.

Something about that bowl of wholesome-looking cereal bursting with crunchy, honey-coated grains, nuts, and seeds has given this cereal a healthy hype it usually doesn't deserve. Commercial granola is, in fact, extremely high in sugar and, worst of all, saturated fat, which comes from the coconut oil it's steeped in. Labels on packaged granola subtly disguise this fact by using a tiny serving size to list nutrients and calories.

Many people assume that because most granolas are made with honey, they must be healthy. Not true. Honey is as much a simple sugar as sucrose or table sugar. The only difference is that it sticks to your teeth! (See Chapter 13.) The bottom line is that granola can be a nutritious

SUGAR CONTENT OF POPULAR CEREALS

Less Than $\frac{1}{4}$ Teaspoon/1 mL per Serving	Cheerios	Puffed Wheat
	Cream of Wheat	Shredded Wheat
	Oatmeal	Wheat Germ
	Puffed Rice	

$\frac{1}{2}$–1 Teaspoon/2–5 mL per Serving	All-Bran	Harvest Crunch
	Bran Buds	Life
	Bran Bites and Raisins	Pep
	Chex, Wheat, Corn, Bran, and Rice	Product 19
		Raisin Bran
	Corn Flakes	
		Rice Flakes
	Corn Bran	
		Shreddies
	Fruit with Fiber, Apple-Cinnamon	Team
	Grape-Nuts	

1–2 Teaspoons/5–10 mL per Serving	Familia	Rice Krispies
	Frosted Mini-Wheats	Total
	Most	Wheaties

2–3 Teaspoons/10–15 mL per Serving	Cap'n Crunch	Honey Nut Cheerios
	Cracklin' Bran	Honey Nut Corn Flakes
	Cocoa Puffs	Instant oatmeal, honey and graham
	Crispy Wheats 'n Raisins	Instant oatmeal, raisin and bran
	Frosted Rice	
	Fruit with Fiber, Dates, Raisins and Walnuts	Instant oatmeal, sugar and spice
	Golden Grahams	Lucky Charms
3 Teaspoons/15 mL or More per Serving	Alpha Bits	Instant oatmeal, cinnamon and spice
	Apple Jacks	Pacman
	Boo Berry	Strawberry Shortcake
	Cocoa Pebbles	Sugar-Crisp
	Count Chocula	Sugar Corn Pops
	Frankenberry	Sugar Smacks
	Frosted Flakes	Trix
	Fruit Loops	
	Honey Comb	

food, but for the most part, only when it's homemade. Try our low-fat recipe on page 175 and vary it as you wish, adding more dried fruit for a sweeter taste.

More Telling Trivia about Cereals

Bran is another nutritional buzzword, and for people in search of high-fibre foods, so-called bran cereals can contain vastly different amounts. Once again it's a case of reading the label. Cereals labelled "100 percent bran" are made from the indigestible outer coating of the wheat kernel and yield the most fibre. Those that contain 40 percent bran are made from the outer coating as well as other parts of the wheat kernel.

Some cereals are high in sodium. If you are on a sodium-restricted diet, be aware of the sodium content of various cereals by reading their labels. Some people—for example, pregnant women—may require extra iron, so for them iron-fortified cereals can be a good idea. To enhance the absorption of iron, accompany the cereal with a food containing vitamin C, such as an orange or its juice.

Some Like It Hot—Some Don't

There are people who, like Daddy Bear, enjoy nothing better at breakfast time than a rib-hugging bowl of steaming hot porridge. Others abhor the taste of hot cereal but live for their daily serving of breakfast-time bran buds steeped in cold milk and topped with fresh fruit. There is no right or wrong in this whole hot-cereal-versus-cold-cereal debate; it is simply a matter of taste. Both hot and cold cereals can be packed with important nutrients. By the same token, there are many products in both groups that are loaded to bursting with sugar, fats, and not much else.

So choose your cereals and read labels carefully. If a cereal is fortified with vitamin A and you already eat plenty of dairy products as well as fruit and vegetables, all of which are rich in this vitamin, this may not be the best cereal for you. On the other hand, if your diet is low in iron, an iron-fortified product is a wise choice.

There is so much variety on the highly competitive cereal market these days that armed with all this nutritional information, your careful scrutiny of package labels should turn up at least one brand that meets your needs.

Other Grains of Truth

There is another important benefit of exploiting all the possibilities of this wondrously varied food group. By eating more bread, potatoes, and grains, we can cut down on protein portions at meals (especially at dinnertime), thus decreasing fat and increasing our fibre intake all in one fell swoop. Another bonus is that grains and cereals are usually easier on the budget than large meat servings.

Look at it this way. It's difficult to decrease our protein consumption and simultaneously reduce calories when we eat meat and salad. If we were to eat a smaller steak, we would finish it and the salad in no time and probably leave the table hungry. But a small quantity of thinly sliced beef stir-fried with broccoli and served on a bed of rice is a lot more filling. It also contains adequate protein, minimal fat, and a whole lot of fibre.

One problem with grains and cereals has been that most of us don't know how to prepare many of the weird and wonderful varieties now on the market. Thanks to the influence of ethnic cuisines, however, we are lately getting more familiar with such exotic but simple-to-cook foods as tabbouleh (made from bulgur), which hails from the Middle East, kasha (cooked buckwheat) from Eastern Europe, and polenta (cooked cornmeal), an Italian specialty.

Good Enough to Wheat

The following grains and cereals all come from wheat.

Bulgur
: Bulgur is a term commonly used for cracked wheat. Buy the whole-grain version, which comes in several different sizes. Bulgur contains B vitamins, trace minerals, and plenty of fibre. It is excellent when it is cooked like rice and served as an accompaniment to meat or fish; it also makes a terrific cold salad when it is soaked in water or stock for a couple of hours and then mixed with vegetables and fresh herbs.

Couscous
: Couscous is the name used for the smallest size of cracked wheat. In the Middle East, where it is a staple, couscous is traditionally steamed and served with small amounts of meat, vegetables, or both as a protein extender.

Wheat Berries
: Wheat berries are the whole wheat kernel and can be eaten as a cooked cereal or baked into bread or muffins.

Wheat Germ	This is the germ of the wheat kernel and is a good source of B vitamins, iron, manganese, zinc, magnesium, phosphorus, copper, potassium, and fibre. Using wheat germ is a great way to add nutrients to food in cooking. Substitute it for breadcrumbs in burgers and casserole toppings and as a coating for baked chicken or fish. It's also easy to mix it into the topping of a fruit crumble. Toasting it lightly in the oven or in a heavy skillet on top of the stove before using it as a topping enhances its flavour. Store wheat germ in the fridge; because of its high oil content, it goes rancid easily. Only buy unrefrigerated wheat germ in a sealed jar; if it is refrigerated, it is all right to buy it in unsealed packages. But avoid the sweetened kind that is sold in jars.
Wheat Bran	Wheat bran, the outer coating of the wheat kernel, is the most concentrated form of insoluble fibre there is. But be careful not to eat too much—this can negatively affect the absorption of calcium and iron in your body.
Barley	Barley contains carbohydrates and trace minerals such as zinc, manganese, magnesium, phosphorus, copper, and iron, plus some B vitamins. Barley tastes wonderful in soups and casseroles.
Buckwheat	Often called buckwheat groats, buckwheat is a source of incomplete protein, fibre, B vitamins, and trace minerals such as iron, potassium, and phosphorus. Roasted buckwheat is called kasha, a delicious Eastern European specialty that can be a savoury dish made with onion and served alone or with meat. It is also a yummy dessert laced with nuts, seeds, and perhaps some dried fruit.

Cornering Corn

The following belong to the corn family.

Cornmeal	Cornmeal is ground corn and is a great source of complex carbohydrates, B vitamins (when enriched), and trace minerals like iron and magnesium. The vitamin A content of cornmeal depends on how yellow it is: the yellower the colour, the more vitamin A it contains. Cornmeal is also a good source of incomplete protein and is therefore extremely nutritious when it is eaten with beans or dairy products. It is terrific in muffins, cornbread, and casseroles but less healthy when it is deep-fried in nachos and other such foods because of their high fat rating.
Popcorn	Popcorn is dried corn kernels and can be one of the most

nutritious of all snacks if it is made with a minimum of fat and salt. The most fat-free way to pop corn is in a hot-air popper. Avoid those ready-to-use packages that come with their own pouch of fat—it contains highly saturated coconut oil. When you pop corn in a pan, use unsaturated oil. After it has popped, add some grated cheese, herbs, or both instead of salt, and—it goes without saying—hold the melted butter!

We Dote on Oats

Oats, which include oatmeal, rolled oats, quick-cooking oats, and oat bran, comprise a particularly important group of grains. This is because the fibre they contain is mainly the soluble type, which is beneficial in regulating cholesterol and blood sugars. The fibre is found in the bran portion known as oat bran.

Oat Bran   Dr. James Anderson of the University of Kentucky Medical College has been conducting research into the benefits of oat bran. His studies on groups of men with high cholesterol levels show that three ounces of oat bran a day lowered their cholesterol by about 19 percent. What is more, while the "bad" LDL cholesterol decreased by this amount, the "good" HDL cholesterol tended to increase or stay the same.

If you combine these results with the findings of the Lipid Research Clinics study (discussed in Chapter 2), which are that a 1 percent reduction in cholesterol decreases the risk of heart disease by 2 percent, you're looking at some pretty good reasons to eat oat bran!

Oat bran can be cooked and eaten as a hot cereal like porridge. It can also be used to replace one-third to one-half the flour and other starch fillers called for in recipes. It is not advisable to use more than this proportion because, unlike flour, oat bran does not contain gluten—the protein required for texture development. Too much oat bran makes food gummy. Because of the fibre it contains, however, oat bran is excellent as a thickener in vegetable purées, soups, and stews in place of cream.

Rice Is More Than Nice

When buying rice, choose either the brown or enriched version whenever possible. Both contain B vitamins, incomplete protein, and trace minerals, but little fibre. Brown rice is rightly shedding its old association with hippies and bean sprouts and emerging as a flavourful, versatile food. It is not only brimming with nutrients but can also taste wonderful if used imaginatively. Because brown rice takes longer to cook than regular rice, you can freeze cooked packages of it to save time later.

Avoid prepackaged, seasoned rice dishes. They are not only expensive but also high in salt and additives. Use your imagination along with a variety of seasonings and vegetables, and you'll find that rice has endless taste possibilities.

Wild rice, harvested mostly by North America's native peoples, is not actually a rice, but a type of grass. It is, however, cooked in a similar manner and has similar nutrients—protein, B vitamins, iron, and manganese.

High on Rye

Rye contains mainly soluble fibre, along with protein, B vitamins, phosphorus, and potassium. Although breads made from 100 percent rye flour do exist, most rye breads are made with a high-gluten product like wheat and only one-third to one-half rye flour, which has a low gluten content. Gluten gives bread its light texture.

Pass the Pasta

Pasta seems to be *the* carbohydrate food of the eighties. And for good reason. Pasta is popular with all age groups. It is amazingly versatile and can be served hot doused in a multitude of sauces or cold as a summer picnic or barbecue accompaniment. Pasta comes in all kinds of shapes, sizes, and flavours. And last but not least, if it is coated in the right sauce, it is low in fat and calories.

The secret to the nutritional content of pasta is in the sauce. For years most North Americans considered pasta to be a plate of spaghetti slathered in a thick crown of often oily meat and tomato sauce that had been simmered for several hours. Not only was this sauce time-consuming to prepare, it also had an unsubtle flavour and had lost some of its nutrients but none of its fat during its lengthy simmering.

Today's trends in preparing pasta sauces are toward lighter versions that are cooked for a short time and rely on good, fresh ingredients enhanced by delicate seasoning. A tomato sauce, for example, laced with fresh basil and some freshly ground pepper tastes wonderful cooked for a few minutes, whether you're using fresh or even canned tomatoes. A fresh tomato sauce that isn't cooked at all (Italians call it *salsa cruda*) is even better, especially at peak tomato season (see page 86).

Pasta is so versatile that you could serve a different version every night of the week with all kinds of sauces—from artichoke and lemon to sliced ham with tomatoes—and never get bored. Such dishes are also a good way to encourage children to eat unpopular vegetables. After all, what eight-year-old is going to refuse broccoli or green beans when they're tossed with his or her favourite noodle and sprinkled with grated cheese?

Pasta has become the order of the day at many restaurants. But avoid menu items loaded with whipping cream. Even if your server assures you that a certain sauce contains only "a little cream," keep in mind that a couple of tablespoons of 35 percent cream likely started out as twice that amount before being reduced during cooking. Order a dish without cream—a generous grating of fresh Parmesan or Romano easily takes its place for taste. Also avoid pasta salads; they are often coated in rich, oily dressings and can be high in fats.

The discussion about fresh versus dried pasta is really a moot point because it is based on personal taste preference. The dried varieties are enriched with B vitamins and iron. Avoid prepackaged pasta meals, which tend to be high in salt and overpriced. You can also make your own pasta; if you do it right, you can produce an excellent, delicate noodle that tastes terrific. The exercise is also a good one in which to include children, who can always benefit from an enjoyable lesson in cooking.

Cooking times for pasta depend on whether it is dried, fresh, or homemade and on what shape it is. The thicker versions, such as large penne, shells, and lasagna noodles, obviously take slightly longer than spaghettini or small fusilli. The traditional way to cook pasta in Italy is until *al dente*, or "firm to the bite." The best way to test for this is to bite into a piece. Throwing spaghetti on the ceiling, as some people suggest, is foolish; you'll wind up with a mess and not much else.

Cook pasta by adding it to a large pot of boiling water. The pot cannot be too large, and you cannot use too much water. Lots of water prevents pasta from sticking; so does stirring at intervals during cooking. When the pasta has cooked, drain it in a colander or sieve. Do not rinse.

Much Ado about Muffins

The old-fashioned, unglamorous bran muffin of yester-year was full of fibre and other nutrients. It also weighed in at a mere 120 calories or so. Not so today's upscale, trendy muffin—it has fallen prey to the crazed dreams of the marketing moguls. Spiked with chocolate chips, loaded with sugar or honey (for some reason, many consumers continue to believe the myth that honey is healthier than sugar), and, worst of all, packed with fat, it can contain as many as 450 calories.

Some of today's gussied-up muffins contain as much as 30 to 35 grams of fat. That's the equivalent of three tablespoons of butter! And then their purveyors have the gall to call them "light!" Such so-called muffins are actually glorified cupcakes, and the only light thing about them is their texture.

The bottom line is that all muffins are not created equal. If you are trying to cut down on sugar, calories, and fat, beware of muffins that aren't basic, low-fat bran. Again, the best policy is to bake your own (see our recipes on pages 176 to 181) or find a baker who makes the old-fashioned kind!

Can She Bake a Cherry Pie?

Because pastry dough doesn't usually taste sweet and has a light texture, many people think it is lower in calories than cake. Again, this is not necessarily true. Most pastry, especially the flaky kind made with layers of dough that sandwich layers of shortening or butter, is extremely high in fat. It's commonly known that a slice of cherry pie is a pretty high-calorie food. But how many of us realize that a lot of these calories come from the pastry as well as the filling?

As for quiche, you can forget this trendy item as a "light meal." Quiche gives you the double whammy of a fat-laden cream filling as well as pastry that's a hiding place for yet more fat.

Another food that masks its calorie count under a "light" image is the increasingly popular croissant. Croissants are made by layering pastry dough with tiny pieces of butter. The result is a light-as-air delicacy that can conceal as much as three tablespoons of fat.

In Search of Cookie Smarts

A love of cookies seems to be universal. It bridges the gaps of age, sex, race, and eating habits. To lump all cookies together in an effort to banish them from our diets would be as impossible as it is unnecessary.

Cookies are here to stay, so choose those that are low in fat and sugar but still tops for taste. But because finding commercially made cookies that fill this bill is a difficult, almost impossible, task, making your own is the best way to obtain nutritious results. An oatmeal cookie made with wheat germ, dried fruit or nuts, and whole-wheat flour, for example, can add valuable fibre, vitamins, and minerals to your diet and that of your children.

Fresh Tomato Basil Sauce

Calories 96
Protein 2 g
Fat 6 g
Carbohydrate 12 g

Serves 4–6.

Called *salsa cruda* in Italy, meaning "raw sauce," this unequalled concoction is a must when tomato season is in full swing. It can be used on pasta or with poultry or fish.

8–10	medium-ripe fresh tomatoes, peeled and seeded	
$\frac{1}{3}$	cup coarsely chopped fresh basil	75 mL
2	cloves garlic, minced	
2	tbsp. virgin olive oil	25 mL
	Salt to taste	
	Plenty of freshly ground black pepper	
	Grated Parmesan cheese	

To peel the tomatoes, cut an *x* into their rounded, non-stem ends and plunge them into boiling water for a few seconds. Plunge them into cold water for a few seconds, then peel off the skin with a sharp knife. To seed them, slice them in half horizontally and squeeze or scoop out the seeds. Chop the tomatoes coarsely. This amount gives about 4 cups/1 L sauce.

Combine the chopped tomatoes with the remaining ingredients, except the Parmesan, in a bowl. Marinate at room temperature for 3–4 hours. Heat slightly if desired, but do not cook. Serve tossed with or on top of your favourite cooked pasta. Serve the Parmesan on the side.

Calories	46
Protein	1 g
Fat	2 g
Carbohydrate	7 g

Quick Tomato Sauce

Serves 6.

Contrary to popular belief, tomato sauce for pasta does not need to be simmered for hours. This sauce is superb made with fresh or canned tomatoes, depending on the season. Add your favourite herb in amounts that suit your palate. This sauce freezes well (an excellent idea when fresh tomatoes are at their peak) and is extremely useful for making quick meals.

2	tsp. corn, safflower, soybean, or sun-flower oil	10 mL
1	medium onion, finely chopped	
2	cloves garlic, finely chopped	
1	28-oz./796-mL can Italian plum tomatoes, chopped	
1	tsp. dried or $\frac{1}{4}$ cup chopped fresh basil	5 mL/50 mL
1	tsp. dried oregano	5 mL

Salt and pepper to taste

Heat the oil in a heavy saucepan. Add the onion and garlic; sauté until soft. Add the tomatoes, basil, and oregano. Bring to a boil, reduce heat, and simmer for about 10 minutes. Season with salt and pepper. Makes about 3 cups/750 mL. Serve with 1 lb./500 g of your favourite cooked pasta.

Note: Add 1–2 tbsp./15–25 mL tomato paste with the tomatoes if canned or fresh tomatoes are watery.

Pasta with Tuna Tomato Sauce

Calories 393
Protein 19 g
Fat 2 g
Carbohydrate 62 g

Serves 6.

Here is a super idea for a protein-packed meal-in-a-hurry that's sure to be a hit all round, especially with children.

1 recipe Quick Tomato Sauce (see page 87)
2 7-oz./198-g cans water-packed tuna, drained
1 lb. pasta   500 g

Heat the tomato sauce in a saucepan. Add the tuna, flaked or left in chunks, according to taste. Heat through.
    Cook the pasta in plenty of boiling, salted water. Drain and top with the sauce. Serve with freshly grated Parmesan and a tossed salad.

Calories 400
Protein 14 g
Fat 8 g
Carbohydrate 66 g

Pasta Primavera

Serves 6.

Any veggies taste magnificent cooked this way; try a combination of green beans, asparagus, and red peppers. Use our Quick Tomato Sauce, and you've got another almost instant dinner that's tops for taste.

1	recipe Quick Tomato Sauce (see page 87)	
1	lb. pasta	500 g
2	carrots, sliced diagonally $\frac{1}{4}$ inch/$\frac{1}{2}$ cm thick	
2	small zucchini, sliced diagonally $\frac{1}{4}$ inch/$\frac{1}{2}$ cm thick	
1	cup snow peas, sliced diagonally	250 mL
1	small bunch broccoli, cut into small flowerets	
$\frac{1}{4}$	cup toasted pine nuts (see note)	50 mL
2	tbsp. chopped fresh parsley	25 mL
$\frac{1}{2}$	cup grated Parmesan cheese	125 mL

Heat the sauce in a saucepan. Cook the pasta in plenty of boiling, salted water. Meanwhile, steam the vegetables until they are only tender-crisp.

Drain the pasta and transfer to a warm serving platter or bowl. Pour the hot sauce over and toss lightly. Top with steamed vegetables and sprinkle with pine nuts and parsley. Serve the Parmesan on the side.

Note: To toast pine nuts, cook them in a small, heavy skillet over low heat, shaking constantly, for 3–4 minutes or until golden brown. Be careful not to burn them.

Calories 403
Protein 35 g
Fat 2 g
Carbohydrate 58 g

Pasta Marinara

Serves 6.

This seafood pasta is simple and quick to make but elegant enough to serve at a dinner party. It is also gorgeous cooked in the oven and then served in a large earthenware casserole. Just bring the tomato sauce to a boil, place it in a casserole, add the fish and seafood, and bake in a hot oven for 4–5 minutes or until cooked. Top the cooked pasta with seafood and sauce served from the casserole at the table. Or follow this method:

18	mussels, scrubbed and with beard removed	
1	recipe Quick Tomato Sauce (see page 87)	
1	lb. firm-fleshed fish (cod, grouper, monkfish, halibut, etc.), cut into chunks	500 g
½	lb. shrimp, peeled and deveined	250 g
1	lb. long pasta (linguini, fettuccine, or spaghetti)	500 g
2	tbsp. chopped fresh parsley	25 mL

Steam the mussels in a little simmering water or dry white wine in a covered pot until they open—about 5 minutes. Discard any that remain closed.

Bring the tomato sauce to a boil in a large, heavy saucepan. Reduce heat; add the fish and simmer for 1–2 minutes or until opaque. Add the shrimp and cook for 1–2 minutes or until opaque.

Cook the pasta in plenty of boiling, salted water until al dente. Drain and transfer to a large, warm serving bowl or platter. Top with the marinara sauce. Arrange the hot steamed mussels attractively on top and sprinkle with parsley.

Calories 323
Protein 12 g
Fat 5 g
Carbohydrate 48 g

Pasta Arrabiate

Serves 6.

Arrabiate means "angry" in Italian, and this dish earns its title because of the delectable zap of fiery chilies.

1	recipe Quick Tomato Sauce (see page 87)	
1	tsp. hot red pepper flakes or $\frac{1}{2}$ fresh, small hot pepper, seeded and finely chopped or to taste	5 mL
1	lb. pasta	500 g
3	tbsp. chopped fresh parsley	45 mL
$\frac{1}{2}$	cup grated Parmesan cheese	125 mL

Stir together the tomato sauce and pepper flakes in a heavy saucepan. Cook until heated through.

Cook the pasta in plenty of boiling, salted water until al dente. Drain and transfer to a warm serving platter or bowl. Toss with the hot sauce and sprinkle with parsley. Serve the Parmesan on the side.

Pasta with Red Peppers

Calories 369
Protein 14 g
Fat 6 g
Carbohydrate 63 g

Serves 4.

Sweet bell peppers in all their gorgeous hues, from palest gold to ruby red, look as good as they taste in this simple recipe that's perfect for autumn when peppers peak. For a more time-consuming but more elegant version of this dish, roast and peel the peppers before making the sauce (see page 48).

2	tsp. corn, safflower, soybean, or sun-flower oil	10 mL
2	cloves garlic, minced	
1	small onion, finely chopped	
2	large sweet red peppers, seeded and sliced	
2	large fresh tomatoes, peeled, seeded, and chopped (see page 86)	
$\frac{1}{4}$	cup chopped fresh basil	50 mL
	Salt and pepper to taste	
$\frac{3}{4}$	lb. pasta	375 g
$\frac{1}{3}$	cup grated Parmesan cheese	75 mL

Heat the oil in a heavy saucepan. Sauté the garlic and onion until soft. Reduce heat slightly and add the peppers; cook 1 minute longer. Add the tomatoes and cook for about 10 minutes, stirring at intervals. Add the basil just before serving. Season with salt and pepper.

Cook the pasta in plenty of boiling, salted water until al dente. Drain. Transfer to a warm serving platter or bowl and top with the pepper sauce. Serve the Parmesan on the side.

Calories 252
Protein 7 g
Fat 19 g
Carbohydrate 10 g

Pesto

Makes about $1\frac{1}{4}$ cups/300 mL, or enough sauce for 1 lb./500 g pasta to serve 6.

This low-fat version of a magnificently aromatic Italian tradition is thick and flavourful. Use as is or thin it out slightly if you wish with a little chicken stock or water. A natural for freezing, pesto is a must to have on hand to add to soups, as a sauce for pasta, or to layer on pizza. If you freeze pesto, omit the cheese and add it when you are ready to use the sauce.

3	cups loosely packed fresh basil, washed and dried	750 mL
3	cloves garlic, minced	
2	tbsp. corn, safflower, soybean, or sunflower oil	25 mL
2	tbsp. virgin olive oil	25 mL
3	tbsp. pine nuts	45 mL
$\frac{3}{4}$	cup grated Parmesan cheese	175 mL
Freshly ground black pepper to taste		

Process all the ingredients in a food processor or blender until blended.

Note: To store pesto, place in a dish and cover the surface directly with plastic wrap to prevent discolouration. Keeps for 1 week in the fridge.

Pesto Noodle Roll-Ups

Calories 589
Protein 34 g
Fat 20 g
Carbohydrate 59 g

Serves 6.

A nifty rolled-up variation on a theme that's old but good.

1	lb. low-fat ricotta cheese	500 g
1	cup grated Parmesan cheese	250 mL
1	cup grated skim-milk mozzarella cheese	250 mL
$\frac{1}{2}$	tsp. dried or 1 tsp. chopped fresh thyme	2 mL/5 mL
$\frac{1}{2}$	tsp. dried or 1 tsp. chopped fresh basil	2 mL/5 mL
$\frac{1}{3}$	cup chopped fresh parsley	75 mL
$\frac{1}{2}$	cup chopped green onion	125 mL
1	egg yolk	

Salt and pepper to taste

12	lasagna noodles, cooked al dente	
$\frac{3}{4}$	cup pesto (see page 93)	175 mL
2	cups Quick Tomato Sauce (see page 87)	500 mL

Combine the cheeses, thyme, basil, parsley, green onion, egg yolk, salt, and pepper in a bowl. Stir to blend.

Divide the cheese mixture into 12 portions and spread evenly on each lasagna noodle. Roll up jelly roll style. Cut each roll in half with a serrated knife and place in a lightly oiled 12-cup/3-L ovenproof dish. Spoon the pesto onto each roll. Cover the dish and bake at 350°F/ 180°C for 20–30 minutes or until bubbly and heated through.

Cook the tomato sauce in a saucepan until heated through. Place 4 lasagna rolls on each plate on a pool of sauce or serve the sauce on the side.

Tuna Broccoli Pasta Salad

Calories 255
Protein 14 g
Fat 9 g
Carbohydrate 32 g

Serves 6 as a main course.

There's nothing like a pasta salad for summer barbecues or as a complete make-ahead lunch, as this one can be. If you are making this beforehand, add the tuna just before serving.

1	small bunch broccoli	
$\frac{1}{2}$	lb. stout pasta (fusilli, shells, penne, or macaroni), cooked al dente and drained	250 g
$\frac{1}{4}$	cup chopped green onion	50 mL
1	7-oz./198-g can water-packed tuna, drained and coarsely flaked	
$\frac{1}{4}$	cup chopped fresh basil	50 mL
2	cloves garlic, minced	
$\frac{1}{4}$	cup lemon juice	50 mL
3	tbsp. corn, safflower, soybean, or sunflower oil	45 mL
2	tbsp. virgin olive oil	25 mL
	Salt and pepper to taste	
3	tomatoes, cut into wedges	

Cut small flowerets from the broccoli and cut smaller stems into thin julienne strips about 1 inch/2 cm long. Blanch the flowerets and stems by plunging them into boiling water for a few seconds or until tender-crisp. Drain and refresh under cold water. Drain again.

Toss the pasta with the broccoli, green onion, tuna, and basil in a large bowl. Whisk together the garlic, lemon juice, and oils in a small bowl. Season with salt and pepper. Pour over the salad, toss well, and garnish with the tomatoes. Serve at room temperature.

Calories 153
Protein 3 g
Fat 8 g
Carbohydrate 18 g

Pasta Veggie Salad

Serves 6 as a side dish with grilled meat or fish.

Use whatever vegetables are in season for this easy-to-make, mouth-watering concoction. For a new twist, use spinach pasta mixed with the regular kind for added colour.

$\frac{1}{2}$	lb. short pasta (fusilli, penne, shells, etc.)	500 g
3	tbsp. virgin olive oil	45 mL
2	tbsp. tarragon, red wine, or white wine vinegar	25 mL
1	tsp. Dijon mustard	5 mL
1	clove garlic, minced	
$\frac{1}{2}$	tsp. dried or 2 tbsp. chopped fresh basil	2 mL/25 mL
	Salt and freshly ground black pepper to taste	
$\frac{3}{4}$	cup snow peas, topped and tailed	175 mL
8–10	stalks asparagus, with coarse stems peeled and cut into pieces on the diagonal	
1	sweet red pepper, roasted (page 48), peeled, seeded, and cut into thin julienne strips	
$\frac{1}{4}$	cup toasted pine nuts (see page 89)	50 mL
3	tbsp. fresh dill, snipped into tiny sprigs	45 mL

Cook the pasta in plenty of boiling, salted water until al dente. Drain and place in a large serving bowl.

Whisk together the oil, vinegar, mustard, garlic, basil, salt, and pepper in a small bowl until well blended. Pour this mixture over the pasta and toss until well coated.

Steam the snow peas and asparagus separately until just barely tender but still crisp, about 1 minute for snow peas and about 3 minutes for asparagus. Refresh under cold water. Add to the pasta and toss.

Add the red pepper to the pasta mixture and toss. Chill. Garnish with toasted pine nuts and dill just before serving.

Note: To make this salad into a main dish, add 2 single poached, skinned, and boned chicken breasts, cut into chunks, or some cooked shrimp, squid, or other seafood.

Oriental Noodle Salad

Calories 443
Protein 29 g
Fat 15 g
Carbohydrate 50 g

Serves 4 as a main course.

The crunch of bean sprouts and cucumber combined with tender yet firm Chinese egg noodles, all laced with a flavoursome soy sauce dressing, make this dish nothing short of superb. Chili oil, available at most Chinese groceries along with the noodles, gives an extra hit of mouth-tingling heat.

$\frac{1}{2}$	lb. dried Chinese egg noodles	250 g
2	tbsp. sesame oil	25 mL
$\frac{1}{4}$	tsp. chili oil or to taste (optional)	1 mL
2	tbsp. low-sodium soy or tamari sauce	25 mL
2	tbsp. red or white wine vinegar	25 mL
$\frac{1}{2}$	tsp. dry mustard	2 mL
2	single chicken breasts, boned, skinned, and poached (see page 50)	
$\frac{1}{2}$	English cucumber, coarsely shredded or cut into small chunks	
$1\frac{1}{2}$	cups coarsely shredded iceberg or romaine lettuce	375 mL
$1\frac{1}{2}$	cups bean sprouts	375 mL
2	tbsp. chopped fresh coriander (also called Chinese parsley or cilantro)	25 mL

Cook the noodles in plenty of boiling, salted water until al dente. Chinese noodles take much less time to cook than regular pasta—about 1 minute. Drain and place in a large bowl.

Whisk together the oils, soy sauce, vinegar, and mustard in a small bowl until well blended. Pour onto the noodles and toss well to coat. Chill.

Cut the chicken into small cubes or shred coarsely. Add to the noodles along with the cucumber, lettuce, and bean sprouts. Toss and sprinkle with coriander.

Calories 197
Protein 4 g
Fat 9 g
Carbohydrate 27 g

Brown Rice Salad

Serves 6–8 as a side dish with meat or fish.

This comes from Frances Beaulieu, artist, avid cook, and designer of the *Sun* recipe cartoon, "Recipix," and is a great dish to serve at parties and barbecues. Rice vinegar is available at both Chinese and Japanese groceries, but you can substitute white wine vinegar if you wish.

$\frac{3}{4}$	cup brown rice	175 mL
2	tbsp. rice vinegar	25 mL
1	tbsp. low-sodium soy or tamari sauce	15 mL
1	tsp. finely grated fresh ginger root	5 mL
$\frac{1}{4}$	cup corn, safflower, soybean, or sunflower oil	50 mL
Pepper to taste		
1	cup quartered mushrooms	250 mL
1	red pepper, finely diced	
1	green pepper, finely diced	
$\frac{1}{2}$	cup finely chopped green onion	125 mL
$\frac{1}{4}$	cup finely chopped fresh parsley	50 mL
1	10-oz./284-mL can unsweetened mandarin oranges, drained	
1	10-oz./284-mL can water chestnuts, drained and sliced	
$\frac{1}{4}$	cup slivered almonds, toasted (see note)	50 mL

Cook the brown rice until tender. Whisk together the vinegar, soy sauce, ginger root, oil, and pepper in a small bowl. Pour this over the rice mixture and toss well. Add the vegetables, green onion, parsley, oranges, and water chestnuts. Mix well and sprinkle with almonds.

Note: To toast almonds, place them in a heavy iron skillet on the stove over low heat. Cook for 3–4 minutes, shaking the skillet at intervals, or until golden brown.

Calories 125
Protein 2 g
Fat 8 g
Carbohydrate 13 g

Tabbouleh

Serves 6 as a side dish.

An aromatic Middle Eastern dish that's delicious by itself or with barbecued meat or fish—and high in fibre to boot. Serve with plain yogurt on the side if you wish.

1	cup medium bulgur	250 mL
1	cup chopped fresh parsley	250 mL
$\frac{1}{2}$	cup chopped fresh mint	125 mL
$\frac{1}{2}$	cup chopped green onion	125 mL
1	clove garlic, minced	
3	tbsp. lemon juice	45 mL
3	tbsp. olive oil	45 mL
Salt and pepper to taste		
2	medium tomatoes, chopped	
1	cup peeled, seeded, and chopped cucumber	250 mL

In a large bowl, pour enough boiling water over the bulgur to cover. Let sit for 1 hour, then drain off any excess liquid. Add the parsley, mint, and green onion.

Whisk together the garlic, lemon juice, oil, salt, and pepper in a bowl. Pour the mixture over the bulgur and toss. Chill.

Just before serving, combine the tomatoes and cucumber with the bulgur mixture. Mix carefully.

Calories 363
Protein 27 g
Fat 13 g
Carbohydrate 10 g

Layered Polenta Bake

Serves 6.

The proteins of cornmeal and cheese are complementary in this sublime version of an Italian peasant dish. What's more, family and guests will be just as complimentary when you serve this with a crisp green salad as a hearty, elegant meal.

1	10-oz./284-g package or 6 cups/1.5 L loosely packed fresh spinach, with coarse stems removed	
1	cup 2% cottage cheese, drained	250 mL
$\frac{1}{8}$	tsp. nutmeg	0.5 mL
1	tbsp. lemon juice	15 mL
	Salt and freshly ground black pepper to taste	
4	cups water	1 L
1	cup fine yellow cornmeal	250 mL
$\frac{1}{3}$	cup freshly grated Parmesan or Romano cheese	75 mL
1	tbsp. dried or $\frac{1}{4}$ cup chopped fresh basil	15 mL/50 mL
$1\frac{1}{2}$	cups grated low-fat cheese (mozzarella, brick, or cheddar)	375 mL
2	cups Quick Tomato Sauce (see page 87)	500 mL

Wash the spinach. Place in a large, heavy pot and steam in water that clings to the leaves until spinach is limp, about 30 seconds. Squeeze with your hands, reserving the liquid for use in vegetable stock. Chop the spinach.

Combine the cottage cheese, nutmeg, lemon juice, salt, and pepper in a small bowl.

Bring the water to a boil in a large, heavy saucepan. Add the cornmeal in a thin stream, whisking constantly. Reduce heat and cook, stirring frequently and adding a little more water if required until the mixture resembles cooked cream of wheat or thick pudding, about 30 minutes. Stir in the Parmesan and basil. Mix well.

Pour half the cornmeal mixture into a 9-inch/2 L round or square ovenproof dish (earthenware works well). Top with the spinach, cottage cheese mixture, half the low-fat cheese, then the remaining cornmeal mixture. Sprinkle with the remaining low-fat cheese.

Bake at 350°F/180°C for 35–40 minutes or until bubbly on top. Brown under the broiler for 1 minute or until golden brown. Serve with the heated tomato sauce on the side.

Eggplant Bulgur Casserole

Calories 103
Protein 4 g
Fat 3 g
Carbohydrate 18 g

Serves 4–6 as a main course.

A yummy, high-fibre, meatless meal. Perfect protein when served with yogurt.

2	medium eggplants (about $1\frac{1}{2}$ lb./750 g), cut into small cubes	
2	tsp. corn, safflower, soybean, or sunflower oil	10 mL
1	medium onion, chopped	
2	cloves garlic, minced	
1	green pepper, cut into small cubes	
1	cup medium bulgur	250 mL
2	cups tomato juice	500 mL
$\frac{1}{2}$	tsp. dried oregano	2 mL
$\frac{1}{2}$	tsp. dried basil	2 mL
Salt and pepper to taste		
$\frac{1}{4}$	cup chopped green onion	50 mL
$\frac{1}{2}$	cup 2% plain yogurt	125 mL

Add the eggplant to a saucepan of boiling water and cook for about 2 minutes. Drain well.

Heat the oil in a large Dutch oven. Add the onion, garlic, and green pepper; sauté until soft. Stir in the bulgur, eggplant, tomato juice, oregano, and basil and bring to a boil. Cover and bake at 350°F/180°C for about 30 minutes, stirring once halfway through cooking. Season with salt and pepper and sprinkle with the green onion. Serve with the yogurt.

Couscous with Chicken and Vegetables

Calories 333
Protein 36 g
Fat 8 g
Carbohydrate 27 g

Serves 6.

A Middle Eastern whole-grain creation laced with the delicate aromas of cumin and coriander. This recipe has three parts—stewed vegetables, steamed couscous, and grilled or barbecued chicken. But don't be deterred: it's worth the effort.

1	tbsp. corn, safflower, soybean, or sun-flower oil	15 mL
1	medium onion, chopped	
1	leek, chopped	
1	celery stalk, diced	
1	green pepper, diced	
2	medium carrots, sliced	
2	small white turnips, diced	
2	cups chicken stock	500 mL
1	cup seeded, chopped fresh tomatoes	250 mL
1	cup cooked chick peas (use canned if you wish)	250 mL
1	tsp. ground coriander	5 mL
1	tsp. ground cumin	5 mL
$\frac{1}{2}$	tsp. paprika	2 mL
$\frac{1}{4}$	tsp. cayenne pepper or to taste	1 mL
1	small zucchini, sliced	
Salt and pepper to taste		
1	cup couscous (not quick-cooking)	250 mL
$\frac{1}{4}$	cup water or skim milk	50 mL
6	single, boneless chicken breasts, skinned	
Fresh parsley sprigs for garnish		

Heat the oil in a large, heavy saucepan and sauté the onion and leek until soft. Add the remaining vegetables, stock, tomatoes, and chick peas. Then add the coriander, cumin, paprika, and cayenne. Bring to a boil, then reduce heat; simmer for 30 minutes. Add the zucchini and cook 15 minutes longer or until the vegetables are tender. Season with salt and pepper.

Soak the couscous for 10 minutes in a bowl in water to cover. Place in a steamer lined with a tea towel and steam for 30 minutes. Spread on a cookie sheet, separating the grains with a fork. Pour the water or milk over, stirring to coat the grains. Bake at 350°F/180°C for 15 minutes.

Grill the chicken for 3–4 minutes per side or until just cooked. Serve the chicken, vegetables, and couscous on separate warm platters garnished with parsley.

Kasha Pilaf

Calories 119
Protein 4 g
Fat 6 g
Carbohydrate 14 g

Serves 6 as a side dish.

A specialty of Eastern Europe. This tasty version combines the nutty flavour of buckwheat with the crunch of almonds. Serve as a side dish with meat, chicken, or fish.

2	tsp. corn, safflower, soybean, or sunflower oil	10 mL
1	medium onion, finely chopped	
1	cup toasted buckwheat (kasha)	250 mL
1	egg, lightly beaten	
$1\frac{3}{4}$	cups water or stock	425 mL
Salt and pepper to taste		
$\frac{1}{2}$	cup slivered almonds, toasted (see page 98)	125 mL

Heat the oil in a Dutch oven and sauté the onion until soft. Add the kasha and egg. Cook, stirring, over medium heat until the egg sets, about 2 minutes. Add the water and bring to a boil. Cover and place in the oven at 350°F/ 180°C. Bake for about 20 minutes or until the liquid is absorbed. Season with salt and pepper. Sprinkle with the almonds.

Note: Toasted buckwheat, or kasha, is available in health food stores and specialty sections of supermarkets.

Calories	276
Protein	20 g
Fat	8 g
Carbohydrate	36 g

Risotto with Fish

Serves 6–8.

A novel version of an Italian rice stand-by, this can also be made with shrimp, mussels, or other seafood.

2½–3	cups fish or chicken stock	625–750 mL
1	tbsp. corn, safflower, soybean, or sunflower oil	15 mL
1	medium onion, finely chopped	
2	cups arborio Italian short-grain rice	500 mL
1	cup dry white wine	250 mL
1	lb. firm-fleshed fish (cod, halibut, monkfish, etc.)	500 g
3	tbsp. finely chopped fresh basil	45 mL
1	cup freshly grated Parmesan cheese	250 mL
Salt and pepper to taste		
3	tbsp. finely chopped fresh parsley for garnish	45 mL

Bring the stock to a boil in a medium-sized saucepan. Reduce heat and simmer.

Heat the oil in a large, heavy saucepan. Add the onion and sauté until soft. Add the rice and cook, stirring, until transparent. Add the wine and bring to a boil. Reduce heat and simmer, stirring, until the liquid is almost absorbed, about 4 minutes. Add 1 cup/250 mL of the hot stock. Simmer, stirring, until almost absorbed, about 10 minutes. Add 1 cup/250 mL more of the stock. Simmer, stirring, until almost absorbed, about 10 minutes. Add the fish and cook for about 10 minutes, gradually adding as much of the remaining stock as is required to cook the rice and still be absorbed. Stir in the basil, Parmesan, salt, and pepper. Sprinkle with parsley.

Calories 100
Protein 4 g
Fat 2 g
Carbohydrate 18 g
(per $\frac{1}{2}$ cup/125 mL)

Pizza Tomato Sauce

Makes about $2\frac{1}{4}$ cups/550 mL, or enough for four
9-inch/23-cm pizzas.

The secret to this rich and smooth sauce is long, slow
simmering and sieving out the seeds. Well worth the time
and effort, this sauce freezes well.

1	28-oz./796-mL can Italian plum tomatoes	
$1\frac{1}{2}$	tsp. olive oil	7 mL
1	small onion, finely chopped	
2	cloves garlic, finely chopped	
1	$5\frac{1}{2}$-oz./156-mL can tomato paste	
1	tsp. brown or white sugar	5 mL
1	tsp. dried oregano	5 mL

Good pinch each dried basil and thyme
Salt and pepper to taste

Process the tomatoes in a food processor or blender until
puréed. Strain through a sieve to remove the seeds.
    Heat the oil in a heavy saucepan. Add the onion and
garlic; sauté until soft. Add the puréed tomatoes, tomato
paste, sugar, oregano, basil, and thyme. Bring to a boil,
reduce heat, and simmer, uncovered, for about 1 hour or
until thick. Season with salt and pepper. Cool before
spreading on pizza dough.

Whole-Wheat Pizza Dough

Calories 701
Protein 20 g
Fat 17 g
Carbohydrate 120 g
(per pizza)

Makes enough dough for two 9-inch/23-cm pizzas.

Pizza is one of the most nutritious, versatile, and popular foods in existence. Fancy it up with artichokes and roasted peppers or go the traditional route with green peppers and mushrooms. This crust is simple to make and freezes well.

$\frac{3}{4}$	cup lukewarm water	175 mL
1	tsp. granulated sugar	5 mL
1	envelope (1 tbsp./15 mL) dry yeast	
2	tbsp. corn, safflower, soybean, or sun-flower oil	25 mL
$\frac{1}{2}$	tsp. salt	2 mL
$1\frac{1}{2}$	cups whole-wheat flour	375 mL
1	cup all-purpose flour	250 mL

Combine the water, sugar, and yeast in a small bowl. Set aside for 5–15 minutes or until foamy. Stir in the oil and blend well.

Combine the salt and flours in a large bowl. Stir in the yeast mixture to form a soft dough that pulls away from the sides of the bowl. Turn the dough onto a floured surface and sprinkle with a little flour. Knead for about 5 minutes or until the dough is smooth and elastic, adding a little more all-purpose flour if required. Place the dough in a large, lightly oiled bowl. Cover with a clean tea towel and let rise in a warm place for 40 minutes to 1 hour or until the dough has doubled in bulk.

Punch the dough down. Knead for about 1 minute, adding a little flour if it is sticky. Cut the dough in half. Roll each piece of dough on a lightly floured surface using a rolling pin or stretching with your hands to form a 9-inch/23-cm round of dough.

Place the dough on lightly oiled baking sheets or pizza pans. Top with Pizza Tomato Sauce (see page 105), grated skim-milk mozzarella, and your favourite toppings. Bake at 450°F/230°C for about 15 minutes or until the crust is brown on the bottom.

Note: For a thicker, softer crust, cover the rolled dough rounds with a clean towel and let them rest on a baking sheet in a warm place for about 30 minutes before adding the toppings.

Calories	96
Protein	2 g
Fat	4 g
Carbohydrate	13 g

Citrus Carrot Bread

Makes about 18 slices.

What a great way to eat those veggies!

$1\frac{1}{4}$	cups whole-wheat flour	300 mL
1	tsp. cinnamon	5 mL
$\frac{1}{2}$	tsp. baking powder	2 mL
$\frac{1}{2}$	tsp. baking soda	2 mL
$\frac{1}{4}$	tsp. salt	1 mL
2	eggs, lightly beaten	
	Grated peel of 1 orange and 1 lemon	
$\frac{1}{4}$	cup unsweetened orange juice	50 mL
1	tbsp. lemon juice	15 mL
$\frac{1}{4}$	cup liquid honey	50 mL
$\frac{1}{4}$	cup corn, safflower, soybean, or sunflower oil	50 mL
1	cup shredded carrots	250 mL
$\frac{1}{2}$	cup chopped walnuts	125 mL
$\frac{1}{2}$	cup raisins	125 mL

Sift together the first five ingredients in a large bowl.

Beat the eggs, orange and lemon peel, orange juice, lemon juice, honey, and oil in a medium-sized bowl. Stir this mixture into the dry ingredients just until the mixture is moistened. Stir in the carrots, walnuts, and raisins. Pour the batter into a lightly greased and floured 9 × 5 × 3 inch/2 L loaf pan.

Bake at 350°F/180°C for about 1 hour or until a toothpick comes out clean. Cool for 10 minutes, then remove from the pan. Cool on a wire rack.

Lemon Loaf

Makes 18 slices.

Perfect tea time or snacking fare with lots of fibre and plenty of taste and texture.

$\frac{3}{4}$	cup all-purpose flour	175 mL
$\frac{3}{4}$	cup whole-wheat flour	175 mL
$\frac{3}{4}$	cup granulated sugar	175 mL
1	tbsp. baking powder	15 mL
$\frac{1}{2}$	tsp. salt	2 mL
2	eggs, lightly beaten	
$\frac{1}{2}$	cup soft margarine, melted	125 mL
$\frac{1}{2}$	cup water	125 mL
3	tbsp. lemon juice	45 mL
	Grated peel of 1 lemon	
1	cup homemade granola (see page 175)	250 mL

Topping		
1	tbsp. all-purpose flour	15 mL
1	tbsp. brown sugar	15 mL
$1\frac{1}{2}$	tsp. soft margarine	7 mL
	Grated peel of $\frac{1}{2}$ lemon	
2	tbsp. homemade granola (see page 175)	25 mL

Sift together the flours, sugar, baking powder, and salt in a large bowl.

Combine the eggs, margarine, water, lemon juice, and lemon peel in a medium-sized bowl. Add this mixture to the dry ingredients, stirring just until moistened. Stir in the granola. Pour into a lighty greased and floured 9 × 5 × 3 inch/2 L loaf pan.

To make the topping, blend together the flour, sugar, and margarine in a small bowl with a fork. Stir in the lemon peel and granola. Sprinkle this mixture on top of the cake batter.

Bake at 350°F/180°C for 45 minutes or until a toothpick comes out clean. Cool for 10 minutes. Remove from the pan and cool on a wire rack.

Nutty Apricot Bread

Calories 131
Protein 3 g
Fat 4 g
Carbohydrate 21 g

Makes about 18 slices.

You'd be nuts not to like this super-healthy snacking cake filled with dried fruit and nuts.

1	cup whole-wheat flour	250 mL
1	cup all-purpose flour	250 mL
1	tbsp. baking powder	15 mL
1	tsp. baking soda	5 mL
$\frac{1}{2}$	tsp. salt	2 mL
$\frac{1}{2}$	tsp. cinnamon	2 mL
$\frac{1}{2}$	tsp. ground ginger	2 mL
$\frac{1}{2}$	cup granulated sugar	125 mL
1	cup chopped dried apricots	250 mL
$\frac{1}{2}$	cup chopped walnuts	125 mL
1	egg	
$\frac{1}{4}$	cup corn, safflower, soybean, or sun-flower oil	50 mL
$\frac{3}{4}$	cup unsweetened orange juice	175 mL
$\frac{1}{2}$	cup skim milk	125 mL

Grated rind of 1 orange

Sift together the first seven ingredients in a large bowl. Stir in the sugar, apricots, and walnuts.

Beat the egg in a medium-sized bowl. Slowly whisk in the oil, orange juice, milk, and orange rind. Pour into the centre of the flour mixture. Stir only until the mixture is moistened. Pour the batter into a lightly greased and floured 9 × 5 × 3 inch/2 L loaf pan.

Bake at 350°F/180°C for about 1 hour or until a toothpick comes out clean. Cool for 10 minutes, then remove from the pan. Cool on a wire rack.

Calories 126
Protein 3 g
Fat 5 g
Carbohydrate 19 g

Bonanza Banana Bread

Makes 18 slices.

Kids will go bananas over this one. Mash those overripe bananas and store them in the freezer until you have the time to make this. It'll be gone in no time!

1½	cups whole-wheat flour	375 mL
2	tsp. baking powder	10 mL
¼	tsp. baking soda	1 mL
½	tsp. salt	2 mL
½	tsp. cinnamon	2 mL
Pinch nutmeg		
½	cup granulated sugar	125 mL
¼	cup wheat germ	50 mL
2	eggs	
⅓	cup corn, safflower, soybean, or sunflower oil	75 mL
1	cup ripe, mashed bananas	250 mL
½	cup carob chips	125 mL

Sift together the first six ingredients in a large bowl. Stir in the sugar and wheat germ; mix well.

Beat the eggs, oil, and mashed bananas together in a medium-sized bowl. Pour into the centre of the dry ingredients and stir only until the mixture is moistened. Stir in the carob chips. Pour the batter into a lightly greased and floured 9 × 5 × 3 inch/2 L loaf pan.

Bake at 350°F/180°C for 50–60 minutes or until a toothpick comes out clean. Cool for 10 minutes, then remove from the pan. Cool on a wire rack.

5   Eat Your Fruits and Veggies

Fruits and vegetables are included in the same food group because they contain similar nutrients. And a pretty impressive list they are: vitamin A, vitamin C, thiamin, folacin, iron, trace minerals (potassium, iodine, copper, and zinc), carbohydrate, and fibre.

Vital Vitamins

The yellowish-orange pigment in fruits and vegetables comes from carotene, also known as provitamin A. Carotene also exists in green vegetables, but its colour is masked by the green chlorophyl. Carotene is converted by the body into physiologically active vitamin A.

Fruits and vegetables are the prime sources of vitamin C—another important vitamin. (See the discussion in Chapter 1.) However, many of the foods we depend on for a natural source of vitamin C are seasonal and thus not always easily available. So many products are fortified with it—in particular, fruit and vegetable juices and drinks. But this practice also has its nutritional hazards.

Fruit drinks fortified with vitamin C may or may not be made with any real fruits or vegetables, so that the only vitamin or mineral they often contain is vitamin C. Unfortunately, such beverages often contain less wholesome ingredients—namely, sugar, colouring, and flavouring. The addition of water, common in many of these drinks, makes them a waste of your food dollar. For example, orange drink contains only vitamin C. Orange juice, on the other hand, contains vitamin C, vitamin A, B vitamins like folic acid, and minerals such as potassium, phosphorus, iron, magnesium, and zinc.

More Reasons to Eat Your Fruits and Veggies

Folacin is an important B vitamin found in vegetables like asparagus, beets, broccoli, Brussels sprouts, and spinach. Fruits that contain folacin include avocados, cantaloupe, and oranges. Iron, a vital mineral, is supplied by such dried fruits as apricots, dates, prunes, and raisins. It also exists in vegetables like lima beans, beet greens, peas, and spinach.

The foods in the fruit and vegetable food group are

FRUITS AND VEGETABLES RICH IN BETA-CAROTENE

Avocados

Beet Greens

Broccoli

Carrots

Chard

Escarole

Kale

Mustard greens

Pumpkin

Spinach

Squash, winter

Sweet potatoes

Watercress

Apricots

Cantaloupe

Mangoes

Nectarines

Papayas

Peaches

Persimmons

Plantain

extremely important because they often contain both soluble and insoluble fibres in combination. Here are a few tips on how to maximize the fibre content of these foods:

• Eat raw fruits and vegetables as often as you can.

• Whenever possible, don't peel fruits or vegetables; otherwise, you are throwing away valuable fibre along with the peel. The peel also acts as a barrier against vitamin and mineral loss from exposure to air and water.

• Given the choice between raw fruits and vegetables and their juices, opt for the whole product—it contains more fibre than juice does. Anyone who has used a juicing machine has likely noticed the fruit and vegetable fibre left behind in the machine's filter. Puréeing fruit and vegetables is fine; it does not remove fibre the way juicing does.

More Fibre and More Water Mean Fewer Calories
One reason to increase the amount of fibre in your diet is that high-fibre foods fill you up without loading on the calories. And the fruit and vegetable group is a terrific source of this benefit. Adding a large spinach salad, doused in a low-fat yogurt dressing laced with herbs, and a stalk of perfectly steamed broccoli to your evening meal is worth its weight in satisfaction at minimal caloric expense.

Blueberries	Asparagus
Cantaloupe	Beet greens
Grapefruits	Broccoli
Guavas	Brussels sprouts
Honeydew melons	Cabbage
Kiwi fruit	Cauliflower
Lemons	Chard
Limes	Kale
Loganberries	Lima beans
Lychees	Mustard greens
Mangoes	Peppers, green and red
Oranges	Spinach
Papayas	Tomatoes
Raisins	Turnips
Red currants	Watercress
Strawberries	

Juices from the above or
enriched with vitamin C

Fruits and vegetables are also high in another filling substance that is particularly low in calories—water. Water fills you up more quickly than whipped cream, and without the unfortunate caloric side effects. Imagine eating a large four- to six-ounce wedge cut from a heavy head of cabbage. Its volume would take up a sizable space in your stomach and fill you up more than a calorie-dense protein food such as a piece of meat.

Another reason to eat plenty of fruit and veg is that the more you eat of them, the less you'll eat of protein foods like meat that tend to be comparatively high in fat. A good time to eat a lot of foods from this food group is at your evening meal, when you need fewer calories and less fuel.

Fruit and Veg Have a Healthy Edge
There is some indication that certain fruits and vegetables can help prevent certain cancers. The specific nutrients that may cause this prevention have not been identified, however, so taking supplements rather than eating the foods themselves is not advisable.

Cruciferous vegetables may reduce the risk of colon cancer. They include cauliflower, cabbage, broccoli, Brussels sprouts, kohlrabi, rutabagas, turnips, and kale. The mechanism by which these vegetables seem to help block the formation of colon cancer is still under investigation.

It is not known whether it is the vitamin A or another substance in carotene-containing foods that may help prevent cancer of the lung, mouth, larynx, bladder, and esophagus. Vitamin A tablets, therefore, are not the answer. Eating foods rich in beta-carotene, however, is certainly a good idea.

It is thought that vitamin C might reduce the incidence of gastric and esophageal cancers. It may also have another benefit—inhibiting the formation in the body of nitroso compounds, which are carcinogenic.

The type of fibre that seems to provide some protection against cancer has not yet been identified. The best way to cover all the fibre angles, therefore, is to eat a good variety of fruits and vegetables.

The Key Is in the Cooking

Fruits and vegetables are the most vulnerable of all foods to nutrient loss during storage and cooking. Most often it is vitamin C and some B vitamins that are lost. Here are some tips on how to treat this food group with nutritional tender, loving care:

- Store vegetables in plastic bags or crispers in the fridge.

- Do not wash or trim produce before storing. Nutrient loss occurs because peeling, slicing, and scraping damages cells and releases enzymes that rapidly reduce vitamin content. It is therefore not a good idea to wash, peel, and slice vegetables in the morning for your evening dinner in order to speed up preparation—you will be losing valuable nutrients on a regular basis. However, doing this on the odd occasion for a dinner party is acceptable.

- Whenever possible, don't peel fruits or vegetables before cooking. Skin and peel are the barriers that prevent nutrients from leaching into cooking water.

- We don't advise you to add baking soda to the water when cooking vegetables to intensify their colour. This destroys some of the thiamin.

- Vitamin C and some B vitamins are most easily lost

when you are cooking fruits and vegetables because they leach into the water. The best way to avoid this can be summed up in one word—*minimalism*. Use as little cooking liquid as possible, and cook foods—covered—for as short a time as possible. Steaming and microwaving are the two best methods. Using the cooking liquid from vegetables in soups and sauces saves valuable nutrients from being thrown down the sink. Covering foods exposed to air before consuming them is another good idea. Eating them raw is, of course, tops!

- When you refrigerate foods, cover them whenever possible to minimize exposure to air, which causes vitamin loss. An opened can of juice, for example, loses its vitamin C after four days, even in the fridge. If you have trouble finishing a large can of juice in this length of time, buy smaller containers of it.

- Leaving cut-up celery, carrots, and other vegetables sitting in a glass of water in the fridge for easy snacking is not the great idea it might seem. Although vegetables stay crisp this way, they also lose most of their water-soluble vitamins, along with their nutrients, to the air and water. A better way to store raw veggies for quick snacks is to cut them up, then store them in a plastic bag or plastic wrap—without water. Even this won't preserve all the nutrients, so make sure you get them from other foods in your diet.

- When you choose fresh fruits and vegetables, use this simple rule of thumb: if the item looks fresh, it has likely retained its nutrients. If it is past its prime, so is its nutritional quality. For this reason, fruits and vegetables that have been frozen at their peak of freshness are a better choice than "fresh" ones of dubious freshness.

- When freezing your own fruits and vegetables, be sure to package them in airtight plastic bags or containers, not to defrost and then refreeze them, and to keep your freezer at the optimum temperature. When buying frozen vegetables, avoid those with calorie-laden sauces. Frozen fruits that don't contain added sugar are a better idea than their sugary counterparts.

- It's a good idea to blanch fruits and vegetables by plunging them into boiling and then cold water before freezing (consult a basic cookbook for instructions); this process destroys certain enzymes that cause the quality of such products to deteriorate.

Although frozen fruits and vegetables are often a good choice, canned foods from this group have serious drawbacks. Canned fruits and vegetables are tempting because they are so easy to use, but they usually contain a lot of salt and sometimes less fibre after undergoing the cooking process. Rinsing canned vegetables can remove some salt, but it washes away flavour and nutrients too. Of course, items like canned artichokes and canned tomatoes are wonderfully handy replacements for the real, fresh thing, which in both cases is strictly seasonal. Canned tomatoes in particular are almost indispensable for much of the year for making pasta sauces and other stand-bys. Buying the new low-salt versions is a good idea. Fruits canned in water or their own juice are a better choice than those canned in syrup. The main thing to remember is that canned fruits and vegetables should not be used exclusively as sources of these foods.

Some Are Not Your Daily Veg

Just as they can be one of the most nutrition-packed of all foods, vegetables can also be sneaky carriers of some substances we can do without—namely, hidden fats.

This is particularly common with vegetable dishes served in restaurants. Items that appear to be a wise nutritional choice are often prepared in such a way that they come to the table laden with hidden fats. Ratatouille, for example, is often made with large amounts of oil, which is easily absorbed by the eggplant, zucchini, and mushrooms. When cooking this dish at home, however, you can grill or fry the same vegetables using only small amounts of oil with healthier as well as tastier results.

Vegetables that have been coated in batter, deep-fried, or both are also the bearers of bad nutritional news. And onion rings and french fries don't even try to hide the fats!

Another instance where a potentially nutritious vegetable intake can have dubious benefit is at the salad bar, and the main culprit here is the dressings. When you add salad dressing from one of those oversized ladles, be careful not to go the whole hog. Pour on a small amount. Marinated salads are already dressed and contain a lot of fat, so avoid them or eat them in moderation. When ordering a salad from a menu, ask for the dressing to be served on the side. Not only does this usually make the salad taste better (so many restaurants drown their salads in dressing), but it is also much healthier and lower in calories. In general, it is wise to check out a salad bar first to see how fresh the salads are; if they're not, they will have lost a lot of their nutrients. Old salad dressings could also be a cause of food poisoning.

When you make a salad at home, serve the dressing separately. And when you garnish cooked vegetables, don't smear them with butter. A dollop of unflavoured yogurt topped with a spoonful of freshly snipped herbs is healthier and tastes delicious.

Calories 199
Protein 12 g
Fat 15 g
Carbohydrate 6 g

Tomato Salad Caprese

Serves 4 as an appetizer.

This dish is near and dear to our hearts because it was
our most popular homemade lunch while we collabo-
rated on this book. Eaten with a loaf of crusty Italian
bread, this salad makes a heaven-sent lunch or light supper that's nutritious, low in calories, and bursting with flavour—especially in late summer, when field tomatoes
and fresh basil are at their peak. Bocconcini can be found
at Italian cheese stores. If unavailable, use part skim-milk
mozzarella.

2	large or 3 medium, ripe, fresh field tomatoes	
6	oz. (4 balls) bocconcini cheese	175 g
2	tbsp. extra-virgin olive oil	25 mL
$\frac{1}{4}$	cup snipped fresh basil	50 mL

Salt and plenty of freshly ground black pepper
to taste

Slice the tomatoes and bocconcini about $\frac{1}{4}$ inch/$\frac{1}{2}$ cm
thick. Arrange the tomatoes on a serving platter or plates
so that they slightly overlap. Place the bocconcini slices
on top of each tomato slice. Drizzle with the oil and
sprinkle with the basil, salt, and pepper.

Calories 277
Protein 32 g
Fat 9 g
Carbohydrate 19 g

Nutritious Niçoise

Serves 2 as a main dish with crusty bread.

This new twist to the traditional Niçoise salad keeps the tuna, omits the olives, and adds a nifty honey-mustard dressing that can be used on almost any salad combo.

Dressing

$\frac{1}{2}$	cup 2% plain yogurt	125 mL
1	tbsp. light or tofu mayonnaise (see page 208)	15 mL
2	tsp. honey	10 mL
1	tsp. lemon juice	5 mL
2	tsp. prepared mustard	10 mL
1	tsp. finely chopped fresh parsley	5 mL
1	green onion, chopped	

Salt and pepper to taste

1	7-oz./198-g can water-packed tuna, drained	
1	cup sliced mushrooms	250 mL

Leaf lettuce

1	tomato, cut into wedges	
1	hard-boiled egg, sliced	

Blend the dressing ingredients in a food processor or blender until smooth. Chill.

Combine the tuna and mushrooms in a bowl. Line each plate with lettuce. Top with the tuna mixture and garnish with the tomato and egg. Drizzle the dressing over the top.

Cranberry Chestnut Salad

Calories 159
Protein 1 g
Fat 6 g
Carbohydrate 25 g

Serves 8.

This is the perfect salad to go with that Thanksgiving turkey—a sweet and sour, soft and crunchy match made in heaven. This fibre-full creation looks as magnificent as it tastes.

1 $\frac{1}{2}$	cups fresh cranberries, coarsely chopped	375 mL
2	tbsp. granulated sugar	25 mL
1	cup sweet chestnuts	250 mL
2	tbsp. lemon juice	25 mL
$\frac{1}{4}$	cup cranberry juice	50 mL
1	tbsp. Dijon mustard	15 mL
Salt and pepper to taste		
3	tbsp. virgin olive oil	45 mL
3	unpeeled tart apples (like Granny Smith), cored and diced	
4	green onions, chopped	
2	bunches watercress	

Toss the cranberries with the sugar in a bowl. Let sit, covered, in the fridge for at least 1 hour.

Slice an x into the flat side of each chestnut with a small, sharp knife. Add to a pot of boiling water and cook for about 5 minutes or until the skin is soft. Peel while still warm, using the same knife.

Whisk together the lemon juice, cranberry juice, mustard, salt, and pepper in a large bowl. Add the oil in a thin stream, whisking constantly until well blended. Add the apples, chestnuts, and green onion and toss. Let sit in the fridge, covered, for at least 1 but no more than 4 hours.

To serve, line a large salad bowl or attractive serving platter with watercress. Place the apple mixture around the edge and the cranberries in the middle.

Spinach Orange Salad

Calories 187
Protein 4 g
Fat 8 g
Carbohydrate 29 g

Serves 4.

An iron-clad creation with a delicious fruity dressing.

4	large navel oranges	
2	small red onions, sliced into rings	
1	tsp. red or white wine vinegar	5 mL
2	tbsp. corn, safflower, soybean, or sun-flower oil	25 mL
1	clove garlic, minced	
	Salt and pepper to taste	
4	cups loosely packed fresh spinach, washed, dried, and with coarse stems removed	1 L

Peel the oranges and slice them thinly crosswise over a shallow dish to catch their juice. Chill the orange slices for 30 minutes. Soak the onion rings in cold water to cover for 30 minutes to remove their sharp taste.

Whisk together $\frac{1}{4}$ cup/50 mL of the reserved orange juice with the vinegar, oil, and garlic. Season with salt and pepper. Drain the onions. To serve, arrange the orange and onion slices on a bed of spinach. Drizzle with dressing.

Calories 128
Protein 4 g
Fat 3 g
Carbohydrate 22 g

Fruity Carrot Salad

Serves 4 as a side salad or appetizer.

Seeing in the dark never looked this good!

$\frac{1}{4}$	cup raisins	50 mL
2	tbsp. unsweetened pineapple juice (from can of tidbits, see below)	25 mL
4	medium carrots (about 4 cups/1 L), peeled and shredded	
1	cup drained unsweetened pineapple tidbits	250 mL
4	tsp. light or tofu mayonnaise (see page 208)	20 mL
$\frac{1}{3}$	cup 2% plain yogurt	75 mL

Soak the raisins in the pineapple juice in a small bowl for a few minutes. Then combine the carrots, pineapple tidbits, and raisins with their soaking liquid in a salad bowl.

Whisk together the mayonnaise and yogurt in a small bowl. Add to the carrot mixture and toss well.

Calories 148
Protein 1 g
Fat 16 g
Carbohydrate 2 g
(entire recipe)

Slim Jim Vinaigrette

Makes about $\frac{3}{4}$ cup/175 mL.

Substituting chicken stock for most of the oil makes this vinaigrette amazingly low in fat. It is also amazingly tasty. This version uses a little soy sauce; if you are trying to cut down on salt, just omit it. If you prefer lemon juice to vinegar, use it instead. If you don't have homemade chicken stock on hand, use a bouillon cube and omit the soy sauce.

1	clove garlic, minced	
1	tbsp. Dijon mustard	15 mL
3	tbsp. cider, tarragon, or wine vinegar	45 mL
$\frac{1}{2}$	cup homemade chicken stock (see page 46–47)	125 mL
1	tbsp. virgin olive oil	15 mL

Salt and freshly ground black pepper to taste

Whisk together the garlic, mustard, vinegar, and chicken stock in a small bowl until well blended. Add the oil in a thin stream, whisking constantly, until well blended. Season with salt and pepper. Store in an airtight jar in the fridge.

Note: Instead of whisking, you can blend this dressing by shaking all the ingredients together in a screw-top jar. If the chicken stock is thick and gelatinous when chilled, bring the dressing to room temperature before using.

Buttermilk Salad Dressing

Calories 208
Protein 6 g
Fat 16 g
Carbohydrate 10 g
(entire recipe)

Makes about $\frac{3}{4}$ cup/175 mL.

Get the calcium and other goodies of buttermilk and yogurt but hardly any fat in this refreshing dressing, which is perfect for coleslaw or assorted blanched vegetables.

1	clove garlic, minced	
1	tbsp. chopped green onion	15 mL
$\frac{1}{4}$	tsp. dried mustard	1 mL
$\frac{1}{4}$	tsp. paprika	1 mL
$\frac{1}{2}$	tsp. dried or 1 tsp. chopped fresh tarragon	2 mL/5 mL
1	tsp. white wine vinegar	5 mL
1	tbsp. corn, safflower, soybean, or sunflower oil	15 mL
$\frac{1}{4}$	cup buttermilk	50 mL
$\frac{1}{2}$	cup 2% plain yogurt	125 mL

Salt and pepper to taste

Process all the ingredients except the yogurt, salt, and pepper in a food processor or blender until smooth. Pour into a bowl, then stir in the yogurt until blended. Season with salt and pepper. Store in an airtight jar in the fridge. It keeps in the fridge for about 1 week.

Fabulous Feta Salad Dressing

Calories 94
Protein 2 g
Fat 6 g
Carbohydrate 1 g
(per tablespoon)

Makes about $\frac{3}{4}$ cup/175 mL.

A zesty dressing with the calcium and bite of feta combined with the Mediterranean flavour of oregano. It's good on any salad but superb on one made with fresh, ripe tomatoes, cucumber slices, and plenty of chopped fresh parsley. It's high in calories but also in protein, so a little of this goes a long way.

$\frac{3}{4}$	cup loosely packed, crumbled feta cheese	175 mL
Juice of $\frac{1}{2}$ lemon		
1	clove garlic, minced	
$\frac{1}{2}$	tsp. dried or 1 tsp. chopped fresh oregano	2 mL/5 mL
Dash Worcestershire sauce		
2	tbsp. virgin olive oil	25 mL
$\frac{1}{4}$	cup corn, safflower, soybean, or sunflower oil	50 mL
Freshly ground pepper to taste		

Process all the ingredients except the oils and pepper in a food processor or blender until smooth. Add the oils in a thin stream, then process again until the dressing is well blended and slightly thickened. Store in an airtight jar in the fridge.

Cottage Blue Cheese Dressing

Calories 263
Protein 19 g
Fat 17 g
Carbohydrate 7 g
(entire recipe)

Makes about 1 cup/250 mL.

A low-fat, top-notch version of an all-time favourite, this dressing is great on a spinach salad or one made with romaine and chopped nuts. Its extra protein makes it a terrific choice for a main-dish salad. Try to use a creamy, low-fat cottage cheese for this, not a dry one. You don't have to skimp on this if you're watching your fat intake.

$\frac{1}{4}$	cup loosely packed, crumbled blue cheese	50 mL
$\frac{1}{3}$	cup 2% cottage cheese	75 mL
$\frac{1}{3}$	cup 2% plain yogurt	75 mL
1	tsp. lemon juice	5 mL
1	clove garlic, minced	
$\frac{1}{4}$	tsp. Worcestershire sauce	1 mL

Freshly ground pepper to taste

Process the blue cheese and cottage cheese in a food processor or blender until smooth. Pour into a bowl and stir in the remaining ingredients. Mix until blended. Store in an airtight jar in the fridge.

Vegetable Stock

Calories *1
Protein *1 g
Fat *1 g
Carbohydrate *1 g

*Less than

Makes about 5 cups/1.25 L.

A must for vegetarians to use in soups and sauces and a great idea for anyone who wants to maximize the nutrients of veggies. Save half-used onions, celery leaves, and any imperfect vegetables to make this stock. Avoid strong vegetables like cabbage, turnips, and cauliflower, which will overpower the flavour.

1	tsp. corn, safflower, soybean, or sun-	5 mL
	flower oil	
1	cup chopped onion	250 mL
1	cup chopped leeks	250 mL
1	cup chopped celery	250 mL
1	cup chopped carrots	250 mL
1	cup chopped tomatoes	250 mL
1	bouquet garni (see page 47)	
8	cups cold water	2 L

Heat the oil in a large, heavy stockpot. Add the onion and leeks; sauté until soft. Add the remaining ingredients and bring to a boil. Reduce heat and simmer, uncovered, for 45 minutes or until the vegetables are tender. Strain. Store in the fridge or freeze in plastic containers.

Cold Summer Veggie Soup

Calories 93
Protein 7 g
Fat 1 g
Carbohydrate 16 g

Serves 6.

The refreshing flavour of buttermilk enhances a bevy of fresh vegetables in this nourishing cold soup.

4	cups buttermilk	1 L
2	cups unpeeled, chopped zucchini	500 mL
2	tsp. Dijon mustard	10 mL
2	tomatoes, peeled, seeded, and finely chopped (see page 86)	
1	green pepper, finely chopped	
$\frac{1}{4}$	cup chopped fresh dill	50 mL
	Salt and pepper to taste	
3	green onions, finely chopped, for garnish	

Process 1 cup/250 mL of the buttermilk with the zucchini and mustard in a food processor or blender until smooth. Pour into a large bowl. Add the remaining buttermilk, tomatoes, green pepper, dill, salt, and pepper. Chill. To serve, garnish each bowl with green onion.

Calories 131
Protein 2 g
Fat 3 g
Carbohydrate 26 g

Carrot Soup

Serves 6.

The taste combination of carrots and orange juice sets this soup apart from most others. What's more, it's loaded with beta-carotene. Substitute $\frac{1}{2}$ tsp./2 mL dried ginger for fresh ginger root if you wish.

1	tbsp. corn, safflower, soybean, or sunflower oil	15 mL
1	tsp. finely chopped fresh ginger root	5 mL
1	medium onion, chopped	
9	medium carrots, scrubbed and thinly sliced	
3	cups vegetable or chicken stock	750 mL
1	cup unsweetened orange juice	250 mL
Salt and pepper to taste		
2	tbsp. chopped fresh parsley for garnish	25 mL

Heat the oil in a large, heavy saucepan. Add the ginger root and onion; sauté until soft. Add the carrots and stock and bring to a boil. Reduce heat and simmer, uncovered, for 25 minutes or until the carrots are tender.

Process the carrot mixture in a food processor or blender until smooth. Return to the saucepan and add the orange juice, salt, and pepper. Cook until heated through. To serve, sprinkle each bowl of soup with parsley.

Calories	87
Protein	4 g
Fat	3 g
Carbohydrate	13 g

Zucchini Soup

Serves 6–8.

This flavourful soup is just as good made with broccoli or cauliflower and is out of this world made with green beans.

1	tbsp. corn, safflower, soybean, or sun-flower oil	15 mL
2	medium onions, finely chopped	
1	leek, finely chopped	
7–8	unpeeled, medium zucchini (about 2 lb./ 1 Kg), thinly sliced	
$3\frac{1}{2}$	cups vegetable or chicken stock	875 mL
2	bay leaves	
$\frac{1}{2}$	tsp. dried or 1 tbsp. chopped fresh thyme	12 mL/15 mL
$\frac{1}{2}$	tsp. dried or 1 tbsp. chopped fresh oregano	2 mL/15 mL
$\frac{1}{2}$	tsp. dried or 1 tbsp. chopped fresh basil	2 mL/15 mL
1	cup 2% milk	250 mL

Salt and pepper to taste

Heat the oil in a large, heavy saucepan. Add the onions and leek and sauté until soft. Add the zucchini, reserving about 12 slices for garnish. Add the stock, bay leaves, thyme, oregano, and basil. Bring to a boil, then reduce heat and simmer, covered, for about 30 minutes. Discard the bay leaves.

Process the zucchini mixture in a food processor or blender until smooth. Return to the saucepan. Add the milk and cook until heated through. Season with salt and pepper. To serve, garnish each bowl with zucchini slices.

Note: If using fresh herbs, add them with the milk at the end of the cooking time.

Calories   63
Protein   2 g
Fat   1 g
Carbohydrate 14 g

Tomato Orange Soup

Serves 6.

Unsurpassed when made with ripe tomatoes fresh from the field at peak season. This soup tastes great hot or cold and is extremely low in calories yet high in vitamins and minerals. This recipe involves no sautéeing in fat; all the veggies are poached. The delectable results speak for themselves.

4	cups homemade chicken stock (see pages 46–47)	1 L
2	lb. fresh or 1 28-oz./796-mL can tomatoes, peeled, seeded, and chopped (see page 86)	1 Kg
1	tbsp. tomato paste	15 mL
1	medium onion, finely chopped	
1	carrot, finely chopped	

Juice and finely grated peel of 1 orange

1	bay leaf	
1	tsp. dried or 1 tbsp. chopped fresh basil	5 mL/15 mL
1	tbsp. frozen unsweetened orange juice concentrate (undiluted) or to taste	15 mL

Pinch sugar
Salt and pepper to taste
Fresh basil leaves or chopped parsley for garnish

Bring the chicken stock to a boil in a large, heavy saucepan. Add the tomatoes, tomato paste, onion, carrot, orange juice, orange peel, and bay leaf. Return to the boil, then reduce heat and simmer, uncovered, for about 20 minutes or until the carrots are tender. Discard the bay leaf.

Process the tomato mixture in a food processor or blender until smooth. Return to the saucepan. Add the basil, orange juice concentrate, sugar, salt, and pepper and cook until heated through. Can be served hot or cold. Garnish with basil or parsley.

Calories	68
Protein	3 g
Fat	1 g
Carbohydrate	15 g

Gazpacho

Serves 6.

A cold soup *par excellence* that tastes just as good without the lashings of olive oil used in the Spanish original. Avoid using a brand of thick tomato juice for this. If the soup turns out too thick, add a little water.

2	large tomatoes, finely chopped	
2	green peppers, finely chopped	
2	red peppers, finely chopped	
1	English cucumber, finely chopped	
1	medium Spanish onion, finely chopped	
1	clove garlic, minced	
1	tbsp. lemon juice	15 mL
2	tbsp. red wine vinegar	25 mL
3	cups tomato juice	750 mL

Pinch cayenne pepper
Salt and pepper to taste
Croutons for garnish (see note)

Set aside 1 tomato, green pepper, and red pepper, half of the cucumber, and 2 tbsp. of the onion.

Process the remaining vegetables and onion with the garlic, lemon juice, vinegar, and tomato juice in a food processor or blender until fairly smooth. Transfer to a large bowl. Season with the cayenne, salt, and pepper; stir in the reserved chopped vegetables. Chill. Serve with croutons.

Note: To make croutons, rub sliced bread (preferably stale) with a cut garlic clove. Cut into small cubes. Place on a baking sheet and bake at 350°F/180°C for 10 minutes or until golden brown and crisp.

Artichoke Spinach Dip

Makes about 3 cups/750 mL. Serves 6–8 as an appetizer.

Canned artichoke hearts work well in this silky-smooth dip packed with vitamins and minerals.

1	14-oz./398-mL can artichoke hearts packed in water	
1	10-oz./284-g package (about 8 cups/2 L loosely packed) fresh spinach, cooked, squeezed dry, and chopped	
1	small onion, finely chopped	
2	cloves garlic, minced	
2	tsp. dried or 2 tbsp. chopped fresh dill	10 mL/25 mL
$\frac{1}{4}$	cup chopped fresh parsley	50 mL
$1\frac{1}{2}$	cups 2% plain yogurt	375 mL
$\frac{1}{3}$	cup light mayonnaise	75 mL
1	tsp. Dijon mustard	5 mL
2	tbsp. chopped fresh chives	25 mL
2	tbsp. lemon juice	25 mL
	Salt and pepper to taste	

Process the first six ingredients in a food processor or blender until puréed. Combine the remaining ingredients except the salt and pepper in a medium-sized bowl. Add the artichoke mixture and mix well. Season with salt and pepper. Chill, covered. Serve with crackers, toast, pita triangles, or raw vegetable crudités.

Tomato Salsa Dip

Makes about $2\frac{1}{2}$ cups/625 mL. Serves 6 as an appetizer or sauce.

This makes a refreshing dip served with crackers or raw veggies and is great on tacos or as a sauce to go with cold meat, fish, or chicken.

2	large, ripe, fresh tomatoes, peeled, seeded, and chopped (see page 86)
⅓	cup finely chopped red onion — 75 mL
¼	cup finely chopped green pepper — 50 mL
½	tsp. minced, seeded jalapeno pepper (canned or fresh) — 2 mL
1	tbsp. lime juice — 15 mL

Salt and pepper to taste

Combine all the ingredients in a bowl and mix well. Chill.

Calories 105
Protein 4 g
Fat 8 g
Carbohydrate 6 g

Avocado Pâté

Makes about 3 cups/750 mL. Serves 6–8 as an appetizer.

Worth every calorie for its abundance of vitamins and minerals as well as the protein and calcium of the cottage cheese and yogurt.

1	small onion, finely chopped
1	clove garlic, minced
1	green pepper, finely chopped
½	cup 2% cottage cheese — 125 mL
½	cup 2% plain yogurt — 125 mL
2	ripe avocados, peeled and mashed

Juice of 1 lime
2 drops Tabasco or hot pepper sauce
Pinch chili powder
Salt and pepper to taste

Combine the onion, garlic, green pepper, cottage cheese, and yogurt in a bowl. Mix well. Mash the avocados with the lime juice with a fork in a separate bowl. Add to the cheese mixture. Stir in the Tabasco and chili powder and mix well. Season with salt and pepper.

Chill. Cover the surface of the pâté directly with plastic wrap to prevent it from turning brown. Serve with crackers or raw vegetable crudités.

Calories 57
Protein 2 g
Fat 2 g
Carbohydrate 10 g

Eggplant Antipasto

Makes about 2 cups/500 mL. Serves 6 as an appetizer.

Eggplant, garlic, raisins, and pine nuts work together to give this nutritious appetizer a harmonious blend of taste and texture. Use as a spread or dip for snacking or as a prelude to a meal.

1	medium eggplant (about $\frac{3}{4}$ lb./375 g)	
2	cloves garlic, peeled and slivered	
1	tomato, peeled, seeded, and chopped (see page 86)	
2	tbsp. raisins	25 mL
1	tsp. low-sodium soy sauce	5 mL
1	tsp. lemon juice	5 mL
1	tsp. olive oil	5 mL
Freshly ground black pepper to taste		
2	tbsp. toasted pine nuts (see page 89)	25 mL
Lettuce leaves		
3	tbsp. chopped fresh parsley for garnish	45 mL
$\frac{1}{4}$	cup chopped green onion for garnish	50 mL

Halve the eggplant lengthwise. Make several slits in the flesh and insert the garlic slivers. Place on a baking sheet and bake at 350°F/180°C for 45 minutes or until tender.

Remove the eggplant from the oven and let it cool. Peel it and finely chop the flesh. Place in a bowl and add the tomatoes and raisins.

Whisk together the soy sauce, lemon juice, oil, and pepper in a small bowl. Pour this over the eggplant mixture and mix well. Cover and refrigerate overnight.

Before serving, stir in the pine nuts. Place on an attractive plate on a bed of lettuce leaves and garnish with parsley and green onion. Serve with warmed pita or toast triangles.

Calories 95
Protein 4 g
Fat 3 g
Carbohydrate 17 g

Ratatouille

Serves 6–8 as a side dish.

A wondrous, herb-laced creation from Provence that is incredibly versatile. Serve it hot with meat or fish or cold and topped with a hot poached egg as a superb summer lunch.

4	tsp. virgin olive oil	20 mL
2	medium onions, chopped	
3	cloves garlic, minced	
1	medium eggplant (about $\frac{3}{4}$ lb./375 g), cubed	
3	small zucchini (about 1 lb./500 g), cubed	
1	small green pepper, cubed	
1	small red pepper, cubed	
1	28-oz./796-mL can Italian plum tomatoes or 2 lb./1 kg fresh tomatoes, peeled and chopped (see page 86)	
3	tbsp. tomato paste	45 mL
3	tbsp. dry red wine (optional)	45 mL
$1\frac{1}{2}$	tsp. dried or 3 tbsp. chopped fresh basil	7 mL/45 mL
$1\frac{1}{2}$	tsp. dried or 3 tbsp. chopped fresh oregano	7 mL/45 mL
$\frac{1}{2}$	tsp. dried or 1 tbsp. chopped fresh thyme	2 mL/15 mL

Salt and pepper to taste

Heat the oil in a large, heavy saucepan. Add the onions and garlic and sauté until soft. Add the eggplant and zucchini and cook over medium heat, stirring, for about 10 minutes. Add the green and red peppers, tomatoes, tomato paste, and wine. Bring to a boil, reduce heat, and simmer for about 10 minutes. Add the herbs and simmer 5–10 minutes longer or until the vegetables are tender but not mushy. Season with salt and pepper.

Note: For a nutritious main course, place 1 cup/250 mL warmed ratatouille in individual ovenproof dishes. Top with a raw egg, sprinkle with 3 tbsp./45 mL grated low-fat cheese, and bake at 350°F/180°C for 10–15 minutes or until the cheese melts and the egg sets.

Calories 46
Protein 1 g
Fat *1 g
Carbohydrate 10 g

*Less than

Carrot Purée

Serves 6–8 as a side dish.

You don't need whipping cream to make a silky-smooth vegetable purée that's bursting with flavour. Here's one example using our low-fat fromage blanc instead of cream.

1½ lb. carrots, scrubbed and sliced	750 g
3 tbsp. fromage blanc (page 154)	45 mL
½ cup skim or 2% milk	125 mL
Salt and freshly ground black pepper to taste	

Steam the carrots until soft. Process together with the fromage blanc and milk in a food processor or blender until smooth. Season with salt and pepper. Serve at once or chill and reheat gently over low heat when needed.

Note: Substitute almost any vegetable you like for the carrots—green beans, squash, and broccoli all work well. Try puréeing turnip or parsnip with cooked fruit such as apples or pears for a delicious change.

Calories 57
Protein 2 g
Fat 1 g
Carbohydrate 8 g

Celery Root Apple Purée

Serves 6 as a side dish.

An excellent example of how a humble root vegetable can reach sublime heights when combined with fruit and made into a purée. Kids will love this too. Use a Delicious or other not too tart apple, or the mixture might curdle. Celery root, also known as celeriac, is at its peak in the fall.

1 celery root (about ¾ lb./375 g), cleaned, peeled, and chopped	
1½ cups 2% milk	375 mL
1 large Delicious apple, peeled, cored, and chopped	
Salt and pepper to taste	

Place the celery root and milk in a large, heavy saucepan. Simmer, covered, for about 10 minutes. Add the apple and simmer 10 minutes longer or until the celery root and apple are soft, stirring once or twice. Drain, reserving the cooking liquid.

Purée the celery root mixture in a food processor or blender, with enough cooking liquid to obtain the desired consistency, until smooth. Season with salt and pepper. Serve at once or chill and reheat gently over low heat when needed.

Calories	72
Protein	2 g
Fat	5 g
Carbohydrate	7 g

Red Cabbage Casserole

Serves 6 as a side dish.

The acid in the yogurt helps the red cabbage retain its gorgeous purple hue. This healthy, low-cal dish is excellent with roast meat or poultry.

1	tbsp. corn, safflower, soybean, or sunflower oil	15 mL
1	small head red cabbage (about 7 cups/ 1.75 L), coarsely shredded	
1	tsp. paprika	5 mL
$\frac{1}{2}$	cup 2% plain yogurt	125 mL
	Salt and pepper to taste	
$\frac{1}{2}$	cup slivered almonds, toasted (see page 98)	125 mL

Heat the oil in a heavy casserole with a lid. Add the cabbage and paprika and cook over medium heat, stirring, for about 5 minutes. Stir in the yogurt. Cover and bake at 325°F/160°C for about 30 minutes. Season with salt and pepper and sprinkle with almonds. Serve with a dollop of yogurt if you wish.

Calories	123
Protein	2 g
Fat	5 g
Carbohydrate	18 g

Low-Fat French Fries

Serves 1.

Baking is the trick to these yummy fries that should satisfy anyone of any age without going overboard on the fat content. Use this recipe as a guide, doubling or tripling the amounts according to your requirements.

1   medium potato, scrubbed and cut into
     french fries
1   tsp. corn, safflower, soybean, or sun-   5 mL
     flower oil
Paprika for sprinkling

Pat the potato dry with a paper towel. Toss in a bowl with the oil to coat. Place on a lightly greased baking sheet and sprinkle lightly with paprika for added browning. Bake at 450°F/230°C for 20–30 minutes or until golden brown, turning at intervals.

Calories	31
Protein	1 g
Fat	3 g
Carbohydrate	2 g

Sautéed Cucumber

Serves 4 as a side dish.

An unusual, healthy vegetable side dish that will make you wonder why you never thought of it before. Leave the peel on for extra fibre; peel it off for elegant occasions.

2   tsp. corn, safflower, soybean, or sun-   10 mL
     flower oil
1   whole cucumber, seeded and cut into
     $\frac{1}{4}$-inch/$\frac{1}{2}$-cm slices
3   tbsp. chopped fresh dill   45 mL
Salt and pepper to taste

Heat the oil in a heavy skillet. Add the cucumber and sauté, stirring, over medium heat until tender-crisp—3–5 minutes. Add the dill, salt, and pepper.

Note: This method of sautéeing also works extremely well using cherry tomatoes instead of cucumber. Add chopped garlic, then the tomatoes, and use chopped parsley instead of dill.

Calories 113
Protein   1 g
Fat *1 g
Carbohydrate 26 g

*Less than

Winter Fruit Compote

Serves 8–10.

Use whatever dried fruits take your fancy, although this version, using prunes and figs, is probably unsurpassed. Those with a sweet tooth can add a little sugar (about 2 tbsp./25 mL) or the equivalent sweetener when simmering the dried fruit. This recipe makes enough for a crowd. Leftovers, if there are any, keep well. Halve these amounts if you wish.

1	cup unsweetened fruit juice (apple, pineapple, orange, etc.)	250 mL
$\frac{1}{2}$	cup port wine	125 mL
12	prunes, cut into chunks	
4	dried figs, cut into chunks	
2	unpeeled medium apples, cut into chunks	
2	unpeeled medium pears, cut into chunks	
1	10-oz./300-g package frozen unsweetened raspberries, thawed and undrained	

Combine the fruit juice, port, prunes, and figs in a large, heavy saucepan or skillet with a lid. Bring to a boil, then reduce heat and simmer, uncovered, for 5 minutes. Transfer the prunes and figs to a large glass bowl using a slotted spoon.

Add the apples and pears to the liquid in the saucepan. Bring to a boil, then cover and simmer for 2 minutes or until the fruit barely begins to turn soft. Add this mixture to the cooked prunes and figs. Cool. Add the raspberries and stir gently to mix well. Chill. Serve with sweetened yogurt.

Three-Fruit Salad

Serves 4.

Peaches, grapes, and blueberries taste as wonderful as they look in this colourful fruit salad.

2	tbsp. unsweetened orange juice	25 mL
2	tsp. lime juice	10 mL
Pinch ground cardamom		
1	tsp. granulated sugar	5 mL
2	ripe peaches, peeled, pitted, and sliced	
1	cup halved seedless green grapes	250 mL
1	cup blueberries	250 mL
Fresh mint leaves for garnish		

Combine the orange juice, lime juice, cardamom, and sugar in a small bowl. Stir until the sugar is dissolved. Place the fruit in a medium-sized glass bowl and pour the juice mixture over. Toss gently to coat the fruit with the dressing. Chill, then garnish with mint leaves before serving.

Apple Citrus Fruit Salad

Serves 4.

The tangy cooked dressing adds zip to this luscious fruit concoction that can easily be made year-round. This is another recipe from Frances Beaulieu, Toronto artist and recipe cartoonist.

$\frac{1}{2}$	cup unsweetened apple juice	125 mL
1	cinnamon stick	
2	cloves	
1	Granny Smith apple, peeled, cored, and sliced	
2	kiwi fruit, peeled, halved, and sliced	
2	navel oranges, peeled and sectioned	
1	pink grapefruit, peeled and sectioned	
$\frac{1}{2}$	cup halved seedless green grapes	125 mL

Combine the apple juice, cinnamon stick, and cloves in a small saucepan. Bring to a boil, then reduce heat and simmer for 10 minutes. Cool. Remove the cinnamon stick and cloves with a slotted spoon. Place the fruit in a large glass bowl. Pour the apple juice mixture over and toss. Chill.

Note: Add about 1 tbsp./15 mL of any juice that may result from sectioning the orange and grapefruit to the cooked apple juice mixture.

Calories	70
Protein	*1 g
Fat	*1 g
Carbohydrate	18 g

*Less than

Super Fruit Sauce

This recipe makes $2\frac{1}{2}$ cups/625 mL. Serves 4–6 as a dessert, 8–10 as a topping for pancakes, with ice cream, or on cereal with low-fat, plain yogurt.

This versatile creation can be made the traditional way with apples, but it is even better made with pears, peaches, or plums. Most fruit will require only the sugar listed in this recipe; some plums and other tart fruit such as rhubarb may require more. Substitute a sweetener if you wish. Omit the lemon juice for extremely tart fruit. This sauce is sensational as a topping for cottage cheese pancakes (page 157) with a dollop of low-fat, plain yogurt. Kids will adore it with ice cream, cereal, or stirred together with a spoonful of chocolate or carob chips. Baked this way, the fruit loses minimal nutrients.

4	cups cored, sliced, unpeeled apples, pears, or other fruit	1 L
1	tsp. cinnamon	5 mL
1	tbsp. brown sugar or honey	15 mL
1	tbsp. lemon juice	15 mL

Place the fruit in an ovenproof dish (earthenware works well). Top with the cinnamon, brown sugar, and lemon juice; cover with a lid or foil. Bake at 350°F/180°C for 35–45 minutes or until the fruit is tender. Process in a food processor or blender until puréed.

Mango Sorbet

Serves 6.

Almost any soft-fleshed fruit works well in this nicest of ices, which is high in vitamins, minerals, and fibre. To purée the mangoes, peel and cut away the flesh, then process in a food processor or blender until smooth.

$\frac{1}{2}$	cup granulated sugar	125 mL
$\frac{3}{4}$	cup water	175 mL
1	tbsp. lemon juice	15 mL
1	tbsp. orange or peach liqueur (optional)	15 mL
3	cups mango purée (from about 3 large mangoes)	750 mL

Combine the sugar and water in a small saucepan. Bring to a boil, stirring, and boil for 2 minutes. Cool, then transfer to a medium-sized stainless steel bowl or metal pan. Stir in the remaining ingredients and mix well. Cover with plastic wrap and freeze until firm.

Remove the sorbet from the freezer. Place in a food processor or blender and process until the mixture is slushy but firm. Return to the freezer until needed. To serve, remove from the freezer about 15 minutes before serving time.

Raspberry Sorbet

Serves 6.

A tangy variation on the sorbet theme.

$\frac{1}{2}$	cup granulated sugar	125 mL
$\frac{3}{4}$	cup water	175 mL
1	tbsp. orange, raspberry, or black currant liqueur	15 mL
2	10-oz./300-g packages frozen unsweetened raspberries, thawed and puréed (see note)	

Follow the method for mango sorbet substituting raspberries for mangoes.

Note: To purée the raspberries, process in a food processor or blender until smooth. To remove the seeds, strain the purée through a fine sieve.

Sorbet Bombe

Calories 98
Protein 1 g
Fat *1 g
Carbohydrate 23 g

*Less than

Serves 12.

The perfect healthy dessert to serve to friends at a dinner party. This beautiful bombe is bound to be a hit!

1   recipe mango sorbet
1   recipe raspberry sorbet
Fresh raspberries and mint leaves for garnish

Remove the sorbets from the freezer. Place the mango sorbet in a food processor or blender and process until slushy but firm. Line an 8-cup/2-L mould or stainless steel bowl evenly with the sorbet and place in the freezer.
    Process the raspberry sorbet in a food processor or blender until slushy but firm. Remove the mango sorbet from the freezer. Fill the hollow in the mango sorbet with the raspberry sorbet. Cover with plastic wrap and return to the freezer.
    To serve, place the bottom of the mould in a larger bowl of hot water for a few seconds or until the bombe loosens. Run a knife around the edge and invert onto a large serving plate. Leave it in the fridge for 15–20 minutes before serving. Garnish with raspberries and mint leaves.

Peach Crêpes

Calories	121
Protein	3 g
Fat	1 g
Carbohydrate	26 g

Makes 8 crêpes.

Elegant, tasty, and low in calories. Use pears, apples, or plums instead of peaches if you wish.

Crêpes

$\frac{1}{2}$	cup skim or 2% milk	125 mL
$\frac{1}{2}$	cup all-purpose flour	125 mL
2	egg whites	
1	tsp. corn, safflower, soybean, or sun-flower oil	5 mL
1	tsp. baking powder	5 mL

Filling

4	ripe peaches, peeled, pitted, and chopped	
$\frac{1}{3}$	cup raisins	75 mL
$\frac{1}{2}$	tsp. cinnamon	2 mL
	Finely grated peel of 1 lemon or orange	
$\frac{1}{4}$	cup unsweetened orange juice	50 mL
1	tbsp. orange liqueur (optional)	15 mL
1	tbsp. granulated sugar for garnish	15 mL

Whisk together the milk and flour in a medium-sized bowl. Whisk in the egg whites, oil, and baking powder until the batter is smooth.

Heat a small, lightly oiled crêpe pan or skillet over medium heat. Add 2 tbsp./25 mL of the batter. Tilt the pan to cover it evenly. Cook over medium heat until the crêpe is set, about 1 minute. Slide the crêpe out of the pan, cooked side down. Repeat with the remaining batter to make 8 crêpes, using a little more oil to coat the bottom of the pan if required.

Combine all the filling ingredients except the sugar in a small saucepan. Simmer gently until the peaches are just tender, about 5 minutes. Set aside $\frac{1}{3}$ cup/75 mL of the filling.

Place an equal amount of filling in the middle of the uncooked side of each crêpe. Roll up and arrange in a lightly greased ovenproof dish. Sprinkle with sugar. Bake at 350°F/180°C until heated through—5–8 minutes. Serve topped with a spoonful of reserved filling.

Poached Pears with Raspberry Sauce

Calories 145
Protein *1 g
Fat *1 g
Carbohydrate 34 g

*Less than

Makes 8 small servings.

A classic recipe for good reason. Be careful to choose ripe pears for this dish.

3	cups unsweetened apple or orange juice	750 mL
3	tbsp. granulated sugar	45 mL
1	tsp. vanilla	5 mL
1	tsp. finely grated fresh ginger root	5 mL
4	ripe pears, peeled, halved, and cored	
	Fresh mint leaves for garnish	

Sauce

1	10-oz./300-g package frozen unsweetened raspberries, thawed	
3	tbsp. honey	45 mL
2	tbsp. orange or raspberry liqueur (optional)	25 mL

Combine the juice, sugar, vanilla, and ginger root in a large skillet. Bring to a boil and cook, stirring, until the sugar dissolves. Reduce heat. Place the pears in the skillet in a single layer and simmer over low heat until tender—8–10 minutes. Remove the skillet from the heat and allow the pears to cool in the syrup.

Place all the ingredients for the sauce in a food processor or blender and process until smooth. Strain the mixture through a fine sieve to remove the seeds.

To serve, pour a pool of raspberry sauce onto individual plates. Top with the pear halves and garnish with mint.

Note: Those who are counting calories can substitute an equivalent amount of sweetener for the honey in the raspberry sauce.

Calories	217
Protein	3 g
Fat	9 g
Carbohydrate	35 g

Fruit Crumble

Serves 6.

Not the traditional version, this low-fat crumble is high in fibre. Use apples, peaches, pears, plums, or whatever fruit is in season and combine it with berries for a tasty combination.

5	cups sliced fruit	1.25 L
2	tbsp. lemon juice	25 mL
1	tsp. cinnamon	5 mL
$\frac{1}{2}$	cup brown sugar	125 mL
1	cup rolled oats	250 mL
$\frac{1}{4}$	cup natural bran	50 mL
$\frac{1}{4}$	cup finely chopped walnuts	50 mL
1	tsp. cinnamon	5 mL
3	tbsp. soft margarine	45 mL

Combine the fruit, lemon juice, cinnamon, and $\frac{1}{4}$ cup/50 mL of the brown sugar in an 8-cup/2-L ovenproof dish. Mix well.

Combine the rolled oats, $\frac{1}{4}$ cup/50 mL of the brown sugar, bran, walnuts, and cinnamon in a bowl and mix well. Cut in the margarine with a pastry blender or fork until the mixture resembles coarse crumbs. Sprinkle it on top of the fruit mixture.

Bake at 350°F/180°C for about 45 minutes or until the fruit is soft and the topping is golden brown.

Note: Those who are counting calories can substitute an equivalent amount of sweetener for the $\frac{1}{4}$ cup/50 mL of brown sugar used in the fruit mixture.

6   From the Dairy

Mom may not have understood exactly why she was
urging you to "drink your milk," but her well-meaning so-
licitation happens to be based on good nutritional common sense. Milk is a source of many vital nutrients—
protein, calcium, vitamin A, riboflavin, niacin, folacin, vitamin B12, and if the milk is fortified, vitamin D.

Milk and milk products are some of the best sources
of calcium, a mineral whose vital importance is being recognized more and more. Calcium helps make muscles,
nerves, blood, and cell membranes function properly.
Calcium is stored in the bones. Should the body not have
enough calcium for the functions we've just described, it
compensates by taking it from the bones. Without
enough calcium, bone mass decreases, and the bones
can become porous. They are then more susceptible to
fractures—a condition known as osteoporosis. (This is
described in more detail in Chapter 1.) The role of calcium in the prevention of heart disease and high blood
pressure is also being studied.

Milk fits into today's fast-paced lifestyle because it is a
food that takes little preparation but is loaded with nutrients. In order to get enough calcium in our diet without
consuming milk or its by-products, our diet would be one
long, intricate balancing act. For example, we would have
to eat about two cups of broccoli to get the same amount
of calcium as we do from one cup of milk. On the other
hand, people who like fish would have an easy alternative—they could get the equivalent calcium from six
sardines!

Milk is also the main food source of the vitamin niacin. Unstable when exposed to light, the niacin in milk
decreases during prolonged exposure to light. It is therefore best not to keep milk in glass or other clear containers. Vitamin A, another of milk's important nutrients,
is found in its fat portion. It is removed along with the fat
during the processing of low-fat milk but is then added
back.

Vitamin D is added to milk to fortify it, making it one
of the best sources of this vitamin. In addition, the vitamin D in fortified milk has the wonderful property of aid-
ing in the absorption of calcium; this makes fortified milk

unique: vitamin D is not added to any other dairy products. Check your milk container when you buy milk to make sure it is fortified. Why miss out on valuable vitamin freebies!

Many Don't Heed Mom's Words

In spite of all the virtues of milk, however, many of us don't consume enough. The reasons are many; some are valid, some aren't.

First, the invalid reasons. Many self-styled nutritionists, some popular reducing diets, and certain extreme forms of vegetarianism denounce milk as being "obscene," bad for you, and the source of almost every health problem known to man or woman. Unfortunately, they often manage to persuade people that these claims are true.

Other people don't drink milk because they consider it too high in calories to be consumed on a regular basis. Whole milk does have a fairly high fat content, and so do cheeses made from it, not to mention those varieties of high-fat cheese made from cream. Skim milk, however, contains a mere 90 calories per eight-ounce glass and is now the basis for some extremely palatable low-fat cheeses that don't taste like waxy cardboard as their unpalatable predecessors did. So instead of avoiding all dairy products in the fear that they are fattening, simply avoid those that are high in fat.

To continue the whole-milk-versus-skim-milk discussion, compare the fat contained in two glasses of whole milk and the same amount of skim. The difference is the equivalent of four teaspoons of butter. Multiply that by seven days, and you have 28 teaspoons of butter hiding in your weekly milk ration. If you don't like the taste of skim milk, try 1 percent milk. If this isn't available, combine half skim milk with half 2 percent. Drinking 2 percent milk itself still saves 14 teaspoons of fat per week over whole milk.

Some people worry about the high saturated fat and cholesterol contents of milk products. Again, they should be concerned about only those foods made from whole milk. Reading the labels on these foods is an important first step in making better choices. The initials B.F. and M.F. stand for butterfat and milk fat respectively. Check the percentage of butterfat in part skim-milk cheeses: amounts can vary widely. And don't let words such as "Natural" on a container of yogurt deceive you into thinking that it's bound to be healthy and therefore low in fat. The high fat content of many yogurts may be more harmful to your health than the preservatives in them.

Some strict vegetarians, called *vegans*, spurn milk and other dairy products as a matter of belief. This avoidance is a personal decision and must be respected. However, these people would be well advised to assess what nutrients they are losing by avoiding milk and to make sure they find them somewhere else. (See the section on vegetarianism in Chapter 10.)

Intolerance to Milk

Many people who complain of stomach problems when they drink milk simply stop drinking it without knowing what their problem is. Milk and milk products are too important a source of nutrients to be so readily renounced. These people should have their problem diagnosed by a doctor or dietitian and then try one of the treatments that will allow them to return to drinking milk.

Adverse reactions to milk can be a result of two conditions. Some people are allergic to milk's protein and thus have a milk allergy; others cannot tolerate its lactose, or milk sugar, and have a lactose intolerance.

It is now recognized that a large number of people—about 10 percent of the population, largely from ethnic groups like Jews, Asians, and blacks—are lactose intolerant. People with lactose intolerance have trouble digesting the lactose in milk and milk products. Instead of producing the right amount of *lactase*, the enzyme that breaks down lactose in the bowel into glucose and galactose, their bodies turn lactose into lactic acid and gas. This causes lactose-intolerant people to become uncomfortably bloated and even to suffer from diarrhea after ingesting milk.

Because there is a growing awareness of this problem, there are many new products available for people suffering from lactose intolerance. For example, you can buy lactose-reduced milk (and even lactose-reduced cottage cheese in some areas); this is milk that has had the lactose predigested by the addition of lactase. You can also buy the lactase enzyme in liquid form and add it to regular milk before drinking it or in tablet form and take it before consuming any dairy product. Foods that are lactase-reduced usually taste sweeter than their regular counterparts because their sugar is in the sweeter form of glucose and galactose.

If you have been diagnosed as lactose-intolerant and you have been following a lactose-reduced diet but still show symptoms, consult a registered dietitian or doctor, who will help you examine your diet to look for hidden sources of lactose. People with lactose intolerance can usually tolerate unprocessed or natural hard cheeses better than such items as processed cheese slices. Some can tolerate yogurt, others cannot.

An allergy to the protein in milk is another story. Because the proteins vary slightly from one dairy product to another, it is important to determine which foods give you problems. People with an allergy to cow's milk should avoid it entirely, but they may not be allergic to products made from goat's milk. The symptoms of a milk allergy can also vary from stomach upset and diarrhea in one individual to hives or breathing problems in another. Again, consult a dietitian or doctor to have your symptoms diagnosed.

Milk in the Raw and Other Bugbears
Many people fall prey to that magical word *natural* and are led to believe that "raw" milk has some valuable properties not contained in the more common pasteurized kind. In fact, raw milk can carry bacteria like salmonella and even viruses. The *Journal of the American Medical Association* has also recently reported that people have died from consuming raw milk. Since there are no nutritional benefits to raw milk, why pass up the benefits of pasteurization, which kills bacteria and disease-bearing organisms?

Other people don't use dairy products because they are concerned about their high salt content. These same people, however, often consume plenty of salt in other foods that are not as dense in nutrients. If you are on a low-sodium diet for medical reasons or don't like the taste of salt, choose cheese labelled low in salt. But beware: unless it is marked otherwise, it may still be high in fat.

Getting the Most out of Milk
Here are some tips for getting the greatest benefit from milk and milk products:

- Use low-fat milk as a snack when mealtimes are far off. Milk can provide the energy you need to keep you going over those few hours.

- Try making tasty drinks using milk as a base.

- Add milk to soups instead of water.

- Add a dollop of yogurt to a bowl of cold soup.

- Use yogurt as a dip for desserts of fresh fruit. For a tasty picnic dessert, mix frozen fruit such as blueberries or strawberries with some cold yogurt. The fruit will keep the yogurt cold and make a tasty combo.

- Use yogurt as a base for vegetable dips.

- Make yogurt salad dressings, which can be poured on more generously than those high-fat versions made with oil, sour cream, and so on. This is a clever way to eat more vegetables too.

- Combine cheeses when cooking to maximize taste while minimizing fat. Use a little old cheddar for strong taste along with a low-fat cheese like mozzarella on pizza and casseroles. Parmesan is also excellent in combination with low-fat cheese because of its intense flavour, especially if you keep it in one piece in the fridge and grate it each time you use it.

- Combine grated low-fat cheeses with wheat germ or whole-wheat breadcrumbs as toppings for casseroles.

- Keep low-fat cheese in the fridge at work to eat as a snack or with a salad or bun as lunchtime protein.

- Use low-fat cheese, cubed or grated, in salads.

- Add powdered milk as a filler to soups and drinks.

- Use low-fat cheese melted on tortilla chips to make nachos or on popcorn for a nutritious snack.

- Low-fat cheese and cottage cheese are terrific protein foods at breakfast time.

- To store cheese, wrap it in a double layer of aluminum foil. It will dry out slightly this way but won't get mouldy. Should the cheese still become dry, moisten a piece of cheesecloth or J cloth, wrap it around the cheese, then wrap foil around it. Leave it in the fridge for 12 to 24 hours—no longer, or the cheese will get mouldy—remove the cloth, and behold! A fresh piece of cheese.

- Die-hard crème fraîche fans can substitute 10 percent cream instead of whipping cream (35 percent) in the recipe on page 154.

- Cream and ice cream contain nutrients from the dairy food group but are a high-fat way of ingesting them. On the other hand, cream and ice cream are more nutritious than a "non-dairy creamer" or "non-dairy" ice cream, which are made from coconut fat and contain none of the goodness of dairy products.

The Lowdown on Yogurt

Stories from Eastern Europe that attribute the amazing longevity of certain individuals to a diet high in yogurt have contributed to its current reputation as some kind of "wonder food" that prolongs life and cures a multitude of ailments. However, yogurt is made simply by adding a live bacterial culture to milk and then leaving it to ferment. Many people who fear taking antibiotics as medication (this is unfounded as long as antibiotics are administered properly) believe that they can replace the "good" bacteria killed off by an antibiotic by eating yogurt. There is no proof of the truth or falsity of the medicinal properties of yogurt.

The fact is that the nutritional attributes of yogurt vary greatly. All yogurt contains appreciable amounts of calcium, riboflavin, and protein. It can, however, depending on the brand, contain high amounts of fat too. Some extremely rich, creamy yogurts rack up more than 8 percent butterfat—almost as much as half-and-half cream, which contains 10 percent; both are close rivals of sour cream for fat content. Low-fat yogurts are another matter. Some brands contain a mere 1 percent butterfat and can be perfectly tasty. To be absolutely sure of the fat content and other ingredients in the yogurt you're eating, you may wish to try making your own. It's easy and delicious.

Then there's the question of how much sweetener yogurt contains. Yogurt that is laced with honey still contains simple sugar, and some of the fruit-flavoured yogurts on the market are extremely high in sugar. The best solution is to buy low-fat, unflavoured yogurt and gussy it up yourself by adding fresh fruit and berries (unsweetened, frozen fruit and canned fruit are also good), a little low-cal sweetener, some vanilla or almond extract, or a few spoonfuls of frozen, concentrated fruit juice.

Frozen yogurt is usually made from yogurt that is fairly high in fat and contains some kind of sweetening agent in goodly amounts. It is therefore not the low-calorie product you might expect it to be. Frozen yogurt is, however, usually lower in fat than ice cream—one scoop of ice cream contains about 150 calories, frozen yogurt about 120. Ice cream's magnificent creaminess comes from butterfat; the creamier the ice cream (usually the premium brands), the more fat it contains.

If ice cream is your way to splurge on calories, then opting for the *crème de la crème* is a good way to treat yourself on occasion. Regular ice cream eaters would be wise to seek out some low-fat brands. Although ice milk is lower in fat, it often contains more sugar to compensate for its lack of creaminess.

Fromage Blanc

Calories 81
Protein 15 g
Fat 1 g
Carbohydrate 2 g
(per ½ cup/125 mL)

Makes about 3½ cups/875 mL.

A terrific, low-fat substitute for whipping cream to use in sauces, soups, or fruit and vegetable purées.

3	cups low-fat ricotta cheese	750 mL
¾	cup 2% plain yogurt	175 mL

Blend the ingredients in a food processor or blender until smooth. Transfer to a jar with a tight-fitting lid and let stand at room temperature for about 6 hours or until thickened. Chill for at least 10 hours before using. Will keep in the fridge for about 2 weeks.

Crème Fraîche

Calories 40
Protein 1 g
Fat 4 g
Carbohydrate 1 g
(per 1 oz./25g)

Makes about 1 cup/250 mL.

This version of crème fraîche uses 10 percent instead of the usual 35 percent cream, but it tastes just as good and is perfect to use as a topping for those occasions when yogurt won't do.

1	cup 10% cream	250 mL
2	tsp. buttermilk	10 mL

Combine the cream and buttermilk in a screw-top jar and shake for about 1 minute. Let the mixture stand, covered, in a warm place until it thickens—4–24 hours, depending on the temperature. Will keep in the fridge for 2–3 weeks.

Calories	69
Protein	2 g
Fat	1 g
Carbohydrate	15 g

Frozen Berry Yogurt

Serves 8.

A refreshing, low-fat, low-calorie dessert that can be made with fresh or frozen berries.

1	10-oz./300-g package frozen unsweet-ened raspberries, thawed	
1	10-oz./300-g package frozen unsweet-ened strawberries, thawed	
3	tbsp. unsweetened orange juice	45 mL
5	tbsp. honey	65 mL
$\frac{1}{4}$	tsp. finely grated orange rind	1 mL
2	cups 2% plain yogurt	500 mL

Fresh mint sprigs or whole berries for garnish

Purée the berries in a food processor or blender. Add the orange juice, honey, and orange rind; process until smooth. To remove the seeds (see note), strain the purée through a fine sieve. Pour it into a bowl and stir in the yogurt. Blend well.

Pour the mixture into an 8-inch/2-L pan. Freeze until firm—3–4 hours. Remove from the freezer 15 minutes before serving. Process in a food processor or beat in a bowl with an electric mixer until slushy but firm. Spoon the mixture into serving dishes or wine glasses. Let sit in the fridge until serving time, then garnish with mint leaves or berries.

Note: Some people prefer the smoother texture of this dish when the seeds are sieved out. The seeds, however, give added fibre and can be left in if you wish.

Cottage Cheese Topping

Calories 84
Protein 8 g
Fat 1 g
Carbohydrate 10 g
(per $\frac{1}{3}$ cup/75 ml)

Makes about $1\frac{1}{3}$ cups/325 mL.

Great as an accompaniment for all kinds of desserts, especially fruit, as well as pancakes and breakfast cereals. It's also wonderful on a fruit salad plate at lunch.

1	cup 2% cottage cheese	250 mL
$\frac{1}{3}$	cup skim milk	75 mL
1	tsp. vanilla	5 mL
2	tbsp. honey	25 mL

Blend all the ingredients in a food processor or blender until smooth. Cover and chill.

Note: Substitute a low-cal sweetener for the honey if you wish.

Cinnamon Yogurt Sauce

Calories 57
Protein 3 g
Fat 1 g
Carbohydrate 10 g
(entire recipe)

Makes about $\frac{1}{2}$ cup/125 mL.

The perfect topping for our cottage cheese pancakes (see page 157), poached or fresh fruit, or your bowl of breakfast granola.

$\frac{1}{2}$	cup 2% plain yogurt	125 mL
$\frac{1}{2}$	tsp. cinnamon	2 mL
1	tsp. honey	5 mL
1	tsp. lemon juice	5 mL

Whisk all the ingredients together in a bowl until blended.

Note: Substitute a low-cal sweetener for the honey if you wish.

Cottage Cheese Pancakes

Calories 45
Protein 3 g
Fat 2 g
Carbohydrate 3 g

Makes 12–15 small pancakes.

The best stack of nourishing hot cakes you'll find anywhere! These pancakes provide a protein-packed breakfast when they are served with a dollop of yogurt and a hefty spoonful of our Super Fruit Sauce (see page 141), and they score as low in fat as they do high in taste and texture. The consistency of the batter depends greatly on the moistness of the cottage cheese. Dry cottage cheese works better than creamed. If the batter is too thick, add a couple of spoonfuls of low-fat, plain yogurt; if it is too thin, add a little more flour. Drain any excess liquid from the cottage cheese before using.

1	cup 2% cottage cheese	250 mL
2	eggs	
2	tbsp. natural bran	25 mL
1	tbsp. wheat germ	15 mL
$\frac{1}{4}$	cup whole-wheat or all-purpose flour	50 mL
$\frac{1}{4}$	tsp. cinnamon	1 mL
Salt to taste		
1	tbsp. corn, safflower, soybean, or sunflower oil	15 mL

Process the cottage cheese and eggs in a food processor or blender until smooth. Combine the bran, wheat germ, flour, cinnamon, and salt in a medium-sized bowl. Mix well. Stir in the cottage cheese mixture and mix well.

Heat the oil in a large, heavy skillet over medium heat. Drop the batter into the skillet with a spoon. Cook the pancakes, one or two at a time, on both sides until golden brown.

7   A Bevy of Beverages

Water, which makes up more than 60 percent of our body weight, is so essential that without it we would die in only a few days. Other nutrients are crucial over the long term; a lack of them takes its toll over a much longer period of time.

Many substances that are soluble in water are carried to the cells or tissues that need them by the bloodstream. Water is also the vehicle that transports nutrients through the digestive tract. At the other end of the system, this important fluid carries waste products out of the body in the urine and feces. Water also comes in handy as a lubricant that the body uses to keep the joints working smoothly and to help digest food. A lack of water in the diet is likely to cause constipation, which can be even more of a problem if a person's diet is high in fibre.

Many of the body's chemical reactions, such as breaking down carbohydrate, protein, and fat, require water. Water is also needed to keep our body temperature at the right level. If it gets too high because of heat from the environment or from a fever, perspiring is the body's way of using water to cool down and regulate its temperature. The same occurs during physical exercise.

Every day the body loses an amazing two to two and a half litres of water in urine and intestinal waste and through the lungs and skin. Thirst is the mechanism that helps the body replace this loss of important fluids. There are occasions when the thirst mechanism fails, and the result is dehydration. For example, prolonged, vigorous exercise or exercising in extreme heat can throw this mechanism off kilter, and we may not feel adequately thirsty. The dehydration that results leads in turn to a lack of fluid for producing sweat, and the body then has no way to cool itself down. In extreme cases, a further rise in body temperature causes heat prostration, which leads to a decrease in blood volume. If this is not corrected by drinking fluids, the circulatory system can collapse, possibly causing death. Exercise enthusiasts should therefore note the importance of consuming liquids as fluid replacement after a strenuous workout. (This discussion is continued in Chapter 9.)

The thirst mechanism can also be thrown off course by the consumption of another fluid—alcohol. Alcohol causes the body to lose water simply because water is needed to get rid of it. In fact, it takes eight ounces of water to purge the body of one ounce of alcohol, so that awful "hung over" feeling is actually a serious case of dehydration. Therefore, if you do consume alcohol, it is wise to drink plenty of water at the same time.

Water, Water, Everywhere

Fortunately for us, meeting our bodies' water requirements is not just a matter of consuming gallons of fluids. Certain foods are also terrific sources of water. Cantaloupe, for example, is 85 percent water; so are apples. Cottage cheese racks up a water count of 80 percent, while hard cheeses contain less than 37 percent. Lettuce is in the lead in the water ratings with a score of 95 percent, followed by spinach with 90 percent. Milk is also largely water—88 percent, to be exact.

Fluids such as juices, coffee, tea, soft drinks, and alcoholic beverages also contribute water to our diet. Because of some of their negative side effects, however, these drinks should be consumed only in moderation, with lots of basic water in between.

Here are some tips for getting into the water-drinking habit:

- Order a glass of water instead of a soft drink at your next meal.

- Keep a pitcher of water flavoured with lemon slices in the fridge for a thirst-quenching cooler.

- Take a thermos of ice water to work instead of coffee, and stop by the water fountain instead of going to the cafeteria for yet another soft drink or coffee.

- When you travel by plane, load up on extra water to combat the dry environment that makes you lose fluids and become fatigued. Coffee, tea, and alcohol only add to your dehydration.

- If you're trying to lose weight, water can be a satisfying, no-calorie filler when the hungries hit.

What Water Will It Be?

The next question to arise is: what water should I drink— tap, filtered tap, distilled, spring, mineral, or well water?

There are many variables to consider. Underground and spring wells are both sources of mineral water. Spring water comes from springs that are above ground. Mineral water can be naturally bubbly or artificially carbonated. Although both kinds of water contain some minerals, neither contains enough to meet a person's mineral requirements. Both mineral and spring water contain negligible amounts of fluoride, unlike tap water, to which fluoride has been added. What is more, bottled waters can be high in the mineral that most of us do *not* need more of—namely, sodium. People who are restricting their sodium intake should check the sodium content of bottled waters, which ranges from 100 to 300 mg per litre. Home water softeners can also add sodium to drinking water.

Distilled water is the condensed steam obtained from boiling water. It is free of minerals and therefore tastes rather bland. Club soda is usually tap water that has been filtered and carbonated. Different waters get their taste from their particular combination of minerals.

Tap and well water vary, depending on their environment and methods of water treatment. How well the components of these waters are monitored depends on the work of local governments and environmental groups. If you are concerned about the quality of your tap water, contact your municipal officials or local watchdog groups.

Methods of water treatment used by local authorities consist mainly of disinfection and filtration. Chlorination, a method of disinfecting water, gives rise to low levels of a group of chemicals called *trihalomethanes*, which may be carcinogenic, so further study is needed to check this possibility. Home filtration units that decrease the levels of chemicals in water can provide a solution to this, but if bacteria is allowed to grow in the filters through careless maintenance, other problems can occur.

Because bottled water harbours fewer chemicals, it is usually assumed to be the best choice of water. However, it is not regularly monitored for chemicals the way tap water is, so its quality is not guaranteed. In addition, methods of disinfecting tap water get rid of contaminants such as bacteria, which may be found in bottled water.

The bottom line is that neither tap nor bottled water is without flaws. The best route to go, therefore, is to alternate the kinds of water you drink. It is also wise to express your concern to the right authorities about the safety of tap water. The more regulations there are controlling the pollution of our waterways and the more controls there are on bottled water, the better for us all.

Face to Face with Caffeine

Caffeine is one of a group of compounds called *methylanxthines*. Consumed by all of us in the form of coffee, tea, and soft drinks, caffeine is, in fact, a stimulant that has become as acceptable a part of our lifestyle as the automobile and sliced bread. Because of its effect on our bodies, however, many of us are now questioning whether overindulging in caffeine could be detrimental to our health.

Caffeine is absorbed in the gastrointestinal tract. Its effects reach their peak 15 to 45 minutes after being consumed, depending on how sensitive a person is to it and on his or her size. Caffeine affects a smaller person more quickly than a larger one, a fact that explains why foods as seemingly harmless as a bar of chocolate washed down with a glass of cola can make a small child irritable and even sleepless.

How fast caffeine is eliminated from the body also varies from person to person and is especially affected by age and the presence of disease.

The stimulant effect of caffeine runs the gamut from increasing alertness in some people to anxiety, irritability, or headaches in others. It can also cause insomnia, a poor sleep pattern, or sleep that leaves a person feeling badly rested. These symptoms occur because caffeine narrows the blood vessels, thereby making the heart work harder to pump the blood through them. In cases of real excess or caffeine sensitivity, heart palpitations can result.

Caffeine can also cause trouble for the digestive system because it stimulates the digestive juices. This can lead to gastrointestinal irritation in predisposed individuals and can easily irritate an empty stomach.

People who are trying to watch their weight should certainly beware of caffeine because it raises blood sugar levels. This can lead to a surge of insulin and a subsequent drop in blood sugar to a level lower than before the caffeine was consumed. The result? That cup of coffee downed in order to squelch hunger pangs can lead to even greater hunger. In addition, the calories in cream and sugar slipped into cups of coffee can quickly add up by day's end. You can reduce the 40 to 50 calories in a

CAFFEINE CONTENT OF VARIOUS FOODS AND MEDICATIONS

Item	Amount	Caffeine Content (mg)
Coffee, drip	5 oz./150 g	140
Coffee, instant	5 oz./150 g	60
Coffee, instant, decaffeinated	5 oz./150 g	3
Coffee, percolated	5 oz./150 g	110
Tea, black, brewed 1 minute	5 oz./150 g	30
Tea, black, brewed 3 minutes	5 oz./150 g	40
Tea, black, brewed 5 minutes	5 oz./150 g	45
Tea, green, brewed 5 minutes	5 oz./150 g	30
Tea, oolong, brewed 5 minutes	5 oz./150 g	40
Cocoa	5 oz./150 g	13
Cola beverages	12 oz./375 g	35–50
Baking chocolate	1 oz./30 g	35
Chocolate powder for milk	1 tbsp./15 mL	10
Anacin	1 tablet	32
Dexatrim	1 tablet	200
Dristan	1 tablet	16
Excedrin	1 tablet	65
Midol	1 tablet	32
Triaminic	1 tablet	30
Cafergot	1 capsule	100
Fiorinal	1 tablet	40

"regular" coffee by using milk instead of cream and eliminating sugar. Avoid coffee whiteners—they are high in saturated fats and are as unhealthy as they are caloric.

Caffeine also has a diuretic effect, meaning that it causes the body to lose fluids. This can be especially harmful to people who are trying to maintain their body's fluid level because they exercise regularly or live or work in environments that are hot or dry.

And there is still more on caffeine's criminal record.

Caffeine seems to have a negative effect on other nutrients in the body, in particular calcium. High caffeine intakes have been shown to result in a negative calcium balance. Caffeine and its connection to Pre-Menstrual Syndrome is a new area of research. One study has linked high caffeine consumption with the presence and severity of PMS, which can cause irritability, anxiety, headache, fatigue, breast tenderness, and food cravings.

Last but by no means least, caffeine is addictive. If you don't believe this, just try cutting it out cold turkey and see how it feels! Symptoms of withdrawal for people who are addicted range from headaches to depression.

So how much caffeine is acceptable? Healthy adults, it seems, can safely drink 200 to 250 mg a day. That's two 5-ounce cups of perked coffee, less if you drink drip coffee. And don't forget to include soft drinks when you do your caffeine count. Pregnant and nursing women should reduce their caffeine consumption even further.

For many of us, the thought of starting the day without that ritualistic cup of coffee is hard to imagine. So if you want to cut down on your caffeine consumption, do it slowly. Try substituting decaffeinated coffee for regular, or mixing half your usual coffee with half decaffeinated. Some people worry about the chemical used to decaffeinate most coffees, methyl chloride. Studies show that it seems to be safe, but if you are still wary, try brands that are decaffeinated by the water process, which uses steam, not chemicals, to extract the caffeine.

Varying your beverages is also wise when trying to cut down on caffeine, and milk, water, and the odd herbal tea might be to your taste. A craving for the stimulation of coffee could also be a helpful indicator of a nutritional lack. For example, skipping breakfast or lunch could be the reason for that dip in energy that makes your body cry out for a cola or coffee. Try a nutritious snack instead.

All about Alcohol

Drinking alcohol is such an integral part of our lifestyle, and the nutritional information on it is often so contradictory, that many people are totally confused. Should they eliminate alcohol from their diets completely or throw caution to the winds and enjoy a few beers like their friends do?

The key once again is moderation.

But it varies. One person's moderation could be another's overindulgence. Three beers a night could be moderate for one person; for another it could be two to three drinks a month. One to two drinks a day—allowing 12 ounces of beer, 5 ounces of wine, and 1.5 ounces of liquor per drink—seems to be the guide to moderate imbibing.

The liver is the place in the body where alcohol takes its sometimes deadly toll. The liver detoxifies alcohol and converts it into energy for the body to use. Excess alcohol makes the liver fatty, and continued excess causes cirrhosis. (However, a person can develop liver disease without being an alcoholic.) Although the combination of bad nutrition and excess alcohol is likely to cause changes in the liver, the liver can return to normal if the alcohol intake is lowered before permanent damage is done.

It is also thought that excess alcohol may be associated with cancer of the liver. Heavy beer drinking has been associated with increased risk of rectal and colon cancer. The Canadian Cancer Society recommends that if you do drink alcohol, limit your drinking to one or two drinks a day.

Last Call for Alcohol

Heavy drinking can have many other bad effects on our health.

Depending on the amount consumed, alcohol creates a greater need in the body for other nutrients. Although a little alcohol stimulates the appetite, too much dulls it. This explains why heavy drinkers often do not eat nutritious foods and do not eat adequate amounts. This, combined with the fact that alcohol causes some nutrients not to be used by the body, explains why many heavy drinkers suffer from malnutrition.

Although alcohol may offer the body enough calories to keep it stable, it may not meet the body's nutritional demands. In addition, the body's need for thiamin (vitamin B1) increases with the amount of alcohol that is consumed; a persistent deficiency of thiamin could result in a disease called beri beri.

Alcohol can also irritate the linings of the stomach and intestines; this can result in decreased absorption of B vitamins. Heavy drinking also seems to affect a person's selenium status. Anyone who suffers from stomach problems should monitor the effect alcohol has on them, because alcohol can be an irritant, especially on an empty stomach.

People with hypoglycemia should be aware that drinking alcohol can cause their blood sugar to fall. This can vary, depending on when the alcohol is consumed and what has been eaten, but abstinence is probably the best policy if you are not symptom-free.

There is a great deal of research going on into many aspects of alcohol consumption. Does drinking a lot of alcohol during pregnancy cause birth defects? Does excess alcohol predispose a person to bone loss, or osteoporosis? Does a lowered intake of alcohol help control high blood pressure? And on the other side of the coin, does a little wine served to the elderly in nursing homes lead to more restful sleep and a greater zest for life?

Certainly alcohol is not all bad. Its moderate use has been shown to increase HDL cholesterol levels in the blood. In predisposed people, however, even moderate consumption can raise triglyceride levels.

Then, of course, there's the matter of weight control.

After being metabolized in the liver, alcohol yields fewer calories per gram than fat but almost twice as many as protein and carbohydrate. Within each gram of alcohol lurk seven calories, accompanied by negligible nutrients. Add the empty calories of a mixer to your drink, and you can rack up a mammoth calorie count and no appreciable nourishment before you can say "gin and tonic!"

When rating alcoholic drinks for calories, remember that light beers can contain anywhere from about 60 to 120 calories per bottle, depending on the brand. Keep in mind too that most calorie charts give the number of calories for a four- or five-ounce glass of wine, which is smaller than the amount that is often served. Note also that cooking with wine and other alcoholic beverages does not add calories to a meal because alcohol evaporates during the cooking process, leaving only its fla-

ALCOHOL AND CALORIC CONTENT OF VARIOUS ALCOHOLIC BEVERAGES

Beverage	Amount	Alcohol (g)	Calories
Cider, fermented	6 oz./175 g	9.4	71
Liqueur	1 oz./30 g	7.0	64
Liquor, 80 proof (gin, rum, whisky, vodka)	$1\frac{1}{2}$ oz./45 g	14.0	97
Liquor, 90 proof	$1\frac{1}{2}$ oz./45 g	15.9	110
Liquor, 100 proof	$1\frac{1}{2}$ oz./45 g	17.9	124
Wine, sweet dessert	$3\frac{1}{2}$ oz./100 g	15.8	153
Wine, dry table	$3\frac{1}{2}$ oz./100 g	9.9	85
Champagne, dry	4 oz./125 g	13.0	105
Beer	8 oz./250 g	8.7	99
Beer, light	8 oz./250 g	7.0–12.0	60–130
Planter's punch	4 oz./125 g	21.5	175
Martini	$3\frac{1}{2}$ oz./100 g	18.5	140
Eggnog	4 oz./125 g	15.0	335

Note: Differences in calories may be a result of carbohydrate content.

vour. If calories are a concern, however, restrict the alcohol in your cooking to dry wine or brandy; avoid sweet liqueurs, which leave behind a lot of sugar.

Another hazard of alcohol if you are trying to lose weight is that it is more readily absorbed on an empty stomach. As your blood alcohol level rises, you likely become hungrier. This combined with your diminishing willpower, caused by the effects of the alcohol on your mind, could cause you to eat more when you're under the influence. One way you can avoid this in social situations is to alternate alcoholic drinks with non-alcoholic ones, for example, drinking a tall glass of soda with lime between beers. The extra fluid will fill you up without adding calories and reducing your mental fortitude!

8   Give Breakfast a Break

You can be sure you're a convert to healthy eating when someone offers you one meal a day and you choose breakfast! If there's one thing we hope this book will teach, it's that eating a nutritious breakfast is an absolute must.

Yet in spite of the crucial role of breakfast in ensuring a balanced diet—and as a result, a healthy body and mind—many if not most people either skip this meal altogether or consider a cup of coffee and slice of toast adequate sustenance at the start of the day. Perhaps the most common reason people give for eating little or no breakfast is that they simply aren't hungry at this time of day. This is a perfect example of how "mind over matter" can become a dangerous thing.

When your mind tells you that you're tired or in a hurry to get to work, you can actually override your body's healthy craving for food until it becomes a habit. Once you learn to override your hunger, you suppress the important ability to regulate your appetite. And if you don't know when your body is hungry, then you won't know when your body is satisfied. The result is that you tend to eat foods that are convenient at times that are convenient, not when your body needs them for nourishment.

And there are more repercussions of this unhealthy syndrome. People who are not hungry at breakfast are, in contrast, usually hungry at night—the very time their bodies do not require much food. Our bodies need fuel to *start* the day, not to end it.

What can be done to save this situation? With a little effort and persistence, it is possible to get our bodies back in touch with their needs, so that they are hungry when they need the nutrients. This means listening to the requirements of our bodies instead of the power of our minds.

The simple practice of eating a substantial breakfast is the best way to change your eating pattern and teach your body how to regulate its appetite. It may be difficult at first, but after a period of sustained breakfast eating, we guarantee that you will begin to feel hungry at the start of the day.

Some people who are not used to eating breakfast will actually feel nauseated when they do. This may be because their blood sugar is low from not eating during the night. But their nausea will gradually decrease as eating breakfast becomes a habit.

Why Waking up Needs Shaking Up

There are several reasons why breakfast is the meal of prime importance.

First, there's the matter of weight control. Being the right weight is highly dependent on your ability to regulate your appetite. If you don't know when you are hungry—and most people have tricked their bodies into believing that rushing out of the house with a cup of coffee inside them is enough—then you won't know when you are full either.

In other words, downing a huge piece of chocolate cake while you're watching the late-night news may be pleasant, but it is biological nonsense when all you have ahead of you is a night's sleep. On the other hand, eating a bowl of porridge topped with nuts, fruit, and milk makes a lot of sense as a prelude to an energy-filled day.

Another reason to eat breakfast to control our weight is that our bodies run at a slower pace during sleep. This means that our metabolic rate—the rate at which our bodies burn calories—is slower after sleeping. Eating a balanced breakfast raises the metabolic rate, so our metabolism is faster after we eat a good breakfast than if we had eaten no breakfast at all. A word of warning here, however: as with everything, moderation is the key; eating too much breakfast can cause problems too.

Still on the subject of weight control, frequent, small meals are less fattening than a few big meals. In other words, the same 1,500 calories downed in one large meal may cause more fat deposition than the same number of calories consumed in six small meals. The ideal eating pattern for losing weight and maintaining good health is to taper off meals from the beginning to the end of the day. Keep in mind the credo: Eat breakfast like a queen, lunch like a princess, and dinner like a pauper.

Should you eat a large, late dinner one night and wake up the next morning with no appetite, stick to the preceding game plan. Eat your usual large breakfast and go easy on the rest of your meals, especially dinner. If you do miss breakfast in such an instance, it's almost guaranteed that you will want a large evening meal, and before you know it, you could be back into the breakfast-skipping syndrome!

What is more, people who eat a good breakfast have fewer cravings for empty-calorie foods later in the day—the sad fate of those unrealistically cheerful snackers on TV commercials who grab a chocolate bar as soon as the "mid-afternoon hungries" hit. Breakfast skippers are also the most likely people to long for chocolate, potato chips, and cola drinks at 4 P.M. when a nutritious snack of yogurt and fruit seems inconvenient and far less tempting.

Breakfast: The Morning Energizer

The body's blood sugar and energy levels go hand in hand. So energy levels throughout the day can be affected by eating or not eating the right breakfast. It may be hard to believe, but a balanced intake at the beginning of the day seems to prevent drastic highs and lows in energy levels later on.

In other words, the "4 P.M. slump" can be eradicated by eating a substantial meal at 8 A.M. Also, if your energy levels are maintained throughout the day, you won't feel as exhausted at night. This is easier to understand when you picture the body functioning without breakfast as a machine running on little or no fuel. It's not surprising that it eventually cuts out. A person who goes for the first half of the day without fuel is bound to be weary by the time evening comes around.

The person who says that he or she is not a "morning person" is probably someone who doesn't make a habit of eating breakfast. But why waste those precious morning hours to sluggishness and droopy eyelids when you could be bursting with energy? Studies show that protein is a crucial breakfast ingredient—it seems to stimulate the mind and give us mental energy. This explains why children who arrive at school without eating breakfast are likely to doze off in the middle of a morning class.

Many people overcome their lack of energy in the morning, when blood sugar and energy levels are somewhat low, by means of a stimulant like caffeine. This source of energy is, however, a poor substitute for good food. Not only is it comparatively short-lived, but it is also lacking in nutrients and so addictive that the body may crave higher and higher doses. In addition, this short surge of energy is followed by a lowering of the blood sugar, which can make you feel more tired and hungry than before you had that hit of coffee, tea, or other source of caffeine.

Keep It All in the Family

Many parents expect their children to eat a good, nutritious breakfast in the morning while they set a bad example and eat little or nothing. And some people, especially women, are so busy getting their family ready to leave home in the morning that they simply skip breakfast. This is the time when everyone most needs nourishing food in order to cope with frenzied mornings.

Instead, make breakfast a family affair. It is a good time for the family to come together, especially with everyone's busy work and school schedules during the week. Also, encourage your children to plan their own breakfasts the night before. If they are part of the decision-making process, they will be more likely to follow through by eating a more substantial morning meal.

Planning breakfast is a good idea even for adults, because it is often the most rushed meal of the day. You could prepare the makings of a tuna melt or grilled cheese sandwich the night before, then put them in the fridge ready to pop under the broiler the next morning while you're getting ready. Brown-bagging it is another nifty idea for people who are rushed in the morning. A cheese sandwich and piece of fruit eaten in the car or at your office desk is better than no breakfast at all.

Breaking with traditional breakfast foods like the fat-laden stand-by of fried eggs, bacon, and buttered toast is also a good way to get more variety into this underrated meal. Kids who eat tuna melts, pizza, or grilled cheese sandwiches in the morning are less likely to get bored with breakfast than those who are faced with the same packaged cereal every day.

Best Ways to Break the Fast

What are the best foods to eat at breakfast?

Ideally, this meal should contain foods from all four food groups and should make up one-quarter to one-third of the day's nutrients. For many people, breakfast is the only meal eaten at home, in which case it is important to pack it with good amounts of fibre, vitamins, and minerals. The meal should also contain some of the following.

Milk and Milk Products

Choose low-fat foods from this group such as a tall glass of skim or 2 percent milk or a cup of low-fat yogurt. Both are also excellent whipped up into a quick blender drink with fruit. Low-fat cheese can count as a serving from this group or from the protein foods—meat, fish, poultry, and alternates.

Meat, Fish, Poultry, and Alternates

Again, go for a low amount of fat and be adventurous. The egg is not the only protein food that has a place on the breakfast table, although it is a favourite of many. Eating a maximum of three egg yolks a week is advised because of their cholesterol content, but you can extend these with plenty of egg whites, especially in omelettes and scrambled eggs.

Bacon and sausages should be eaten in moderation and with an eye to fat content. Side bacon is basically saturated fat, salt, nitrites, and not much more. Back, or Canadian, bacon is much leaner and is all right if it is consumed occasionally; the same is true for sausages, which are high in fat. When you cook these meats, cook them so the fat drips off.

Why not try fish at breakfast? Along with the traditional kipper, albacore tuna, complete with its omega-3 fatty acid, is excellent on a melt (the cheese gives you the dairy component) or in a whole-wheat pita.

Breads and Cereals

Choose whole-grain breads and cereals where possible or, as second best, enriched versions of refined breads. Be careful when you select muffins, quick breads, or breakfast pastries. That good-looking Danish is probably loaded with fats as well as sugar. The same goes for most store-bought granolas (see also Chapter 4) and for the lashings of butter you might be tempted to smear on that healthy hunk of whole-wheat bread. Remember: breakfast is supposed to pep you up; lots of fat will get your day off to a sluggish start.

Fruits and Vegetables

A piece of fresh fruit is the ideal choice from this food group—a better choice than juice because of the fibre. For people who are creatures of habit and cannot start the day without a glass of juice, this is second best. Dried fruits are great additions to hot and cold cereals, especially for people who are trying to boost their iron intake.

What's on the Morning Menu?

Eating breakfast away from home, either in a restaurant or in a hotel, presents its own set of problems. And because most dining establishments are still stuck in the bacon-and-eggs, pancakes-with-syrup, or buttered-toast-with-jam routine, it can be tricky to eat a healthy breakfast. Here are some tips:

- When ordering eggs, opt for poached or boiled rather than fried or scrambled, which are usually high in fat. If you order an omelette, see if it can be cooked with minimal butter and if it can be made with one whole egg and extra egg whites.

- Order low-fat milk.

- Order toast unbuttered, and if you want, with butter on the side. Buttering toast yourself can really reduce your fat intake. Ask for whole-wheat or other whole-grain toast or bread rather than white.

- Fresh fruit may not be listed on a restaurant menu but is often available on request.

- When you are travelling, if your hotel room has a fridge, stock it with nutritious items not offered on the breakfast menu—low-fat cheese, fresh fruit, and low-fat milk.

- For the nutritional content of fast-food breakfasts, see the chart on pages 196 to 201.

Healthy Munching at Brunch
Brunch is becoming an increasingly popular midday meal, especially on weekends. But this pleasant custom has some unique hazards. Here is some advice on how to avoid them:

- Never go to a brunch (especially one of those lavish buffet affairs consisting of everything from lobster thermidor to Black Forest cake) starving! Don't skip breakfast in anticipation of a big brunch, especially if you have slept late, in which case your body will be even hungrier. Remember that you can always skip your evening meal.

- When you select food from a lavish brunch buffet table, remember these key words—discernment and moderation. Don't load up your plate with everything from soup to nuts. Choose small amounts of nutritious foods from all the food groups, and arrange them on your plate in an appetizing way. You can always return to the buffet for more, and you will savour your food more if you take small servings. Survey the buffet table before choosing your food, and opt where possible for dishes with the least amount of fat. A series of small, carefully chosen assortments is your best bet for brunch.

Calories 141
Protein 10 g
Fat 10 g
Carbohydrate 3 g

Scrambled Tofu

Serves 4.

A delicious way to extend eggs and minimize your cholesterol intake.

2	tsp. soft margarine	10 mL
1	clove garlic, minced (optional)	
2	cups well-drained, mashed tofu	500 mL
4	eggs, lightly beaten	
Salt and pepper to taste		
1	green onion, chopped	

Heat the margarine in a heavy skillet and sauté the garlic until soft. Mix together the mashed tofu and eggs in a bowl. Add to the garlic in the skillet. Cook, stirring, over medium heat for 3–4 minutes. Season with salt and pepper and sprinkle with green onion. Serve at once.

Calories 296
Protein 14 g
Fat 7 g
Carbohydrate 45 g

Banana Milkshake

Serves 1.

A great way to start the day for adults and children alike. Try using whatever fruit you have on hand with or without the banana. Peaches, pears, papayas, and mangoes taste wonderful.

1	ripe banana, peeled and sliced	
$\frac{3}{4}$	cup skim milk	175 mL
1	egg	
$\frac{1}{2}$	tsp. vanilla	2 mL

Blend all the ingredients in a food processor or blender until smooth. Serve at once.

Great Granola

Calories 200
Protein 6 g
Fat 9 g
Carbohydrate 27 g
(per $\frac{1}{2}$ cup/125 mL)

Makes 12 cups/3 L.

Lower in fat and sugar than the commercial versions, this granola is absolutely delicious and extremely high in fibre. It's also great in baking or as a topping for yogurt and fresh fruit.

5	cups rolled oats	1.25 L
$\frac{1}{2}$	cup unsweetened shredded coconut	125 mL
1	cup chopped walnuts	250 mL
$\frac{1}{2}$	cup natural bran	125 mL
1	cup oat bran	250 mL
$\frac{1}{2}$	cup wheat germ	125 mL
$\frac{3}{4}$	cup sunflower seeds	175 mL
$\frac{1}{2}$	cup honey	125 mL
$\frac{1}{4}$	cup corn, safflower, soybean, or sunflower oil	50 mL
2	tsp. vanilla	10 mL
1	cup raisins	250 mL

Combine the first seven ingredients in a large bowl. Heat the honey, oil, and vanilla in a small saucepan over low heat until blended. Pour this mixture over the dry ingredients, stirring to coat well.

Spread the mixture in a thin layer on one or two large cookie sheets. Bake at 350°F/180°C for about 20 minutes, stirring at intervals until lightly browned. Cool completely, mix in the raisins, and store in an airtight container in the fridge.

Calories 267
Protein 6 g
Fat 7 g
Carbohydrate 49 g

Muesli for One

Serves 1.

Birchermuesli, a high-fibre cereal based on raw oats, was first made by a Swiss doctor and can be bought ready-made in most health food stores. This version is easy to make the night before.

$\frac{1}{4}$	cup rolled oats	50 mL
2	tbsp. unsweetened fruit juice	25 mL
$\frac{1}{2}$	ripe apple or pear, coarsely grated	
2	tbsp. dried fruit (raisins, chopped apricots or prunes, etc.)	25 mL
1	tbsp. sunflower seeds or chopped nuts	15 mL
2	tbsp. 2% milk or 2% plain yogurt	25 mL

Place the oats in a bowl. Pour the fruit juice over and let sit in the fridge overnight. In the morning, top the oats mixture with the grated apple, dried fruit, and sunflower seeds. Add the milk or yogurt.

Calories 144
Protein 4 g
Fat 5 g
Carbohydrate 22 g

Fruity Oatmeal Muffins

Makes 1 dozen.

Use your favourite fruit, dried or otherwise, to make these delicate muffins even better.

1	cup rolled oats	250 mL
$1\frac{1}{4}$	cups buttermilk or sour milk	300 mL
1	cup all-purpose flour	250 mL
1	tsp. baking powder	5 mL
1	tsp. salt	5 mL
$\frac{1}{2}$	tsp. baking soda	2 mL
1	egg	
$\frac{1}{3}$	cup brown sugar	75 mL
$\frac{1}{4}$	cup corn oil	50 mL
1	cup blueberries, cranberries, or raisins	250 mL

Combine the oats and buttermilk in a large bowl. Let stand. Combine the flour, baking powder, salt, and baking soda in a separate bowl. Stir well to blend.

Beat the egg, sugar, and oil together in another bowl. Stir it into the oats mixture. Add the dry ingredients and fruit, stirring just until blended. Spoon into greased muffin cups. Bake at 400°F/200°C for 18–23 minutes.

Note: If you wish, substitute $\frac{1}{2}$ cup/125 mL dried apricots or prunes soaked for 30 minutes in a little hot water, port, or fruit juice for the blueberries.

Calories 193
Protein 4 g
Fat 5 g
Carbohydrate 34 g

Orange Oat Bran Muffins

Makes 1 dozen.

Tender, light, and moist with a wonderful orange flavour plus the nutritional bonus of oat bran—the cholesterol-reducing fibre.

1	cup all-purpose flour	250 mL
1	cup oat bran	250 mL
$\frac{1}{3}$	cup granulated sugar	75 mL
1	tsp. baking powder	5 mL
1	tsp. baking soda	5 mL
$\frac{1}{4}$	tsp. salt	1 mL
$\frac{1}{2}$	tsp. cinnamon	2 mL
1	egg	
$\frac{3}{4}$	cup buttermilk or sour milk	175 mL
$\frac{1}{4}$	cup corn oil	50 mL
1	tbsp. grated orange rind	15 mL
2	tbsp. orange juice	25 mL
1	cup raisins or chopped dates	250 mL

Combine the first 7 ingredients in a bowl and stir well to blend. Beat the egg with the buttermilk, oil, orange rind, and orange juice in a separate large bowl. Add the dry ingredients, stirring just until blended. Stir in the raisins. Spoon the mixture into greased muffin cups. Bake at 400°F/200°C for 18–23 minutes.

Banana Bran Muffins

Makes 12 large or 15 small muffins.

The best possible use for those overripe bananas and a favourite with kids, for whom it makes the perfect snack.

$1\frac{1}{4}$	cups all-purpose flour	300 mL
$\frac{1}{2}$	cup natural bran	125 mL
$\frac{1}{3}$	cup wheat germ	75 mL
1	tsp. baking powder	5 mL
1	tsp. baking soda	5 mL
$\frac{1}{4}$	tsp. salt	1 mL
1	egg	
$\frac{1}{3}$	cup brown sugar	75 mL
$\frac{1}{3}$	cup corn oil	75 mL
1	cup mashed banana (3 bananas)	250 mL
$\frac{1}{2}$	cup buttermilk or sour milk	125 mL
2	tbsp. molasses	25 mL
1	cup raisins or chopped dates	250 mL

Combine the first 6 ingredients in a bowl. Stir well to blend. Beat the remaining ingredients together in a separate large bowl. Add the dry ingredients, stirring just until blended. Spoon into greased muffin cups. Bake at 375°F/ 190°C for 20–25 minutes.

Note: Add $\frac{1}{2}$ cup/125 mL chopped nuts if you wish.

Three-Bran Refrigerator Muffins

Calories 136
Protein 3 g
Fat 3 g
Carbohydrate 25 g

Makes 5 dozen large or 6 dozen small muffins.

Have this batter on hand to bake fresh muffins that are ready when you are. This incredible muffin combines top-notch taste and texture with the double whammy of both insoluble and soluble fibre in the wheat and oat bran. This recipe makes *a lot*, so you might wish to halve it.

2	cups boiling water	500 mL
2	cups natural bran	500 mL
5	cups all-purpose flour	1.25 L
2	tbsp. baking soda	25 mL
1	tsp. salt	5 mL
1	cup soft margarine	250 mL
$2\frac{1}{2}$	cups granulated sugar	625 mL
$\frac{1}{2}$	cup molasses	125 mL
4	eggs	
4	cups buttermilk	1 L
2	cups All-Bran	500 mL
2	cups oat bran	500 mL
2	cups raisins	500 mL

Pour the boiling water over the natural bran in a bowl. Let stand. Meanwhile, combine the flour, baking soda, and salt in a separate bowl. Stir well to blend.

Cream the margarine, sugar, and molasses in a very large bowl until light and creamy. Add the eggs and buttermilk, beating until smooth. Stir in the natural bran. Add the flour mixture, All-Bran, and oat bran, mixing until well blended. Stir in the raisins. Spoon into greased muffin cups and bake at 400°F/200°C for 18–23 minutes.

Store unused batter in airtight containers in the fridge until you are ready to use it. This mixture keeps for up to 2 months. To use, take the batter directly from the fridge and bake the muffins at 375°F/190°C for 20–25 minutes.

Note: Substitute $2\frac{1}{2}$ cups/625 mL each of whole-wheat and all-purpose flour for 5 cups/1.25 L all-purpose if you wish.

Carrot Pineapple Muffins

Calories 169
Protein 3 g
Fat 7 g
Carbohydrate 25 g

Makes 1 dozen.

Moist and tender with a hint of cinnamon.

1	cup all-purpose flour	250 mL
$\frac{3}{4}$	cup whole-wheat flour	175 mL
1	tsp. baking powder	5 mL
1	tsp. baking soda	5 mL
1	tsp. cinnamon	5 mL
$\frac{1}{2}$	tsp. salt	2 mL
1	egg	
$\frac{1}{2}$	cup liquid honey	125 mL
$\frac{1}{3}$	cup corn oil	75 mL
1	cup grated carrot	250 mL
1	cup crushed unsweetened pineapple with juice	250 mL

Combine the first 6 ingredients in a bowl. Stir well to blend. Beat the remaining ingredients together in a large bowl. Add the dry ingredients, stirring just until blended. Spoon into greased muffin cups. Bake at 400°F/200°C for 20–25 minutes.

Note: Add $\frac{1}{2}$ cup/125 mL chopped nuts or raisins if you wish.

Cheesy Cornmeal Muffins

Calories 167
Protein 9 g
Fat 6 g
Carbohydrate 18 g

Makes 1 dozen.

These mini-cornbreads make a yummy savoury snack and are great with a bowl of hot soup or chili.

1	cup all-purpose flour	250 mL
1	cup cornmeal	250 mL
3	tbsp. granulated sugar	45 mL
$4\frac{1}{2}$	tsp. baking powder	22 mL
$\frac{3}{4}$	tsp. salt	3 mL
$1\frac{1}{2}$	cups grated low-fat cheddar cheese	375 mL
1	egg	
1	cup milk	250 mL
$\frac{1}{4}$	cup corn oil	50 mL

Combine the first 6 ingredients in a bowl. Stir well to
blend. Beat the egg, milk, and oil together in a large
bowl. Add the dry ingredients, stirring just until blended.
Spoon into greased muffin cups. Bake at 400°F/200°C for
18–23 minutes.

Calories 198
Protein 17 g
Fat 5 g
Carbohydrate 22 g

Pita Pizza

Serves 1.

Most children never refuse pizza, so why not serve this
protein-packed, simple-to-make creation at breakfast
time? Have pita bread and pizza sauce on hand in the
fridge or freezer, and all you have to do—or better still,
your children—is grate the cheese and pop it into the
oven.

3	tbsp. Pizza Tomato Sauce (see page 105)	45 mL
1	whole-wheat pita bread	
$\frac{1}{2}$	cup grated low-fat cheese	125 mL

Optional toppings (sliced mushrooms, chopped
green pepper, zucchini slices, etc.)

Spread the pizza sauce over the pita. Sprinkle evenly with
low-fat cheese and top with toppings if you wish. Place
on a baking sheet. Bake at 450°F/230°C for about 15
minutes or until the crust is brown on the bottom and the
cheese is golden brown and bubbly.

9   Fit and Well Fuelled

Eating well is the crucial first step in feeling and looking good. But this goal would be impossible without one important factor—regular physical activity.

In the days when women worked their hands to the bone cooking, cleaning, and scrubbing laundry, when men did heavy chores around the house, and when both often worked together ploughing the fields, strenuous exercise was an integral part of everyday life. Not only that, the automobile had not yet come along to relieve people of what was then a normal activity, namely, walking.

Today's lifestyle, especially for urban folk, allows little time or opportunity for good, healthy exercise. We must consciously seek it out, either by increasing our everyday activity levels or by participating in structured exercise.

Why Fitness Feels Good

The health benefits of physical exercise are many, but the most important are the prevention and, to a lesser extent, the treatment of disease.

The primary goal of exercise is to increase endurance, strength, or both. Endurance or aerobic exercise is important because it conditions the heart and lungs, thereby enhancing the capacity of the body's cardiovascular system. The use of the body's large muscles during aerobic exercise requires oxygen. This stimulates circulation, which in turn causes the heart to work harder. In order for the body to use oxygen more efficiently, aerobic activity must last for 20 to 30 minutes at a time, three to four times a week.

Activities like walking, skipping, jogging, swimming, and cycling are all considered aerobic activities, as are active sports. Sports in which there is a lot of starting and stopping, however, are not considered as effective aerobically as those in which the activity is continuous.

In order for the cardiovascular system to benefit from aerobic exercise, the heart must be working at 70 to 85 percent of its maximum rate. An easy way to determine your maximum heart rate is to subtract your age from 220. Multiplying this number by 0.7 gives you your 70 percent level. Multiplying it by 0.85 determines the *maximum* your heart rate should reach during exercise. For example, if you are 35 years old, your maximum heart rate should be 185 beats per minute (220 − 35). Your lowest heart rate during exercise should be 130 (185 × 0.7) beats per minute for aerobic benefit; your highest, 157 beats per minute (185 × 0.85). You should *never* do any exercise that increases your heart rate above 85 percent of your maximum.

There are two kinds of aerobic activity. High-intensity aerobics raise the heart rate above 70 percent of a person's maximum. Low-intensity aerobics raise a person's heart rate, but to only 60 to 70 percent of maximum. The difference lies in a person's fitness level—a high-intensity activity for a person who is not physically fit may be a low-intensity activity for someone who is.

One of the most persuasive reasons to get physically fit is that exercise, in particular the aerobic variety, has been shown to increase HDL cholesterol—the cholesterol that helps lower the risk of heart disease. Exercise is also being used in the treatment of cardiac patients to develop new circulation in areas of the body that are affected by blocked arteries, such as the heart. Exercise can help promote the development of small blood vessels, which act as alternative pathways to blocked arteries.

Exercise is beneficial for diabetics because it allows the use of blood glucose to fuel the muscles without requiring insulin. Therefore, diabetics who exercise regularly require less insulin, either from their own bodies or from injections.

It is thought that regular, weight-bearing exercise helps retain calcium in the bones. This prevents the bones from becoming thin, a process that happens in osteoporosis. Exercise is also an asset in keeping the body's joints in good shape. Good muscular control means less wear and tear on various joints. Having weak upper arm muscles, for example, could put more stress on your shoulder joints. Developing strong quadriceps in your upper leg, on the other hand, means that you place less physical stress on your knees. But as with everything, moderation is the key. Overdoing it can make your joints tired and sore.

Regular bowel movements are another bonus of regular exercise.

Feel as High as You Jump

There is one benefit of exercise for which there isn't conclusive scientific proof but to which any fitness enthusiast will likely swear. This is the physical and emotional "high," or feeling of extreme well-being, that occurs after exercising.

This does not usually occur the first time a person exercises, but rather once he or she makes it a regular activity. Some researchers believe that *endorphins*, substances produced by the body to counteract pain, could be responsible for this exercise "high." Because it is thought that the body can become addicted to a certain level of endorphins, this theory could explain the often addictive aspect of working out. It might also explain the depression that runners feel when they stop running and why a person who has stopped regular exercise for a period of time has trouble taking it up again.

If all this is true, then in order to remain motivated by the elation of exercising and not let your body's endorphin level slide too far, it is best to exercise at least three to four times a week. Should you be forced to stop exercising for an extended period of time, return to it with more frequent workouts or swimming sessions to build up those endorphins and their accompanying good feeling.

Another major benefit of exercise is its positive effect on stress. Our bodies react in the same manner to both emotional and physical types of stress. When faced with stress, we react with a "fight or flight" readiness for action, much as animals behave when they are faced with physical danger. This situation causes our bodies to release adrenalin, which helps prepare us for action—to fight or flee. The muscles also tense up, and the blood sugar level climbs to fuel them.

Such a survival mechanism has its place in the animal kingdom, but we humans make poor use of it; we might sometimes futilely slam a door with surprising force or lift a heavy object to throw it across the room! Most often, however, we react to stress by doing little more than stewing in our own hormones; we're tense and ready for action but only able to sit and worry or pace the room. The result is often a sore neck, a headache, or both.

Enter exercise. Physical activity is a fruitful way to use our readiness for action caused by stress. And anyone who has gone to a workout class mad at the boss and come out with a much calmer perspective will testify to this! The reason is that moving our bodies with some effort gets rid of adrenalin and reduces those feelings of tension and anxiety. Naturally, this doesn't solve the core problem, but it does help us deal with the situation with a clearer head. Using long walks, jogging, or swimming as a way of combatting stress is a good habit to get into.

In the same vein, exercise can act as a physical pick-me-up. If you've had a tiring day at work and are thinking of lying down, try doing some exercises instead. A short series of stretches and some aerobics will raise your energy level and might give you the green light to go out and boogie!

The ABCs of Exercise

Walking is one of the best ways to exercise. Brisk walking and speed walking (using your arms to propel yourself) can elevate your heart rate and really benefit cardiovascular fitness training. It is also tops for burning fat. In addition, walking is not as jarring on the joints as jogging or running and does wonders for toning the muscles in the upper legs and buttocks.

As with any type of exercise, speed walking should be preceded by some stretching to help prevent muscle injury and conclude with a cooldown, which could consist of a slower pace at the end of the walk as well as a few stretches. While walking, move your arms or carry weights in your hands to help raise your heart rate.

Start your walking routine with a pace that's comfortable and slowly build up speed until you're moving at a good clip.

Fitness and Fuel

When and what should you eat in relation to exercise?

Do not exercise right after eating. During a taxing degree of physical exertion, the body requires oxygen to be supplied to the muscles by the bloodstream. After eating, blood gathers in the abdominal region to aid in the digestive process. Exercising soon after eating causes excessive demand on the blood supply, which physical exertion draws to the muscles. The result can be muscle cramps, a stitch in one's side, and even digestive upset.

Avoid eating foods such as fat before exercising. They take longer to digest than other foods and cause blood to pool in the abdomen for a longer time. Avoid eating simple sugars alone as a pre-exercise snack. Unlike fats, they may digest quickly and thus not compete in the body for blood, but they can cause a surge of insulin to be released. This results in a blood sugar level that is even

ESTIMATED ENERGY COST OF VARIOUS ACTIVITIES

Activity	Calories Used per Hour
Watching TV	75
Sleeping	75
Playing softball	130
Doing desk work	180
Cleaning windows	200
Gardening (raking)	200
Ironing	250
Skating	250
Playing tennis (beginner)	250
Playing table tennis	300
Playing golf (and carrying clubs)	400
Chopping wood	450
Gardening (digging)	550
Walking (4.5 mph or 7.5 km/h)	450
Jogging or walking (5 mph or 8.3 km/h)	540
Swimming (2 mph or 3.3 km/h)	550
Aerobics classes (vigorous)	550
Cycling (13 mph or 21.5 km/h)	650
Cross-country skiing	750
Rowing (vigorous)	850
Running (8 mph or 13.3 km/h)	950

Note: The above is based on the energy expended by a 150-lb./59-Kg person. People who weigh less will expend slightly less, while those who weigh more will expend more.

lower than before you ate that chocolate bar or orange, and there goes your energy! High-fibre foods are another pre-exercise no-no because they slow down digestion, leaving less oxygen available for the muscles. They could also cause stomach upset.

Eating a snack of complex carbohydrates, however, is highly recommended. Starchy foods like whole-grain bread or pasta, eaten at least two hours before exercising, do not cause a surge of insulin. They can also be combined with a small amount of protein food for more sustained energy, as in a snack of low-fat cheese and crackers.

To Drink or Not to Drink?

Fluid replacement is important after and sometimes during athletic activity. The amount of fluid to be replaced depends on a couple of things, namely, how strenuous the activity is and the temperature of the environment. On a hot day, your body loses more fluid, and you need to drink more after or during exercise. Don't wait until you get thirsty to have some kind of drink afterward. Your body does not immediately recognize that it needs fluid, and if fluids are not replaced, dehydration can occur.

It is best not to drink just before indulging in exercise; liquid in the stomach causes blood to pool there just as food does. And sugar solutions like juice cause this to occur to a greater extent than water. However, during an extended period of activity, fluids must be replaced, but in small amounts. A maximum of eight ounces of fluid should be consumed at one time. After exercising, if you have perspired a lot, drink a couple of glasses more than your thirst demands.

Cold water is the best liquid to consume during exercise because it competes less for a share of the blood supply. Sugar solutions like juice and sports drinks should be diluted with water. Sports drinks, already somewhat diluted, are best mixed with an equal amount of water; juices should be diluted much more.

After that workout, think twice about knocking back a cool one. Alcohol is not the ideal fluid replacement because it causes fluid loss through urination. If you cannot forgo a few beers after exercising, drink a couple of glasses of water first. Beware also of drinks high in sugar; if you're trying to lose weight, a few glasses of juice could even out that "energy in—energy out" equation!

Some people worry about sodium loss during exercise. If you perspire heavily during an exercise session, some salt may need to be replaced. But moderate perspiration does not cause loss of any sodium that the body needs, because most of us already consume more salt than we need. Taking salt tablets is not a good idea for the same reason. An extra shake of the salt shaker at the next meal is adequate. People who think they need some salt replacement because they perspire excessively should consult a doctor about their salt intake.

Don't Let Leisure Go to Waist

There are many reasons to exercise to control weight.

Studies have shown that people who diet and exercise lose more fat than those who merely diet. This is an ideal regimen—after all, the goal of dieting is to lose fat. Exercise also helps prevent loss of lean body mass during dieting. And because fat is bulkier than muscle, people who lose more fat look leaner than those who lose lean body mass as well as fat. People who exercise while dieting may even gain a little weight at first because muscle weighs more than fat. But they will likely lose inches—and who can argue with that?

Exercise also helps dieters because of its effect on their bodies' metabolic rate. The *basal metabolic rate*, or BMR, describes the energy required to sustain processes in the body and maintain body temperature. When an individual starts dieting, the body initially allows weight loss to occur. However, it soon begins to perceive this weight loss as some kind of starvation and switches on the survival mechanism by slowing down the metabolic rate. Suddenly the reducing diet becomes the maintenance intake for the body. The dieter is then faced with a choice: either reduce food consumption or increase activity in the form of exercise.

The choice seems an easy one. Who wants to keep lowering their intake of food? Not only that, people who drastically lower their caloric intake are likely to miss out on certain nutrients. In addition, lean body mass, or muscle, requires more energy than fatty tissue. This means that leaner people require more calories to maintain their weight than fatter people who weigh the same. This helps explain why men, who have more lean body mass than women, lose weight more quickly.

Studies have shown that active, slim people eat more than sedentary, overweight people. The reason for this is partly that exercise burns calories, but it is also thought that the metabolic rate increases for several hours after exercising.

There is now a new area of research that is comparing exercise intensity and the burning of fat. It used to be thought that aerobic activities, which create a demand for oxygen by the large muscles, burned body fat. It now appears, however, that high-intensity aerobics—those that elevate the heart rate above 70 percent of a person's maximum—might not promote the burning of fat. Carbohydrate, which is stored in the liver and muscle as glycogen, is needed for fuel during high-intensity exercise. Thus a diet rich in complex carbohydrates helps fuel the body for high-intensity aerobics.

However, low-intensity aerobics—those that keep the heart rate below 70 percent of maximum—cause fat to be used as fuel. It takes about 12 minutes of low-intensity exercise before fat begins to be broken down. Therefore, in order to burn fat, a workout should be long enough to have some effect, that is, 25 to 30 minutes. Because this type of exercise does not promote cardiovascular fitness, the best idea is to combine both low- and high-intensity programs throughout the week. One goal could be to lose body fat first when you are dieting and then to concentrate on cardiovascular fitness once your body is better able to withstand the stress.

Some research shows that body weight has a *set point*. This is the weight at which the body seems to want to stay and to which some people find their body wants to return after losing weight. Exercise seems to change the set point. By exercising regularly, it appears that the body adjusts to a new, lower weight.

Another bonus of exercise is that diminished appetite usually follows. So if you are trying to reduce your food intake, go for a walk on the way home for dinner. Be warned, however, that if you are not eating properly, no amount of exercise will control your appetite. In fact, if your timing of meals is off, exercise can exaggerate the bad effects.

Best Ways to Work That Body
Here are a few tips on how to work more exercise into your life:

- Before starting on any exercise program, check whether

it is the best one for you. If you have a bad back, for example, consult a doctor before joining up for aerobics classes or weight-lifting. Before joining any type of fitness club, check the instructors' qualifications, size of classes, and so on.

- Take stairs instead of an elevator whenever possible.

- If you drive to work, park your car a few blocks from where you normally park and walk the rest of the way.

- Walk small children to school instead of driving them, if the distance isn't too great. This increases activity levels for all of you.

- If your lunch hour permits, go for a 15-minute walk before eating lunch.

- Go on a family hike or bicycle ride on weekends instead of watching TV or going to a movie.

- If you own a bike, equip it with a carrier and use it to do shopping and other errands instead of driving.

- If you are a music lover, listen to your favourite music on your headphones while taking a brisk walk instead of lounging around.

Too Much of a Good Thing
As with all good things, too much exercise can have negative results. For example, women who overdo it might experience a hormonal change that leads to irregular periods. This change can also affect their calcium status, as it does at menopause. Women athletes such as marathon runners should therefore be concerned about their predisposition to thinning of the bones.

Athletes should also pay attention to their consumption of iron. Iron is an essential compound of hemoglobin in the blood. Because hemoglobin is necessary for transporting oxygen, an iron deficiency can seriously impair athletic performance. Research has shown that certain types of exercise can affect an athlete's iron status. It has been found that red blood cells, which contain hemoglobin, break down when the body pounds against hard surfaces during strenuous exercise. Proper shoes, good running surfaces, and moderate distance can help protect against this breakdown. Athletes, especially those who are cutting down on their consumption of red meat, should be wary and choose a diet rich in iron.

10 Different Strokes for Different Folks

One person's meat is indeed another's poison, and our society's eating styles reflect this timely variation on an old adage.

Today a growing number of people are choosing to live alone and must adapt their eating styles accordingly. Many others have decided to eschew meat, but finding a nourishing meatless diet, particularly one containing adequate protein, needs special care. And for the burgeoning number of elderly people, this is a time of life when eating right is a primary concern. Here are some pointers for people in these three groups.

Sweet Solo

Almost one in ten people in our society lives alone. Most of these people are under 34 or over 65 years old. And the single person who stands alone by the kitchen counter eating spaghetti straight from the can at mealtime is, unfortunately, all too common.

The main nutritional concern for such people is the lack of variety in their diets. A balanced diet contains more than 50 nutrients, which have to come from a diversity of foods. The keys to achieving this balance are planning meals and carefully shopping for food. In an effort to avoid waste, many singles wind up with little or nothing in the fridge. There are, however, ways to minimize waste and still have food in the house even if you are shopping and cooking for one.

When you shop for food, it is particularly important to choose items that give good nutritional value for your dollar. One way to do this is to shop with a detailed list. Checking "best before" dates is crucial—single people have no other family members to finish the carton of yogurt that, according to the label, has only two days to go. And buying a large package of perishable food on special may not be so economical for the person who lives alone.

Storing foods carefully is another way to retain nutrients and avoid waste. A couple of good ideas are to label frozen foods and store them in see-through containers so you can tell at a glance what is in them.

Dairy products need not pose problems for singles.

Milk is cheaper bought in plastic bags and can be frozen this way. Freezing milk causes it to change in appearance because it separates somewhat, but this does not affect the taste. Skim-milk powder and small cans of low-fat evaporated milk are handy to have around. So is UHT (ultra-high temperature) milk, which can be stored at room temperature until opened, after which time it must be kept in the fridge. Cottage cheese is a versatile milk product to keep on hand for all meals and can be bought in small containers. When you buy other types of cheese, go for small packages and freeze the excess if you wish.

It's a good idea to keep canned fish, cold cooked chicken, and eggs on hand to supply the protein components of a quick meal. When you buy meat at the supermarket, ask the meat manager to sell you the portion of meat you need if no appropriate packages are available. If the item is on special in a larger amount than you need for a meal, separate it into portions at home, wrap them individually, label them with the date, and freeze them. You can also cook the whole batch and then freeze it in portions for ready-cooked, frozen meals.

Many singles, fed up with eating a couple of slices of bread and finally throwing out the rest, give up buying bread altogether. This is an instance where the freezer comes in handy. Just freeze a loaf of sliced bread and use it a slice or two at a time. Freezing muffins or buns is also a good idea. As for grains, you can cook and then freeze individual portions of slow-cooking types, such as brown rice, to warm up later.

Fruits and vegetables are often sadly lacking in a single person's household because of their short shelf life. Buying a few fresh fruits and vegetables at a time is the best solution. Frozen fruits and vegetables are convenient, especially when packaged in bags rather than boxes; they can then be taken directly from the freezer in the amounts needed. Leftover cooked vegetables can be marinated in a tasty dressing to be eaten the following day as a cold salad. It is advisable to buy juices in small containers because the vitamins in an opened container of juice last only four days.

Make Mine Meatless

In many countries, vegetarianism is a way of life. Sometimes the reason is religious; just as often it's simply that there is a shortage of animal meat. In North America, recent concern about eating meat, especially the red variety, along with meat's soaring prices, has led to an increased interest in vegetarianism.

There are several types of vegetarianism. Vegans are vegetarians who eat only foods of plant origin. Lacto-vegetarians eat dairy products in addition to plant foods. Lacto-ovo-vegetarians eat eggs, dairy products, and plant foods. Pesco-vegetarians exclude meat but eat fish and plants. A pollo-vegetarian is someone who does not eat red meat but eats poultry as well as plant foods.

Vegetarians, in particular those who do not eat fish or poultry, risk missing out on certain nutrients unless their diet is carefully designed. The most important of these nutrients is protein. As explained in Chapter 3, there must be a proper balance of amino acids in a meal in order for the body to use the protein those foods contain. If the protein in a particular food lacks any amino acid, then the food must be complemented with another protein that contains that amino acid. Any complete protein can accomplish this; so can an incomplete protein that contains the missing amino acid.

In societies where vegetarianism is the norm, complementary proteins are built into the traditional diet. In many regions of India, for example, legumes such as lentils cooked in yogurt are a dietary staple, and in parts of Italy so is a soup made of pasta and beans. Not so in North America. A vegetarian member of a family (frequently a teenager who has decided to renounce meat) often eats everything served at dinner—minus the meat. The person then faces the serious hazard of missing out on essential protein; this is a particularly bad situation for a growing teen with high nutrient requirements.

Vegetarians who eat other foods in addition to plants can balance their protein intake by varying the complete protein eaten at each meal. For example, they can eat an egg for breakfast, drink a glass of milk with lunch, and slip yogurt into their salad dressing at dinner.

Vegans, on the other hand, have only a couple of choices. Soybeans and products made from them, such as tofu, are the only foods that contain complete plant protein. Although soybeans are extremely versatile, eating them at every meal is not necessarily a desirable choice. The only other way for vegans to round out their protein intake is to learn which incomplete proteins are complementary (that is, which ones provide the others' missing amino acids) and to consume them at the same meal. One rule of thumb is that similar foods lack the same amino acids. Legumes, for example, tend to lack the amino acid methionine, whereas grains are often low in lysine. Thus, by combining incomplete proteins like beans and pasta, you can prepare yourself a plateful of complete protein.

There are some other special dietary needs of which the vegetarian should be aware.

Infants and children require increased protein in order to grow, and this can pose problems if they are vegetarians. Soy products such as milk and tofu, as well as nut butters, can help supply some of this extra protein. It is also important that anyone who is still growing maintains an adequate caloric intake; otherwise, the body begins to break down protein for fuel, a process that could hamper growth and the repair of tissues.

On the other hand, vegetarians, particularly teenage vegetarians who do not eat balanced meals, are in danger of snacking on sweet, starchy foods between meals and becoming overweight. They might then go on a diet, which can lead to an even lower nutritional intake. The moral for vegetarians who tend to gain weight is: be sure to eat balanced meals that contain some complete protein and to ward off that snack attack with something nutritious.

Vitamin B12 is another nutrient often lacking in the vegetarian diet because it does not occur naturally in plant foods. This vitamin is found in dairy products and eggs, so it is the vegan who is mainly at risk here. Vegans should seek out foods fortified with vitamin B12, such as fortified soy milk and nutritional yeasts, or take a supplement. This is particularly important during pregnancy and breast-feeding to ensure the health of the baby. After weaning, the vegan baby should be given a B12 supplement. For more information on this vitamin, see Chapter 1.

It can be tricky for vegetarians to meet their mineral requirements, iron in particular. The iron consumed in a vegetarian diet is non-heme iron, which the body does not easily absorb. Iron absorption is further impeded by high amounts of other components in the vegetarian diet, such as phytates and oxalates. One way vegetarians can facilitate the absorption of iron is to increase their consumption of vitamin C.

Calcium is another mineral that may be lacking in the vegetarian diet, particularly that of vegans, who should take special care to find good plant sources of calcium (see Chapter 1). In addition, their absorption of calcium can be adversely affected if their diets are too high in insoluble fibre. This is of special concern to pregnant, breast-feeding, and post-menopausal women as well as adolescents, whose diets may also be low in vitamin D. They should drink fortified milk, which contains this nutrient. Although vitamin D can be manufactured if there is sufficient sunshine, it can easily be deficient in the diet of vegetarians who do not consume dairy products.

Fast Food: Feast or Famine?
With the speedy pace of today's lifestyle, fast foods are becoming a bigger and bigger part of many people's diets. Often rightly frowned on as being nutritionally lacking, fast food in some shape or form is here to stay. The realistic approach, therefore, is to make some informed choices and get the most nutrition possible out of these foods. Making such choices will, one hopes, help influence the fast-food chains to improve the nutritional quality of their products.

The following tips could be helpful when deciding which fast food to feast on.

When you order a hamburger, go for the regular single patty rather than double or jumbo-sized burgers. A three-ounce beef patty is a perfectly adequate amount of protein at a meal, and this way of consuming it is high enough in fat that no one needs a double whammy! A hamburger, however, is still a better choice than a piece of fried fish or chicken. These items, because they may be fried in animal fat, are considerably higher in saturated fat.

French fries are best avoided altogether. The best choice of potato is the baked variety, with the skin intact for added fibre and without fat-laden toppings. Best toppings are steamed veggies and some grated or cottage cheese. Cheese sauce is likely to be high in fat. Avoid potato skins, which are usually deep-fried.

Watch out for milkshakes—they can add 300 to 400 calories to your meal. Instead drink low-fat milk, fruit juice, or a sugar-free drink.

Pizza can be one of the most nutritious forms of fast food. Keep the amount of fats to a minimum by avoiding meat toppings like pepperoni, sausage, and bacon. Picking them off a cooked pizza is not the answer, because the fat will have already seeped into it. Avoid high-sodium items like anchovies and olives, and load up

NUTRIENT CONTENT OF FAST FOODS

Chain	Food	Fat (g)	Sodium (mg)	Calories
Arby's	Butter croissant	10	225	220
	Croissant, mushroom and Swiss cheese	25	630	340
	Croissant, bacon and egg	30	550	420
	Croissant, sausage and egg	50	745	530
	Club sandwich	30	1,610	560
	Ham and cheese sandwich	17	1,350	380
	Roast beef sandwich	15	880	350
	Super roast beef sandwich	28	1,420	620
	Turkey sandwich	24	1,220	510
Burger King	Cheeseburger	17	730	350
	Cheeseburger, double	32	990	530
	Chicken sandwich	50	775	690
	French fries, regular	11	230	210
	Hamburger	13	525	290
	Hamburger, Whopper	36	990	630
	Hamburger, Whopper, with cheese	45	1,435	740
	Hamburger, Whopper, double beef	52	1,080	850
	Hamburger, Whopper, double beef with cheese	60	1,535	950

The Enlightened Eater

Chain	Food	Fat (g)	Sodium (mg)	Calories
	Onion rings, regular	16	450	270
	Pie, apple	12	335	240
	Shake, chocolate	10	280	340
	Shake, vanilla	11	320	340
	Whaler sandwich	25	745	540
	Whaler sandwich with cheese	30	885	590
Domino's	12″ Pizza, 2 slices	5	660	340
	16″ Pepperoni pizza, 2 slices	15	1,080	440
Kentucky Fried Chicken	Chicken breast filet sandwich	22	1,093	436
	Chicken, fried drumstick, extra crispy	9	263	155
	Drumstick, original recipe	6	207	117
	Side breast, extra crispy	18	564	286
	Side breast, original recipe	12	558	199
	Thigh, extra crispy	23	549	343
	Thigh, original recipe	17	566	257
	Wing, extra crispy	14	312	201
	Wing, original recipe	9	302	136
	Kentucky Nuggets (6)	20	810	282

Nutrient Content of Fast Foods (continued)

Chain	Food	Fat (g)	Sodium (mg)	Calories
	Coleslaw	8	225	121
	French fries	7	434	184
	Mashed potatoes	1	268	64
	Roll	1	118	61
Harvey's	Hamburger	6	*	437
	Cheeseburger	8	*	505
	French fries	7	*	478
	Wiener	6	*	344
McDonald's	Egg McMuffin	15	885	327
	English muffin with butter	5	318	186
	Hash brown potatoes	7	325	125
	Hot cakes with butter and syrup	10	1,070	500
	Sausage, pork	19	615	206
	Scrambled eggs	13	205	180
	Big Mac	33	1,010	563
	Cheeseburger	14	767	307
	Chicken McNuggets (6)	19	525	314
	McNugget sauce Barbeque	Less than 1	309	60

Chain	Food	Fat (g)	Sodium (mg)	Calories
	Honey	Trace	Trace	50
	Hot mustard	2	259	63
	Sweet and sour	Less than 1	186	64
	Cookies, Chocolaty Chip	16	313	342
	Cookies, McDonaldland	11	358	308
	Ice cream in cake cone	5	109	185
	Ice cream in sugar cone	4	110	170
	Pie, apple	14	398	253
	Pie, cherry	14	427	260
	Shake, chocolate	9	300	383
	Shake, strawberry	9	207	362
	Shake, vanilla	8	201	352
	Sundae, caramel	10	195	328
	Sundae, hot fudge	11	175	310
	Sundae, strawberry	9	96	289
	Filet-o-fish sandwich	25	781	432
	French fries, regular	12	109	220
	Hamburger	10	520	255
	Quarter Pounder	22	735	424
	Quarter Pounder with cheese	31	1,236	524
Swiss Chalet	French fries	8	*	462

Chain	Food	Fat (g)	Sodium (mg)	Calories
	Chicken, half	14	*	699
	Chicken, quarter	5	*	308
	Sauce	Less than 1	*	24
	Bun	Less than 1	*	110
	Coleslaw	Less than 1	*	65
	Salad and dressing	Less than 1	*	30
Taco Bell	Burrito, bean	11	*	350
	Burrito, beef	21	327	466
	Burrito, combination	16	300	404
	Cheeseburger	12	330	278
	Enrichito	17	1,304	373
	Frijoles and cheese	6	*	232
	Hamburger	7	231	221
	Taco	9	*	162
	Tostada	6	101	179
	Tostada with beef	15	138	291
Wendy's	Cheeseburger, single	34	1,085	580
	Cheeseburger, double	48	1,414	800

Chain	Food	Fat (g)	Sodium (mg)	Calories
	Cheeseburger, triple	68	1,848	1,040
	Chili con carne	8	1,065	230
	French fries	16	112	330
	French toast, 2 slices	20	850	400
	Hamburger, single	26	774	470
	Hamburger, double	40	980	670
	Hamburger, triple	51	1,217	850
	Omelette with mushrooms, onions, green peppers	15	200	210
	Omelette with ham, cheese, mushrooms	25	570	290
	Potato with chicken à la king	5	820	350
	Potato with chili and cheese	25	610	510
	Potato with sour cream and chives	25	230	460
	Potato with stroganoff and sour cream	25	910	490
	Potato with cheese	40	450	590
	Potato with bacon and cheese	35	1,180	570
	Shake, chocolate	16	247	390

* Values are not available.

with lots of veggies like green peppers, onions, mushrooms, and extra tomato. Some pizza places use low-fat mozzarella—an excellent idea.

Chinese fast food can be high in nutrients if you avoid fatty items like egg rolls and deep-fried, battered foods. Stir-fries are usually a better choice, especially if the chef goes easy on the oil. Steamed rice is healthier than fried, which is usually high in sodium and fat. Ask to have the MSG omitted from your food to lower the sodium, and try seasoning food with rice vinegar instead of a salty soy sauce.

Fried chicken is a fast way to load up on unwanted fat and sodium—one piece can rack up more than 300 calories! If you do feel compelled to eat it, avoid small pieces coated in extra crispy, fat-laden batter, and choose those with a large amount of chicken compared to breading. If you have the choice, go for barbecued or rotisserie chicken and peel off the skin. But avoid the sauces that accompany all of these kinds of chicken.

Fast-food breakfasts—usually fried eggs with bacon and buttered toast—are not a good way to start the day. Instead grab a bran muffin and a piece of low-fat cheese, both of which are probably faster and healthier to boot!

Last but not least, remember one thing. Fast-food chains are in the business of giving people what they want. If we insist on salads, baked potatoes, and meat that isn't loaded with fat but insist that they also be fast, the chains will respond by selling food that meets these requirements. It can be fast and still be good food!

Let's Create a Stir-Fry

The homemade stir-fry is probably the easiest, most versatile, and healthiest of fast-food meals. It is ideal for a solo lunch or dinner, takes only minutes to make, and can incorporate whatever your fridge might hold. Use our stir-fry chart along with the following pointers and recipes for sauce to come up with your favourite creation. Serve over rice or noodles.

- Cut all the ingredients into uniform sizes ahead of time and keep them close at hand. Speed is of the essence when stir-frying. Arrange them on plates in categories as shown in the chart.

- Use a wok for best results, but a large, heavy skillet will do.

A	B	C	D
Your Pick of Protein (About 3 oz./90 g)	**Veggies with Verve** (About $\frac{1}{2}$ cup/ 125 mL)	**Tender Veggies** (About $\frac{1}{4}$ cup/ 50 mL)	**Topping It Off** (About 1 tsp./ 5 mL)
Chicken, cubed or slivered	Asparagus, sliced diagonally	Bean sprouts	Toasted peanuts
Turkey, cubed or slivered	Bamboo shoots, cut into julienne strips	Bok choy leaves	Toasted sesame seeds
Lean meat, cubed or slivered	Bok choy stems, sliced diagonally	Chinese cabbage, shredded	Toasted cashews
Firm-fleshed fish, cubed	Broccoli flowerets; broccoli stems, cut diagonally	Green onion, cut into matchsticks	Toasted pine nuts
Shrimp, peeled and deveined	Carrots, cut into julienne strips	Lettuce, shredded	Toasted slivered almonds
Scallops	Celery, sliced diagonally	Spinach, shredded	Green onion, chopped
Tofu, pressed and cubed	Cauliflower flowerets		Fresh coriander (also called Chinese parsley or cilantro), chopped
	Green beans, topped and tailed		
	Green or red peppers, cubed or cut into julienne strips		
	Onion, sliced		
	Snow peas, topped and tailed		
	Turnip, cubed or cut into julienne strips		
	Water chestnuts, sliced		
	Yellow squash, cubed or cut into julienne strips		
	Zucchini, cubed or cut into julienne strips		

Note: Quantities are for one serving.

- Heat the wok over medium-high heat until very hot, almost smoking. Then add 1 tsp./5 mL corn, safflower, soybean, or sunflower oil. Swirl it around the wok and heat 1 minute longer. If you wish, substitute chicken stock for oil for lower fat content.

- Add the protein ingredient from Column A. Stir-fry, tossing quickly with a slotted spoon, wok flipper, or chopsticks, for 1–5 minutes or until browned on all sides. (Shake the wok gently if you are frying tofu so it does not break.) Remove with a slotted spoon.

- Drizzle 1 tsp./5 mL oil or chicken stock into the wok and heat for 1 minute. Add the vegetables from Column B. Stir-fry for about 3 minutes or until they are tender-crisp. (It is a good idea to first blanch hard vegetables like broccoli, cauliflower, and carrots by plunging them into boiling water before adding them to the stir-fry.)

- Return the protein ingredient to the wok along with tender vegetables from Column C.

- Push the stir-fry to the sides of the wok. Add a sauce (see recipes on page 213). Cook until the sauce thickens.

- Add toppings from Column D. Toss. Serve at once.

- For a more aromatic stir-fry, add $\frac{1}{2}$ tsp./2 mL minced fresh ginger root, 1 minced garlic clove, or both to the wok before adding the protein ingredient from Column A.

Basic Meal in a Pouch

Calories 329
Protein 23 g
Fat 12 g
Carbohydrate 20 g

Serves 1.

Baking fish, chicken, or vegetables in a pouch with your favourite seasoning and a little white wine or stock is a great way to prepare a nutritious meal that takes only minutes. It's perfect for single people who like to dine well on their own.

Foil or parchment paper
Corn, safflower, soybean, or sunflower oil for brushing

1	4-oz./125-g fish fillet or boneless, skinned chicken breast	
2	tbsp. finely chopped onion, leek, celery, fresh ginger root, or a combination of all four	25 mL
1	tsp. finely chopped fresh herbs (parsley, dill, tarragon, thyme, or basil)	5 mL
1–2	tbsp. dry white wine or fish or chicken stock	15–25 mL

Salt and pepper to taste

Cut a square of foil or parchment paper large enough to hold the fish or meat. Brush it with oil and place the fish or meat, vegetables, and herbs on one half. Sprinkle with the wine or stock, salt, and pepper. Seal the package by crimping the edges.

Bake at 400°F/200°C for 10 minutes per 1 inch/2 cm of thickness for fish or for 20–25 minutes for chicken. To serve, place the pouch on your plate and open it at the table to release the aromas. Serve with steamed veggies, bread, rice, or potatoes.

Note: It is easy to cook your vegetables in the same pouch as the fish or chicken. Just enclose broccoli flowerets, carrot juliennes, snow peas, etc. along with a little extra wine or stock.

Low-Fat Fettuccine Alfredo

Calories 390
Protein 23 g
Fat 5 g
Carbohydrate 54 g

Serves 1.

This is as close as you can come to the silken-smooth original without using cream. A terrific way to pamper yourself when you're making dinner for one.

$\frac{1}{3}$	cup 2% cottage cheese	75 mL
2	tbsp. grated Parmesan cheese	25 mL
Freshly ground pepper to taste		
3	oz. fettuccine noodles	75 mL

Blend the cottage cheese and Parmesan in a food processor or blender until smooth. Cook the mixture in a small saucepan over medium heat until heated through, stirring constantly. Do not boil, or the mixture will separate. Season with pepper.

Cook the fettuccine in plenty of boiling, salted water until al dente. Drain and toss with heated sauce.

Note: For a delicious vegetable variation on this theme, top the cooked fettuccine and Alfredo sauce with 1 cup/ 250 mL assorted veggies steamed until tender-crisp— julienne carrots, zucchini, snow peas, or broccoli flowerets.

Calories 285
Protein 36 g
Fat 7 g
Carbohydrate 18 g

Chinese Soup for One

Serves 1 as a meal.

This delicate soup includes all the food groups, is a cinch to make, and is amazingly low in calories. The flavours of fresh ginger root and coriander leaves give it a magnificent fragrance and taste that will have you making it as a satisfying lunch or supper on a regular basis. Use whatever vegetables or noodles you have on hand, but don't forgo the homemade stock, which you can keep on hand frozen in plastic containers.

1	cup homemade chicken stock (see pages 46–47)	250 mL
1	tsp. peeled, finely grated fresh ginger root	5 mL
1	small single chicken breast, skinned, boned, and diced	
$\frac{1}{4}$	cup pressed tofu (see page 210), diced	50 mL
$\frac{1}{4}$	cup drained canned Chinese straw mushrooms	50 mL
$\frac{1}{4}$	cup sliced bok choy or Chinese greens	50 mL
	Handful Chinese rice vermicelli or dried egg noodles	
1	green onion, chopped	
1	tsp. chopped fresh coriander (also called Chinese parsley or cilantro)	5 mL

Bring the stock to a boil in a medium-sized saucepan. Add the ginger root, chicken, tofu, mushrooms, and bok choy. Simmer for 1–2 minutes or until the chicken is cooked. Return the soup to the boil and add the vermicelli; cook until al dente. Pour into a bowl and sprinkle with green onion and coriander.

Tofu Mayonnaise

Calories 469
Protein 33 g
Fat 31 g
Carbohydrate 22 g
(entire recipe)

Makes about 1 cup/250 mL. Keeps in the fridge for up to 5 days.

Make sure the tofu is at its freshest for this silken mayonnaise that is just as tasty as the real thing. It's terrific with freshly steamed asparagus, in any salad, or on sandwiches and is a fabulous way to get the taste of mayo without all the fat.

1	cup drained, mashed tofu	250 mL
2	tbsp. corn, safflower, soybean, or sunflower oil	25 mL
2	tbsp. lemon juice	25 mL
1	tbsp. Dijon mustard	15 mL
Salt and pepper to taste		
1	tbsp. fresh herbs (basil, tarragon, chives, or parsley) or $\frac{1}{2}$ tsp. dried (optional)	15 mL/2 mL

Blend all the ingredients in a food processor or blender until smooth. Store in the fridge in an airtight container.

Spinach Tofu Dip

Calories 469
Protein 33 g
Fat 31 g
Carbohydrate 22 g
(entire recipe)

Makes about 2 cups/500 mL.

Your party guests will never know that this is a low-fat dip made with tofu. Ideal for dipping raw vegetable crudités or spreading on whole-grain toast rounds and crisp crackers. This recipe comes from Susan Joseph, who owns and operates her Slimcook cooking school in Bethesda, Maryland.

3	cups lightly packed fresh spinach, washed, dried, and with stems removed	750 mL
1	cup drained, mashed tofu	250 mL
$\frac{1}{2}$	English cucumber, peeled and seeded	
1	tbsp. sesame oil	15 mL
3	tbsp. lemon juice	45 mL
2	cloves garlic, minced	
$\frac{1}{2}$	cup 2% plain yogurt	125 mL
$\frac{1}{4}$	cup finely chopped green onion	50 mL

Salt and pepper to taste

Blend the first six ingredients in a food processor or blender until smooth, then transfer the mixture to a bowl. Stir in the yogurt and onions until blended. Season with salt and pepper.

Calories 215
Protein 18 g
Fat 11 g
Carbohydrate 16 g

Tofu Stir-Fry

Serves 4.

The tofu must be pressed (see below) before going into this tasty vegetarian stir-fry that is full of protein and other goodies.

2	cups drained tofu	500 mL
2	tsp. corn, safflower, soybean, or sun-flower oil	10 mL
1	small onion, sliced	
1	clove garlic, minced	
1	cup sliced mushrooms	250 mL
1	medium zucchini, cut into thin julienne strips	
1	sweet red pepper, cut into thin julienne strips	
1	cup bamboo shoots, cut into thin julienne strips	250 mL
2	tsp. low-sodium soy sauce	10 mL
$\frac{1}{2}$	tsp. sesame oil	2 mL

Freshly ground pepper to taste

To press the tofu, cut the slabs into 2 or 3 slices. Place absorbent tea towels underneath and on top of the tofu slices. Place a cookie sheet or cutting board on top of the covered tofu. Place 2–4 1b./1–2 Kg of weight on top (canned food works well) and leave for 20 minutes to 1 hour. Cut the tofu into small cubes.

Heat the oil in a wok until it is very hot. Sauté the onion, garlic, and mushrooms until the onions are soft. Add the zucchini, red pepper, and bamboo shoots and stir-fry for about 1 minute. Stir in the soy sauce and sesame oil. Then add the tofu, stirring gently or shaking the wok to mix the ingredients without breaking the tofu. Cook until the tofu is heated through. Add pepper to taste. Serve over rice or Chinese noodles.

Calories 263
Protein 30 g
Fat 11 g
Carbohydrate 13 g

Tofu Eggplant Lasagna

Serves 6–8.

Tofu does a superb imitation of noodles in this flavourful, protein-packed meatless meal.

1	1-lb./500-g package tofu, drained and pressed (see page 210)	
1	medium eggplant, cut into $\frac{1}{4}$-inch/$\frac{1}{2}$-cm slices	
1	tsp. salt	5 mL
1	tbsp. corn, safflower, soybean, or sunflower oil	15 mL
$1\frac{3}{4}$	cups Quick Tomato Sauce (see page 87)	425 mL
$\frac{1}{2}$	cup loosely packed chopped fresh basil	125 mL
2	medium tomatoes, sliced	
$1\frac{1}{2}$	cups sliced mushrooms	375 mL
1	medium onion, sliced	
1	lb. low-fat ricotta cheese	500 g
1	tsp. freshly ground black pepper	5 mL
$\frac{1}{2}$	cup grated Parmesan cheese	125 mL
$1\frac{1}{2}$	cups grated low-fat mozzarella cheese	375 mL

Cut the tofu into thin slabs. Sprinkle the eggplant with salt and let it sit in a colander for 5 minutes. Pat dry with paper towels. Oil a large cookie sheet and arrange the eggplant slices in a single layer. Broil for 1–2 minutes per side or until golden brown.

Mix the tomato sauce and basil in a bowl. Spoon enough tomato sauce into a 12-cup/3-L ovenproof dish to cover the bottom. Arrange half the eggplant slices on top. Top with half the tomatoes, mushrooms, onion, and more tomato sauce. Layer half the tofu slices on top. Spread half the ricotta on the tofu layer. Sprinkle with pepper and half each of the Parmesan and mozzarella. Repeat with the remaining ingredients.

Bake, covered, at 350°F/180°C for about 30 minutes. Remove the cover and bake 15 minutes longer. Brown under the broiler if you wish.

Lemon Maple Tofu Cheesecake

Calories 336
Protein 16 g
Fat 18 g
Carbohydrate 33 g

Serves 12.

This is one of the most amazing facsimiles ever tasted. As good as regular cheesecake without the caloric side effects.

1½	cups walnut pieces	375 mL
½	cup rolled oats	125 mL
3	tbsp. soft margarine, melted	45 mL
3	tbsp. honey or maple syrup	45 mL
1½	lb. tofu, well drained	750 g
2	eggs	
	Juice and grated rind of 1 lemon	
½	cup maple syrup	125 mL
1	tsp. grated fresh ginger root	5 mL
	Pinch salt	

Icing

½	lb. tofu, drained	250 g
	Rind of 1 lemon	
	Juice of ½ lemon	
2	tbsp. maple syrup	25 mL
1	cup blueberries, sliced strawberries, or raspberries	250 mL

Spread the walnut pieces on a cookie sheet in a single layer. Toast at 400°F/200°C for 5–7 minutes and cool. Reduce the oven temperature to 350°F/180°C.

Process the rolled oats in a food processor or blender using a few on-off turns. Add the toasted walnuts and process until just coarsely chopped. Transfer the mixture to a bowl and stir in the melted margarine and honey. Pat into an 8- or 9-inch/2- or 2.5-L springform pan. Bake at 350°F/180°C for 12 minutes. Cool.

Press the tofu (see page 210) for 30 minutes—no longer—and process in a food processor or blender until smooth. Add the eggs, lemon juice and rind, maple syrup, ginger root, and salt and process until smooth. Pour this mixture into the cooked crust and bake at 350°F/180°C for 50 minutes or until the cake has set. Let it cool in the pan.

Purée all the icing ingredients except the berries in a food processor or blender. Remove the rim of the spring-form pan and spread the icing on the cake. Arrange the berries on top of the icing.

Stir-Fry Sauces

Basic Stir-Fry Sauce	$\frac{1}{4}$	cup chicken stock	50 mL
	1	tsp. low-sodium soy sauce	5 mL
	1	tsp. dry sherry	5 mL
	1	tsp. cornstarch	5 mL

Combine all the ingredients in a small bowl. Add to the stir-fry at the end of the cooking time as described in the stir-fry pointers (see pages 202 and 204).

Szechuan Spicy Sauce Substitute chili oil for regular oil for a spicy flavour when stir-frying the ingredients. A spicy sauce can also be made by adding a pinch of minced dried chili pepper to the basic sauce.

Oyster Sauce Substitute prepared oyster sauce, available at Chinese groceries, for soy sauce in the basic sauce recipe.

Five-Spice Sauce Add a pinch of Five Spice powder, available at Chinese groceries, to the basic sauce.

Sweet and Sour Sauce Substitute pineapple juice for chicken stock in the basic sauce.

11 Spanning the Age Spectrum

From babyhood to old age, the principles of good nutrition as outlined in this book have a common application. But there are some special needs in the space of a lifetime that make some pretty particular demands on how and what we eat.

Eating for Two

The development of the human fetus puts some especially high nutrient requirements on the pregnant woman because a baby's birth weight and nutritional status depend on the mother's food intake during pregnancy. Equally important, however, is her state of health prior to becoming pregnant because in many cases, the fetus has begun to develop before the woman is even aware of her condition. A pregnant woman's good health is particularly vital if she suffers from nausea and vomiting, which can result in a low nutrient intake during early pregnancy.

The nutritional demands of the teenage years require that the pregnant teenager be particularly careful to meet the growth requirements of both herself and her baby.

These days, a maternal weight gain of 25 to 30 pounds is thought to be optimum for the baby to be born with a good birth weight and for a healthy placenta and amniotic fluid to develop in the mother. It is not advisable for the mother to restrict her weight gain because this can result in insufficient nutrient intake and a small baby.

Some women who believe they are overweight think that pregnancy is a time to watch their diet and perhaps lose some body fat. However, the fetus needs a wealth of nutrients to develop bones, muscles, and blood supply, and they must be supplied by the mother, so she should not use pregnancy as a time to diet. One consolation for the overweight pregnant woman is that her weight gain may not be as high as that of a thin one. How the mother-to-be gains weight is also important. A good average pattern for weight gain is about five pounds in the first 20 weeks of pregnancy and about one pound a week until the birth.

If your eating habits before pregnancy were far from ideal, then this is a good time to improve them. Not only will it mean a healthier baby, but good parental eating habits are also the best example for a growing child. After all, a mother who never eats fruit can hardly expect her child to buy that story about "an apple a day!"

Here are some foods that pregnant women should be wary of.

Caffeine   The effects of caffeine on the fetus are not completely known. What is known, however, is that it crosses the placenta to the fetus, so until more is known about its effects, moderation is recommended. An occasional caffeine-containing food is certainly all right. Regular doses of herbal teas may not be a good idea; their toxic effects have been documented, along with severe diarrhea and allergic reactions. More research is needed in this area.

Alcohol   Alcohol can cross the pregnant woman's placenta, and studies show that alcoholic mothers sometimes give birth to babies with deformities, mental retardation, or both. Women who consumed alcohol before they knew they were pregnant may be reassured by the fact that, although safe levels of alcohol consumption have not been determined, the occasional drink does not seem harmful to the fetus. But because there is no conclusive evidence of this, avoid alcohol if motherhood is in your immediate plans.

Smoking   Smoking during pregnancy can cause babies to be born with a lower birth weight; it also increases the risk of premature birth. Need we say more?

The pregnant woman should eat the basic balanced diet recommended in this book—but with some extras.

Energy and caloric needs during pregnancy vary from one woman to another, but you should consume an average of 100 extra calories a day in the first three-month period and about 300 extra calories a day during the second and third. What these calories consist of is also important; they must contain the nutrient bonuses of iron, calcium, and folic acid.

Extra calcium is best consumed by boosting your intake of dairy products and other calcium-rich foods (see the chart on page 12).

The pregnant woman needs a lot of fluids because of increased blood volume and kidney function and will find herself thirstier than usual. Drinking more water and eating plenty of high-fibre cereals, vegetables, and fruits will help—they not only add fluid to the diet but also help prevent constipation, an unpleasant hazard of pregnancy.

North Americans are used to eating too many salty foods. And although the practice of restricting salt during pregnancy has lately been discontinued, the mother-to-be is advised to use salt in moderation for the same reasons that anyone else should (see the chart on pages 16–17).

Many pregnant women have cravings for foods that are low in nutrients but high in sugar or fat. Women who are regularly overcome by the overwhelming desire for a huge slice of banana cream pie or a bag of pretzels do, however, have some healthier options. The best way to deal with cravings (and giving in to them on occasion is not harmful) is to eat a number of mini-meals throughout the day. This will maintain your energy level and help reduce your cravings.

Eating mini-meals is also a good routine for pregnant women experiencing severe nausea. Small, frequent amounts of food—healthy snacks like a small bran muffin or some low-fat yogurt topped with blueberries and wheat germ—can prevent extreme hunger and seem to reduce that queasy feeling. Women who are nauseated first thing in the morning should keep some crackers beside the bed to eat on waking up and then wait a few minutes before getting out of bed. It is also advisable not to drink and eat at the same time if nausea is a problem.

Skipping breakfast is just as unhealthy for pregnant women as it is for other people and can lead to uncontrolled weight gain in some women.

Best Foods for Baby

Breast-feeding is, without a doubt, the best way to feed a newborn baby for nutritional, immunological, and psychological reasons.

Breast-feeding is beneficial nutritionally because a mother's milk is uniquely suited to her particular baby and has the wonderful quality of changing its composition to suit her baby's stages of development. For example, the milk of a mother whose baby has just been born has a different nutritional balance than the milk of a mother whose baby is four months old. Breast milk is the easiest food for a baby to digest and seems to protect the infant against iron deficiency. It also allows better absorption of fats than cow's milk does. In addition, it is difficult to overfeed a breast-fed infant, who will stop sucking on the breast once he or she is satiated; a bottle can be forced on a full baby more easily.

The immunological advantages of breast-feeding result from antibodies in the mother's milk that help the newborn fight germs. Colostrum is the first secretion to come from the nursing mother's breast. Being rich in antibodies, it is especially important because it ensures that the baby concentrates on growing without the obstacle of illness. A breast-fed baby is generally unlikely to catch any diseases that the nursing mother cannot catch. This fact is worth considering by the mother who plans to wean her baby and realizes that flu or cold season is not the ideal time!

In general, breast-fed babies have fewer gastro-intestinal and respiratory infections than babies who are bottle-fed.

Breast-feeding is also a good idea if there is a family history of allergies. Babies whose parents have any kind of allergy can develop food or airborne allergies but are less likely to if they have a strong nutritional head start by being breast-fed. (Babies are never allergic to breast milk itself.) With maturity, infants are better able to handle the allergic load of new foods and the environment.

A baby can, on the other hand, have an allergic reaction to something the mother has eaten. The mother should then manipulate her diet to pinpoint the offending food. The mother of a bottle-fed baby, however, is faced with a more serious problem if she finds her baby is allergic to certain formulas, because she no longer has the option to begin to breast-feed.

One of the main benefits of breast-feeding is the psychological bond it promotes between baby and mother. It also seems to have a soothing effect on the baby that bottle-feeding does not.

Breast-feeding speeds up the process that returns the uterus to its pre-pregnancy size. It can also be a time-saver in the middle of the night by dispensing with that whole business of warming up bottles. And it makes travelling easier, because the nursing mother has no bottles or cans of formula to pack!

The Fine Art of Breast-Feeding
Although breast-feeding might seem like a simple process, many women find it fraught with problems. Here are some important guidelines to help the milk flow freely.

The nursing mother produces milk, which stays in the breast ready for the infant. The amount of milk produced depends on how much the baby nurses. If the baby empties the breast, the mother produces more milk. If the mother's breasts are not emptied, milk production decreases.

At the beginning of a feeding, milk is produced extremely slowly as the baby sucks. The mother's body then releases a hormone called *oxytocin*, which causes her milk to flow more freely. This is called the *let-down*. If there is no let-down, the baby has to work hard for little result and will likely tire before the breast is emptied. The result is decreased milk production and more frequent feedings.

This brings us to the primary rule for nursing mothers—"Relax and get your rest!" Fatigue and nervousness can both prevent the let-down from occurring, a fact that might explain why a mother's supply of milk is sometimes diminished on coming home from hospital, when the demands of other children or of chores around the home add to the strain of being a new mother. This could be the beginning of a frustrating experience for all concerned. But nursing should be a priority at this time. For the first three to four weeks of breast-feeding, the nursing mother would do well to think of herself as a cow at pasture. Once the breast-feeding pattern is established, it is likely to continue without problems. A well-fed baby whose mother is calm and confident will sleep better at night, and so will the rest of the family—including mom!

How often does a baby need to breast-feed? This varies from child to child, but a breast-fed baby does eat more often than a bottle-fed one because mother's milk is more digestible. Frequent feedings also help stimulate the breast supply.

Managing the Maternal Menu

The ideal diet of the breast-feeding mother is similar to that of the pregnant woman, and because breast milk contains iron, she should continue to tuck into those iron-rich foods.

Her caloric needs depend on the amount of milk she produces, and some of them can be met by the breakdown of extra fat deposited during pregnancy. The pregnant woman should lose weight gradually so that she does not jeopardize her milk supply, and the best way she can achieve this is with that old stand-by—a nutritious diet.

Quick weight loss is not advisable during breast-feeding for several reasons. A severe reducing diet not only lacks important nutrients, it also tires the nursing mother, whose taxing role at this time requires all kinds of extra energy and stamina. Another reason is the possible hazard of PCBs (polychlorinated biphenyls)—environmental pollutants found in some foods, air, and water. If the mother has been exposed to PCBs, they will have been stored in her adipose (fatty) tissue. When it breaks down during rapid weight loss, PCBs could be released into her breast milk. Although the chances of being seriously contaminated are rare (for example, by eating fish from polluted water), should you be concerned, get your breast milk tested.

Plenty of fluids are essential for the nursing mother's milk production, but they can also add up to a lot of calories. The mother who drinks three to four glasses of whole milk a day is ingesting 240 more calories a day, or 43,000 in six months, than the woman who drinks fat-free milk—that's more than 12 pounds in extra weight that the mother can likely do without! The woman who drinks 2 percent milk can add up an additional six pounds in the same six-month period. Juice is another liquid source of calories and should not be consumed in large doses if weight loss is to occur. Plenty of water, combined with fresh fruit for fibre, vitamins, and minerals, is a much better choice.

The new mom should also be careful not to miss out on meals because of her changed routine. If it is difficult to fit in regular meals between nursing, napping, and doing the odd chore around the house, then frequent small meals could be the answer. But above all, don't forget to eat, or you will run out of energy in no time!

The nursing mother should stay away from large amounts of alcohol because it can hinder the let-down reflex during breast-feeding and could affect her infant's health. Some people believe that small amounts, on the other hand, such as the occasional beer, may stimulate milk production. High consumption of caffeine by the nursing mom can not only make her too jumpy to nurse well, it can also make her baby restless and unable to sleep.

Smoking is thought to have a negative effect on both production and let-down of breast milk, not to mention any bad effects it might have on the infant. It is also wise for the woman who is breast-feeding to consult a physician or pharmacist before taking any drugs; they could be transferred to her milk and have adverse effects on her newborn child.

If the nursing mother decides to go back to work, she can continue breast-feeding two or three times a day. This could be first thing in the morning, on coming home from work, and then at bedtime. In order for this arrangement to work well, the breast-feeding pattern must be well established. During the day, the baby can be bottle-fed formula or stored breast milk. Breast milk that the mother has expressed can be stored for up to 48 hours in the fridge or frozen for a maximum of two months.

The Perfect Formula
Commercially prepared formulas are the closest foods to breast milk available; they have a similar ratio of ingredients. There are two main types of formulas—those with a base of cow's milk and those with a base of soy. Even formulas with a base of cow's milk contain protein that is more like that of breast milk, and their fats are easier to digest than the fats in cow's milk. Both types of formula have added vitamins and minerals and supply all the necessary nutrients until the baby is four to six months old. Then the infant requires extra iron, which can be given in the form of an iron-fortified formula, an iron supplement, or iron-enriched infant cereals.

If there is a family history of allergies and your infant has been showing signs of them, it is not advisable to switch from a cow's milk formula to the soy-based version, because soy products are also allergenic. Speak to your physician about what less allergenic products are available.

Be careful to feed your infant formula according to instructions. Different products require different concentrations, and giving a baby a formula full strength when it should be diluted could cause dehydration.

If possible, feed your baby formula until the age of 12 months. Cow's milk is hard for an infant to digest, and cases of internal bleeding have been documented. When cow's milk is introduced, it should be whole milk, at least until the age of two, because it provides the fat required for healthy development.

On Solid Ground

It is not advisable to give babies solid food before the age of four to six months. Even if your baby is hungrier and needs to be fed more often for a week or two, as often happens at around three months when there is a growth spurt, resist the temptation to offer solid foods. Not only will the infant exhibit the *extrusion reflex* (sticking out of the tongue) during the first few months of life, making him or her spit out solid food, but breast milk and formula also contain all the necessary nutrients in perfect balance during this stage of development.

When you introduce solids, don't be in a hurry to offer all kinds of different foods at once. Start with one or two new items at a time to ensure that your baby does not have intolerances or allergies. In order to do this, serve foods individually, not in mixtures. Start new foods a little at a time over three to four days so you can observe any problems. Some signs of intolerance are obvious, but because an infant cannot tell you that he or she has stomachache, this might be manifested by sleeplessness or crying. Watch for patterns when trying to pinpoint such problems.

It is wiser to feed babies infant cereals than adult varieties. Some adult cereals like cream of wheat are fortified with iron; others are not. All infant cereals, however, are fortified with important vitamins and minerals, especially iron, and should be fed to babies up to one year old.

Is Homemade Always Best?

There is often little nutritional difference between homemade and store-bought baby food. It is, however, cheaper to make your own baby food and a good idea as long as you are careful to maximize nutrients. Commercial baby food is made with ingredients of peak nutritional quality, so they are a better choice in some cases.

Use fresh ingredients, and cook foods in ways that minimize loss of vitamins and minerals (see Chapter 5). Then purée and freeze them in ice cube trays for single serving portions. As your baby develops teeth, you can chop food to a coarser texture. Don't add sugar or salt to your baby's food, and when feeding your baby dishes eaten by the rest of the family, avoid strong spices; he or she may not like the taste.

When you buy commercial baby food, read the labels. A "beef dinner" could be quite different from beef alone and could be extended with cereal, making it lower in protein. Similarly, plain and simple fruits are a better choice than an infant "dessert." In general, avoid foods containing more than a trace of salt and sugar, whether they are homemade or not.

It is also best not to feed your baby homemade spinach or carrots before the age of six months because of the nitrate levels in these foods. Commercial processing removes nitrates. Because of the danger of botulism, honey is not recommended as a food for babies less than one year old. Nor is it wise to feed allergenic foods like wheat, cow's milk, eggs, fish, nuts, or chocolate to a baby with allergy-prone parents. Another no-no is putting your baby to bed with a bottle: the sugar in juice and the lactose in milk can cause cavities.

Into the Mouths of Babes
It is during childhood that a lifetime's eating habits are formed.

These habits are crucial to developing strong bodies and minds that can help prevent disease, so starting children on the path to healthy eating is a must. To ensure this, adults must first set the example and then involve the child in their own nutrition. Letting children make some decisions about what foods they eat, having them help plan meals, especially their school lunches, and even including them in some of the cooking are great ways to do this.

Children need to eat the same kinds of foods as adults, but in different amounts. How much depends on their stage of development as well as activity levels. The biggest growth spurt happens in the first year of life, and this explains why a child's appetite may become smaller at the start of the second year. This is a time to offer small portions of food and let your child eat as much as he or she wants.

A parent must keep in mind that a child's appetite varies from day to day and from season to season. The key is to offer a variety of foods and not to be discouraged if a new food is rejected. Don't offer a new food when your child is tired or not feeling well, and serve new foods in small amounts. If an unfamiliar vegetable, for example, is met with outright rejection, try serving it later in a more attractive disguise, such as puréed in a soup containing alphabet noodles. If a child refuses the meal at hand, it is not a good idea to offer substitutes.

Bargaining with children can be another way to teach them to accept a variety of nutritious foods. If, for example, a child usually refuses whole-grain bread, make an arrangement whereby you agree to alternately buy white and whole-wheat loaves to use in sandwiches for school. The child will feel that he or she is part of the decision-making process and will likely develop a taste for whole-grain breads at the same time.

Sometimes outside influences, such as television commercials that tempt children with surprise gifts tucked into the packages of yet another new, sugary breakfast cereal, can be a real problem. When a food of questionable nutritional quality is cleverly advertised this way, it is hard to convince a child that it is not a desirable food to eat. Stick to your guns and refuse to buy it without appearing too moralistic, and use the opportunity to teach your child not to believe everything he or she sees on TV. Complain to the television station or food company about the misuse of persuasive advertising as a way to try and change it.

Snacking is extremely important for children because they tend to eat small meals, so try to make snacks as nutritious as possible. Don't go to the extreme of never allowing a potato chip or candy to pass your child's lips— this could create a greater desire for such "forbidden fruit."

Try to avoid giving sugary snacks to kids; they cause cavities when plaque on their teeth combines with the sugar to form acids. Every time sugar is eaten, these acids stay in the mouth for 20 minutes, wreaking havoc. Sticky, chewy, sugary foods are the worst for this, and they include dried fruit as well as many kinds of candy.

Best snacking foods are fresh fruits and vegetables along with their juices, nuts and seeds, whole-grain crackers and cereals, and popcorn, especially when they are eaten with milk, plain yogurt, or low-fat cheese. Cutting down on the fat and sugar in cake and cookie recipes is another good idea. Calling muffins cupcakes and baking them in fancy paper cups is a nifty way to make healthy eating fun.

Here are more ideas for easy, nutritious snacks that children can help prepare: peanut butter logs made of sliced bananas smeared with peanut butter; banana popsicles made by dipping whole bananas in orange juice and nuts and freezing them; seasoned popcorn made by sprinkling home-popped corn with grated cheese; fruit kebabs made by placing whole or chunks of fresh fruit on wooden skewers and then dipping them in low-fat yogurt blended with fresh fruit, vanilla, or a little honey. As for the ever-popular cookie, see our great recipes on pages 238 to 240.

Obesity, the most glaring nutritional problem in today's society, must be prevented during childhood. By applying the principles of this book along with an understanding that small people need small portions, even a child with a genetic tendency to be overweight can be helped to avoid obesity.

Studies have shown that in many cases, overweight children do not consume more calories than lean children; they just burn fewer calories by being less active. Nagging such children about being overweight only causes a bad self-image and could cause them to seek solace in food. A more productive approach is to encourage children to be physically active by involving them in family sports, outings, etc. Dieting during childhood is definitely out—this is a time when young people need plenty of nutrients for growth. It is better for the overweight child to grow while remaining at the same weight; the child therefore becomes leaner without compromising growth.

Teen Years: A Time for Growth
During their teens—a time of growth and development when nutrient requirements increase substantially—many young people, especially girls, unfortunately do not pay much attention to nutrition. This is a time when young people need more calcium because of a growth in skeleton size and when most consume too little iron for their bodies' needs.

Teenage boys generally fare somewhat better in this regard than girls. Although they may not pay any more attention to nutrition, they are likely to get more nutrients simply by eating larger amounts of food.

A time of increasing independence, this can also be a period during which teens learn to make food choices that are often different from their parents'. It is now that the habit of skipping breakfast frequently begins—one that leads to low energy levels during the school day. A big breakfast and sizable lunch not only increase mental alertness during school but also help control the overeating that is common when teenagers arrive home and raid the cookie jar.

The teens are a time when it is easy to gain weight. After sitting all day in school, a walk or planned aerobic activity before going home are good ways to provide energy for homework and speed up the metabolic rate.

School lunches are another hazard for this age group because they are often not nutritious enough. Parents and their children can put pressure on schools to make cafeteria food more nutritious and to add low-fat milk and fresh fruit to the pop and potato chip selection in vending machines. The latter is usually a surprisingly popular move with teenagers, who often pick a nutritious fast-food alternative when given the choice.

Girls Will Be Girls

For girls, the teens are a time when growth spurts and a developing body can make them feel they are getting fat. In fact, it is normal for some weight gain to precede a growth spurt. However, girls often turn to fad dieting, and the resulting lack of nutrients can stop growth from taking place. At a time when a girl's self-image might be somewhat low, it is best for parents not to harp on her weight, but to discourage fad diets and be caring advisors, not dictators.

If a girl's weight begins to act like a yo-yo at this age, her concern about being overweight can get worse, and bulimia or anorexia nervosa could result. Both conditions are characterized by excessive dieting and obsessive exercising.

Bulimia and anorexia nervosa are both increasingly common diseases, and 90 percent of those afflicted are female. An anorexic, although emaciated, believes that she is overweight. Her fanatical dieting can cause loss of periods, lowered heart rate and metabolism, loss of hair, and electrolyte imbalance. In the most serious cases, she starves to death. Even if the anorexic stops her dieting, health problems can show up years later. Because of hormonal changes, the calcium status of an anorexic is similar to that of the post-menopausal woman.

Bulimia is characterized by binge eating followed by self-induced vomiting and the use of laxatives. Because these practices do not rid the body of many calories, body fat does not change drastically, and the person does not usually lose weight. Any weight loss that does occur is caused by loss of water and can result in dehydration. Electrolyte imbalance can also follow. Bulimics also commonly experience bloating, constipation, and the wearing away of dental enamel.

Because of the pressures to be thin and beautiful that our society exerts on women, they are more likely to succumb to the diet demons than teenage boys. This is, however, an age when boys might be tempted to build up their muscles with protein powders and expensive supplements. They would do better to concentrate on eating a balanced diet while exercising their muscles by means of training, which is much more effective and inexpensive!

Babies of the Boom
Those people who are pushing or past 40 know only too well that this is a time when the body refuses to take abuse lying down!

Suddenly you find yourself getting older and feeling it. Your body is starting to speak up loud and clear when you mistreat it by overeating, drinking to excess, or not getting enough sleep. For the first time, perhaps, you cannot eat whatever you want without it showing on your stomach or hips. And overnight you, who used to be able to drink two cups of coffee before going to bed, realize it was that after-dinner cappuccino that kept you awake till 3 A.M.!

This is an age when eating correctly and exercising begin to be an absolute must to keep you feeling vital and stop your weight from creeping up. It's a time of reckoning, but also a time when preventive action is usually not too late.

Getting Older and Better
Youth may be wasted on the young, but there is no reason why age should not be accompanied by wisdom in the important matter of eating well. After all, the older one gets, the more crucial it is to maintain energy levels and a feeling of physical well-being.

Many elderly people, however, consider themselves past the age when eating a nutritious diet is a top priority. They are often more concerned about what they should *not* eat for all kinds of medical reasons rather than taking a positive attitude about what foods would be good for them. This is unfortunate because, along with pregnancy and breast-feeding, the senior years are a time when nutrient requirements are more important than at any other stage of adulthood.

Certainly the metabolic rate slows down with increasing age, so that elderly people need fewer calories to maintain their weight. Less physical activity adds to this reduced need for calories. But the requirement for nutrients is in no way reduced, so packing these nutrients into a smaller quantity of food is the name of the game.

Many elderly folk have psychological reasons for lapsing into the "tea and toast" syndrome or other unhealthy eating habits. One reason might be a lack of motivation to cook for oneself after a lifetime of eating with a family or spouse. Feelings of loneliness and isolation at this stage of life can even lead to a lack of appetite. Many women complain that after years of cooking for a family and finding it a chore, they simply don't feel like preparing food. Whatever the reason, not having the will or the energy to think about meals could lead to malnourishment and all that goes with it.

Seek out a friend or group of friends to get together at mealtimes to solve the aversion to eating alone. Potluck meals, to which each person brings a course, are a good way of sharing the work and the cost of cooking as well as making mealtime a pleasant, social event. Picnicking outdoors in warm weather is also a good idea; the fresh air can be a terrific stimulant to conversation as well as appetite.

If you are forced to eat alone against your wishes, try reading a book, listening to the radio, or watching a favourite program on TV while you eat. This can help take your mind off the fact that you are alone. Set a proper place for yourself, perhaps pour a glass of wine to go with dinner, and even eat by candlelight—enjoy yourself!

The Right Vittles Can Keep You Vital
There are some physical conditions that often accompany aging that can be an obstacle to a nutritious diet. Here are some ideas on how to overcome them.

Osteoporosis, or loss of calcium from the bones, can occur in the jaw. This brings with it problems with teeth and difficulty chewing certain foods—raw fruits and vegetables, some meats, and whole grains, to name a few. A simple cure could be to ensure that your dentures fit well. If you still have a problem, roast, boil, or stew meats and then slice them thinly, cook vegetables in soups, and eat ripe, stewed, or canned fruit; these are all good ways to prepare nutrition-packed foods for easy chewing.

It is particularly important at this age to consume an adequate amount of protein. If the "tea and toast" routine becomes a substitute for proper meals, the muscles can begin to waste away. A lack of iron in the diet often makes an elderly person, whose meals should include some iron-rich foods, tired and listless. (See the discussion of iron in Chapter 1.)

To combat the increase in blood pressure that often accompanies the aging process, many elderly people follow sodium-restricted diets. But aging is also usually accompanied by reduced sense of taste and smell, so the lack of salt can render food almost tasteless.

Medication is another factor that can interfere with an elderly person's eating habits. Diuretics, for example, create an increased need for potassium-rich foods (again, see Chapter 1). And a drug like tetracycline should not be taken with dairy products. If you are taking medication, consult your physician or pharmacist about whether the drug should be taken with, before, or after meals and whether you should be avoiding or increasing certain foods while on the medication.

It is easy for people in this age group to become overweight because of their lower metabolic rates and decreased activity levels. You can combat this tendency by cutting down on foods that are high in empty calories and increasing activity wherever possible (more on this in Chapter 12).

If a physician has advised you to follow a special diet and you are having difficulty doing so, ask to be referred to a dietitian.

Smart Shopping Tips for Seniors

Many of the food shopping pointers that we gave for singles in Chapter 10 also apply to seniors. Here are some more.

• An "emergency" shelf is an excellent idea in case there actually is an emergency. Perhaps you are unable to shop for food because of bad weather; the person who usually gives you a ride to the supermarket can't make it; or someone drops by unexpectedly. Foods on this shelf should include dairy products like skim milk powder, evaporated low-fat milk, UHT milk, and perhaps some instant pudding mix. Canned meat and fish, baked beans, dried legumes such as kidney beans, and peanut butter are protein stand-bys. Crackers, noodles, whole-grain cereals, and muffin or biscuit mixes are carbohydrate foods that keep well. Canned fruit and vegetables, canned juices and soups, as well as dried fruit complete the picture.

- A shopping list based on a careful reading of weekly specials advertised in the newspaper can be a big help. Evaluate whether an item on special is worth a detour. If you're saving only a small amount, it might not be worth the extra cost in transportation.

- Read labels on food packages to assess value for money as well as nutritional content of ingredients. In order to do this easily, don't forget to take your glasses when you are food shopping if you have eyesight problems.

- Shop with a friend and divide things up if sizes are too large. For example, milk is cheaper in the large plastic bags than in single cartons.

Tuna Melt

Serves 4 as a snack.

Calories 195
Protein 22 g
Fat 4 g
Carbohydrate 17 g

A fabulous, quick, and easy lunch or supper dish eaten with a green salad, this is also excellent at breakfast. You can vary this theme by using thickly sliced whole-grain bread, a pita, or an English muffin as your base and substituting cooked chicken or steamed vegetables for the tuna.

1	7-oz./198-g can water-packed tuna, drained	
2	green onions, chopped	
3	tbsp. finely chopped green or red sweet pepper	45 mL
4	small mushrooms, sliced	
2	tbsp. light mayonnaise, 2% plain yogurt, or tofu mayonnaise (page 208)	25 mL
	Salt and pepper to taste	
2	bagels, sliced in half horizontally	
4	slices tomato	
4	slices low-fat cheese	

Combine the tuna, green onions, green or red pepper, mushrooms, mayonnaise, salt, and pepper in a small bowl.

Toast the bagel halves. Layer each half with a tomato slice and a quarter of the tuna mixture and top with a slice of cheese. Bake at 350°F/180°C for 4–5 minutes or until the cheese melts. Brown under the broiler for 1–2 minutes or until lightly browned.

Macaroni and Cheese with Spinach

Calories 444
Protein 24 g
Fat 15 g
Carbohydrate 52 g

Serves 4.

Kids will never guess that this is low in fat! A wonderfully healthy version of an old favourite.

2	tbsp. soft margarine	25 mL
1	small onion, finely chopped	
1	clove garlic, minced	
3	tbsp. all-purpose flour	45 mL
$2\frac{1}{2}$	cups skim milk	625 mL
Pinch cayenne pepper		
$\frac{1}{2}$	tsp. nutmeg	2 mL
Salt and pepper to taste		
1	cup grated low-fat cheese	250 mL
2	cups elbow macaroni, cooked and drained	500 mL
1	10-oz./284-g package fresh spinach, cooked, well drained, and chopped	
$\frac{1}{2}$	cup grated Parmesan cheese	125 mL

Melt the margarine in a medium-sized saucepan. Add the onion and garlic and cook over medium heat until soft. Stir in the flour and cook, stirring, for about 1 minute. Whisk in the milk, stirring until the sauce is smooth and thickened. Season with cayenne, nutmeg, salt, and pepper. Stir in the cheese and cook until it melts.

Place half the macaroni in a medium-sized ovenproof dish. Top with a layer of spinach. Spoon half the sauce over the spinach. Top with the remaining macaroni and sauce. Sprinkle with Parmesan. Bake at 350°F/180°C for about 20 minutes or until golden brown on top.

Calories 208
Protein 14 g
Fat 5 g
Carbohydrate 33 g

Cheesy Baked Potato

Serves 1.

The stuffed baked potato is one of the most versatile and delicious ways to cook the noble spud. Served with a salad, this and the following 3 recipes are perfect for anyone needing an easy, nutritious meal. Kids love them! And they're also perfect for singles. Be sure to eat the skin for extra fibre.

1	large baking potato	
1	tbsp. 2% plain yogurt	15 mL
3	tbsp. 2% cottage cheese	45 mL
$\frac{1}{4}$	cup grated low-fat cheese	50 mL
$\frac{1}{4}$	tsp. dried or 1 tsp. chopped fresh basil	1 mL/5 mL
Salt and pepper to taste		
1	small tomato, sliced	
1	tbsp. finely chopped green onion	15 mL

Scrub the potato and prick it with a fork. Bake at 375°F/190°C for about 1 hour or until tender. Slice in half horizontally and scoop out the pulp, leaving some attached to the skin for support.

Mash the pulp in a bowl with the yogurt, cottage cheese, and half the low-fat cheese. Mix in the basil, salt, and pepper. Divide this mixture between the potato halves. Place two slices of tomato on each half and sprinkle with the remaining low-fat cheese.

Bake on a baking sheet or in an ovenproof dish at 375°F/190°C for 20 minutes or until the cheese melts. Place under the broiler to brown if you wish. Sprinkle with green onion.

Summery Baked Potato

Calories 196
Protein 12 g
Fat 4 g
Carbohydrate 30 g

Serves 4.

Use whatever veggies you have on hand for this yummy version.

4	large baking potatoes	
1	cup grated low-fat cheese	250 mL
1	small red onion, finely chopped	
1	small green pepper, finely chopped	
2	tbsp. 2% plain yogurt	25 mL
1	tbsp. finely chopped chives or green onion	15 mL
1	egg, beaten	

Salt and pepper to taste

Scrub the potatoes and prick them with a fork. Bake at 375°F/190°C for about 1 hour or until tender. Slice a lid off each potato about 1 inch/2 cm from the top. Scoop out the pulp from the lid and centre of each potato, leaving some attached to the skin for support.

Combine half the low-fat cheese with the remaining ingredients in a bowl and spoon this mixture into the potato shells. Sprinkle the remaining low-fat cheese on top of each one. Place the potatoes on a baking sheet. Bake at 375°F/190°C for 20 minutes or until the cheese melts. Brown them under the broiler if you wish.

Calories	248
Protein	18 g
Fat	3 g
Carbohydrate	29 g

Baked Potato Florentine

Serves 4.

Popeye would love this one!

4	large baking potatoes	
$\frac{1}{4}$	cup finely chopped green onion	50 mL
3	cups lightly packed fresh spinach, cooked, well drained, and chopped	750 mL
1	egg, lightly beaten	
1	cup grated low-fat cheese	250 mL
$\frac{1}{4}$	tsp. ground nutmeg	1 mL
Salt and pepper to taste		
$\frac{1}{4}$	cup grated Parmesan cheese	50 mL

Scrub the potatoes and prick them with a fork. Bake at 375°F/190°C for about 1 hour or until tender. Slice a lid off each potato about 1 inch/2 cm from the top. Scoop out the pulp from the lid and centre of each potato, leaving some attached to the skin for support.

Mash the pulp in a bowl. Mix in the green onion, spinach, egg, low-fat cheese, nutmeg, salt, and pepper. Spoon this mixture into the potato shells. Sprinkle with Parmesan. Place the potatoes on a baking sheet. Bake at 375°F/190°C for 20 minutes or until the cheese melts. Brown them under the broiler if you wish.

Calories 405
Protein 31 g
Fat 18 g
Carbohydrate 30 g

Salmon Baked Potato

Serves 4.

You can also use tuna for this tasty dish.

4	large baking potatoes	
$\frac{1}{3}$	cup skim milk	75 mL
1	medium Spanish onion, finely chopped	
1	tbsp. lemon juice	15 mL
2	tbsp. chopped fresh parsley	25 mL
1	7.5-oz/213-g can salmon, drained and with skin removed	
Salt and pepper to taste		
$\frac{1}{2}$	cup grated low-fat cheese	125 mL
$\frac{1}{4}$	cup grated Parmesan cheese	50 mL

Scrub the potatoes and prick them with a fork. Bake at 375°F/190°C for about 1 hour or until tender. Slice a lid off each potato about 1 inch/2 cm from the top. Scoop out the pulp from the lid and centre of each potato, leaving some attached to the skin for support.

Mash the pulp in a bowl with the remaining ingredients except the low-fat cheese and Parmesan. Spoon this mixture into the potato shells. Combine the low-fat and Parmesan cheeses in a small bowl and sprinkle them on top of the stuffed potatoes. Place the potatoes on a baking sheet and bake them at 375°F/190°C for 20 minutes or until the cheese melts. Brown them under the broiler if you wish.

Calories 99
Protein 4 g
Fat 6 g
Carbohydrate 9 g

Tofu Nuggets

Makes about 15 balls.

A nutritious substitute for fried chicken that children of all ages will enjoy. Make a meal of them with a crisp tossed salad.

1	cup tofu, drained and pressed (see page 210)	250 mL
$\frac{1}{2}$	cup brown long-grain rice, cooked	125 mL
2	tbsp. low-sodium soy sauce	25 mL
$\frac{3}{4}$	cup ground almonds	175 mL
$\frac{1}{4}$	cup wheat germ	50 mL
$\frac{3}{4}$	cup sesame seeds	175 mL

Place the tofu in a bowl and mash well. Blend half the cooked rice with the tofu in a food processor or blender until they form a thick paste. Transfer to a bowl and stir in the remaining rice, soy sauce, almonds, wheat germ, and $\frac{1}{4}$ cup/50 mL sesame seeds. Blend well.

Roll this mixture into 1-inch/2-cm balls. Roll each ball in the remaining $\frac{1}{2}$ cup/125 mL sesame seeds to coat. Bake on a lightly greased baking sheet at 350°F/180°C for about 45 minutes or until golden brown.

Calories 235
Protein 11 g
Fat 6 g
Carbohydrate 40 g

Tofu Fruit Pudding

Serves 2.

This is one of the tastiest ways to introduce tofu to children. It tastes better than any commercial pudding mix and is, of course, much healthier. This recipe combines the protein of tofu with the fibre, vitamins, and minerals of fresh fruit.

$\frac{3}{4}$	cup drained, mashed tofu	175 mL
$\frac{3}{4}$	cup sliced fresh, ripe, tender fruit	175 mL
	(banana, peach, nectarine, or mango)	
1	tsp. honey	5 mL
1–2	tsp. lemon juice	5–10 mL

To remove the excess moisture from the tofu, wrap it in a clean tea towel and squeeze gently. Blend the tofu with the remaining ingredients in a food processor or blender until smooth. Pour into individual serving dishes and chill.

Note: If using banana, serve at once, or the pudding will turn brown.

Chewy Carob Squares

Calories 171
Protein 4 g
Fat 8 g
Carbohydrate 22 g

Makes 12–16.

Crunchy, chewy, and healthy all at the same time, these have a yummy peanut butter and carob topping plus a fibre-full cookie base.

$\frac{1}{4}$	cup wheat germ	50 mL
3	cups rolled oats	750 mL
$\frac{1}{3}$	cup soft margarine	75 mL
$\frac{1}{4}$	cup honey	50 mL
$\frac{1}{2}$	tsp. vanilla	2 mL
$\frac{1}{4}$	cup raisins	50 mL

Topping			
	$\frac{1}{2}$	cup carob chips	125 mL
	$\frac{1}{3}$	cup chunky peanut butter	75 mL

Combine the wheat germ and rolled oats in a medium-sized bowl. Melt the margarine together with the honey and vanilla in a small saucepan and mix well. Pour into the rolled-oat mixture and mix well. Stir in the raisins. Pat into an 8-inch/2-L square baking pan. Bake at 400°F/200°C for 10–15 minutes. Cool completely.

Melt the carob chips in a small, heavy saucepan. Stir in the peanut butter until blended. Spread this mixture over the cooled crust. Cool, then cut into squares.

Calories 94
Protein 2 g
Fat 5 g
Carbohydrate 13 g

Great Granola Bars

Makes 12–16.

These are a must as part of anyone's brown-bag lunch and the perfect between-meal snack. A granola bar that's as nutritious as it's cooked up to be!

$\frac{1}{4}$	cup soft margarine, melted	50 mL
2	tbsp. brown sugar	25 mL
$\frac{1}{2}$	tsp. vanilla	2 mL
1	egg	
$2\frac{1}{2}$	cups homemade granola (see page 175)	625 mL

Combine the margarine and sugar in a medium-sized bowl and blend well. Add the vanilla and egg and beat until smooth. Stir in the granola. Pat the mixture into a lightly oiled 8-inch/2-L square baking pan. Bake at 400°F/ 200°C for about 15 minutes or until golden brown. Cool completely before cutting into bars.

Calories 100
Protein 1 g
Fat 5 g
Carbohydrate 12 g

Nutty Oatmeal Cookies

Makes about 3 dozen.

These cookies are so tasty, they could turn anyone into a monster! But go easy on them because they are fairly high in fat and sugar. This recipe uses a food processor, but you can also make them by hand.

$\frac{1}{2}$	cup soft margarine	125 mL
$\frac{1}{3}$	cup corn, safflower, soybean, or sunflower oil	75 mL
$\frac{3}{4}$	cup lightly packed brown sugar	175 mL
1	tsp. vanilla	5 mL
$\frac{1}{4}$	cup boiling water	50 mL
$1\frac{3}{4}$	cups whole-wheat flour	425 mL
$\frac{1}{2}$	tsp. salt	2 mL
1	tsp. baking soda	5 mL
2	cups rolled oats	500 mL
$\frac{1}{2}$	cup chopped walnuts	125 mL

Process the margarine, oil, sugar, and vanilla in a food processor or blender until well blended. Add the boiling water and process until blended. Add the flour, salt, baking soda, and rolled oats and process with several on-off turns until they are mixed.

Transfer the mixture to a bowl and stir in the walnuts. Shape into 1-inch/2-cm balls. Place on a lightly greased or paper-lined cookie sheet and flatten completely with a floured fork. Bake at 325°F/160°C for about 18 minutes or until golden brown.

Oatmeal Chocolate Chip Cookies

Calories 124
Protein 2 g
Fat 6 g
Carbohydrate 17 g

Makes about 4 dozen.

Fibre and flavour all in one delectable package! All kids seem to love chocolate chip cookies, so give them one that's more nutritious.

$\frac{2}{3}$	cup soft margarine	150 mL
$\frac{1}{2}$	cup granulated sugar	125 mL
$\frac{1}{2}$	cup lightly packed brown sugar	125 mL
2	eggs	
$1\frac{1}{2}$	cups whole-wheat flour	375 mL
1	tsp. baking soda	5 mL
$\frac{1}{2}$	tsp. salt	2 mL
3	cups rolled oats	750 mL
1	cup chopped walnuts	250 mL
$\frac{1}{2}$	cup chocolate chips	125 mL

Cream together the margarine and sugars until light and creamy. Beat in the eggs one at a time.

Sift together the flour, baking soda, and salt in a medium-sized bowl, then stir them into the creamed mixture. Stir in the rolled oats, walnuts, and chocolate chips and mix well. Drop the dough in spoonfuls onto a lightly oiled or paper-lined cookie sheet. Bake at 350°F/180°C for 10–12 minutes or until golden brown.

Peanut Butter Cookies

Calories 64
Protein 2 g
Fat 4 g
Carbohydrate 7 g

Makes about 3 dozen.

The best we've tasted, these are a high-fibre version of an old favourite.

$\frac{1}{3}$	cup soft margarine	75 mL
$\frac{1}{2}$	cup natural peanut butter	125 mL
$\frac{1}{3}$	cup granulated sugar	75 mL
$\frac{1}{3}$	cup lightly packed brown sugar	75 mL
1	egg	
1	tsp. vanilla	5 mL
$\frac{1}{2}$	cup natural bran	125 mL
$\frac{1}{2}$	cup all-purpose flour	125 mL
1	tsp. baking soda	5 mL
Pinch salt		
$\frac{1}{3}$	cup blanched, unsalted, chopped peanuts	75 mL

Cream together the margarine, peanut butter, and sugars in a large bowl until smooth and fluffy. Blend in the egg and vanilla.

Combine the bran, flour, baking soda, and salt in a separate bowl. Stir into the peanut butter mixture and mix well. Stir in the peanuts. Shape the dough into 1-inch/2-cm balls on an ungreased cookie sheet and flatten with a floured fork. Bake at 350°F/180°C for 10–12 minutes or until golden brown.

12   Do or Die-t

Let's wipe the weight control slate clean.

First, let's dispel all thoughts of what is usually called dieting—that mind-numbing process of self-denial that can obsessively govern each movement of fork to mouth day after day, month upon month, year in and year out. Next, let's see what weight control really means. The good news is that although there is no magic formula for losing weight, the subject is much less complicated than the diet gurus would have us think.

Weight control is simply a matter of making the right food choices, feeling good physically and mentally, and developing realistic attitudes about our bodies and how they are fuelled.

Lean, Not Mean
What does being overweight really mean?

We have only to look at a Rubens painting or photos of that curvaceous sex goddess Marilyn Monroe to realize that standards of body weight have changed over the years. In North America today, ideal looks are unfortunately epitomized by bony fashion models so thin and lacking in curves that they seem almost emaciated. No wonder anorexia and bulimia are two diseases of our age.

One of the reasons for our obsession with weight is a misconception of how the body is made up. Contrary to popular belief, our bodies do not consist mainly of fat. Lean body mass, or muscle, bones, water, and other substances all make up our body weight. Tables showing what we "should" weigh that do not take into account physical variations like body frame and muscle mass should therefore be used only as guidelines—nothing more.

The best way to determine who needs to lose weight is to assess who is "overfat" rather than who is over-weight according to a chart. And one of the best ways to check on fat is the old-fashioned "pinch test." If you can pinch more than an inch around your midriff, then you are a candidate for streamlining by shedding weight.

But we should not dismiss the dangers of being legitimately overweight.

One out of two North Americans is overweight. Such people tend to die younger than people of average weight, especially if they were fat at an early age. In addition, the consequences of being overweight often take years to surface as disease. Heart disease, hypertension, diabetes, and degenerative arthritis are all prevalent in our society and tend to strike overweight people progressively over a matter of years. These people are also at risk of developing certain cancers, including cancer of the colon, endometrium, and breast, all of which seem to be linked with diets high in fat.

"Yo-yo" diets, on which weight is quickly shed and then just as quickly regained (often in spades), have become a growing trend over the past few decades and also carry serious risks. People who lose and gain large amounts of weight are likely to develop medical problems such as gallstones, not to mention the nutritional hazards that such diets usually entail.

Why certain people become overweight is a complex question that is the subject of extensive research and much debate. What seems clear amid the controversy is that genetic factors and environment both play a part.

If a child has one overweight parent, the likelihood of the child being overweight is 50 percent. If both parents are overweight, the likelihood jumps to 70 percent. However, in a family whose weekend ritual is going for walks, the chances of offspring being overweight are certainly lower than in one whose favoured activity is eating out! Developing healthy attitudes toward food as a family and encouraging physical activity both help prevent weight problems, particularly if there is a genetic predisposition to amass body fat.

Another misconception is many people's firm belief in the almighty power of the scale. The scale is certainly a helpful tool in determining body weight, but it does not accurately measure changes in body fat. A person's weight often depends on fluctuations in bodily fluids. If you drank 16 ounces of water and then stepped on the scale, you would weigh one pound more—a gain of fluid, not fat. Body fluids and electrolytes can easily affect your weight if you are on a weight-loss program. The best way to determine weight is to step on the same scale in the same place wearing the same weight of clothes once a week.

The Animal in Us

To discover the ideal eating plan that will keep us at an optimum weight, each of us must get back to basics. This means rediscovering the animal in us. Animals eat when they are hungry and stop eating when they have had enough, provided, of course, that they have an adequate source of food. When it is time to hibernate, they sensibly put on fat.

Human beings, whose bodies have the same ability to regulate weight and appetite as animals, carry with them a complicating factor that can cause problems, namely, the mind.

The human mind can override the body's basic need for food with cerebral notions such as dining out to celebrate, nibbling on hors d'oeuvres at a cocktail party, or downing a package of chocolate chip cookies to quell pre-exam nerves! In fact, our habit of using food as a means to socialize or solve a psychological problem has made sustenance its secondary function. The result is the nutritional mess in which we find ourselves today.

But all is not lost. We can return to a more animal-like approach to eating that allows us to listen to our bodies with sensitivity and feed ourselves with the care and nurturing we all deserve. But first, we have to rediscover the animal regulation of appetite in order to know when we are hungry and when we are full.

If you don't eat when your body is hungry, you will not know when it is full. Responses to this vary from "I know when I'm hungry—for sure not in the morning" to "Whether I'm full depends on the meal, the company, how I'm feeling, and what my day's been like." In a nutshell, most people believe they cannot change their eating patterns, even though these patterns are based on habit and the power of the mind rather than on the body's physical need for food.

The main task when tackling weight control, therefore, is to develop eating habits that are in harmony with your body's need for food. First, you must learn to eat when you are hungry and not eat when you are full. Next, you must establish an eating pattern and stick to it. The result will be a nutritious way of eating that is easy to maintain and does not obsess you as most ways of dieting do.

It's all a matter of listening to our bodies' cues. The reason that fad diets don't work is that nearly all of them run counter to our bodies' need for food. This sets up a battleground on which our bodies fight the regimen being forced on them and explains why most people on such diets last for only a short time.

The body has another mechanism that must be considered when discussing weight loss. This is its desire to maintain the status quo. The healthy body wants to stay at the weight it is, overweight or not. In fact, it is a sign of illness to lose weight easily with no appetite changes. Because of this, hunger that results from an attempt to lose weight is actually a positive sign—a sign of good health.

Perpetual dieters, whose days are dominated by feelings of hunger, are eventually unable to cope, quit the diet, and often seek solace from their frustration by eating even more than before they began their diet. In these cases, dieting can actually be a cause of gaining weight!

On a healthy weight-loss program, however, you should eat often and stave off hunger. You will be hungry before meals and satisfied afterward. If you are eating properly, you will be hungry after a meal only at a time when your weight is dropping—a sure sign of success!

For most people, the first week of a weight-loss program is the time the hungries really hit and the biggest weight loss happens. For others, the drop in weight and accompanying hunger occur only after two weeks of a change in eating habits. It is thus important to realize that weight loss varies from person to person and from week to week and that the long-term shedding of pounds during healthy weight loss averages out. It is also crucial to develop a positive attitude to hunger when you are losing weight and to realize that it is a happy sign of impending weight loss—not a cue to throw in the tea towel!

Feast or Famine?
What is a proper weight loss?

A healthy rate at which to shed weight is an average of two pounds a week. This is small compared to the amounts advocated by some diets, but still substantial, especially if you visualize the equivalent two pounds of butter or lard!

Keep in mind that the goal of losing weight is to shed fat, not just to weigh less. The quick weight loss that results from crash dieting is often loss of water combined with lean body mass and fat—a loss that returns almost as fast as it disappeared. Fat takes time to accumulate and time to lose, and there are no miracles that can make it otherwise. People who state that they can gain and lose weight in the blink of an eye are kidding themselves that this is loss of fat. And those who tout diets that will help you do this may be kidding themselves as well as hoodwinking you!

Equating Eats with Energy

Body fat is nature's way of storing excess energy, or calories. An increase in body fat causes an increase in body weight. How much fat we store is a matter of how the energy equation balances out:

Energy intake equals energy expenditure: fat stores are stable.

Energy intake is greater than energy expenditure: fat stores increase.

Energy intake is less than energy expenditure: fat stores decrease.

This is what these equations mean. One pound of body fat is equal to 3,500 calories. In order to gain or lose one pound of body fat a week, the body must have an excess or deficit of an average of 500 calories per day. To gain or lose two pounds a week requires an excess or deficit of 1,000 calories per day, or 7,000 calories a week. Therefore, an excess or deficit of 100 calories a day would mean a gain or loss of 36,500 calories, or 10 pounds, over a period of one year. In order to determine your caloric needs, you must consider your present weight and activity levels.

A person who weighs more than 200 pounds can lose weight with a much higher intake of calories than someone who weighs 130 pounds. Chances are, too, that the 200-pound person will stick to the higher calorie intake better than to a severe reducing diet that could doom him or her to failure.

A good reducing program must include all the daily nutrient requirements while cutting down on calories. This requires a minimum of 1,200 calories a day. If nutrients are lacking, weight loss will go hand in hand with fatigue, feelings of malaise, and a lacklustre, sickly appearance—not great when your aim is to look as good as you feel! Crash diets that cause these symptoms create dips in energy levels and often cause the dieter to give up the regimen. A nutritious weight-loss program, however, has the opposite effect and makes the dieter feel

AVERAGE ENERGY REQUIREMENTS OF INDIVIDUALS

Sex	Weight	Calories per Day
Male	150 lb./59 kg	2,450
	160 lb./63 kg	2,600
	170 lb./67 kg	2,800
	180 lb./71 kg	2,950
	190 lb./75 kg	3,100
	200 lb./79 kg	3,300
	225 lb./89 kg	3,700
	250 lb./98 kg	4,100
Female	100 lb./39 kg	1,450
	110 lb./43 kg	1,600
	120 lb./47 kg	1,750
	130 lb./51 kg	1,900
	140 lb./55 kg	2,050
	150 lb./59 kg	2,200
	160 lb./63 kg	2,350
	170 lb./67 kg	2,500
	180 lb./71 kg	2,600
	190 lb./75 kg	2,750
	200 lb./79 kg	2,900
	255 lb./89 kg	3,272

Note: The above are averages based on ages 25 to 49. Energy needs of younger individuals are greater, whereas those of older individuals are slightly lower.

and look healthy while he or she gradually sheds weight.

There are exceptions to the 1,200-calorie-per-day rule of thumb. One is if the dieter has an orthopedic problem in the back or joints and must lose some weight before he or she can become more active. A vitamin or mineral supplement would likely be advised to accompany such a low calorie intake.

Each person's daily energy requirement or calorie intake also depends on his or her basal metabolic rate and activity levels (see the chart opposite).

Today's lifestyle has caused a dramatic shift in the energy equation. All manner of devices, from the automobile to the electric clothes dryer, have made our way of life more sedentary than it was in the past, and we must adjust our activity levels accordingly (see Chapter 9 for a discussion of the benefits of exercise).

Compounding this problem is the body's reaction to a person's effort to lose weight. When a person embarks on a weight-loss program, the body shifts into a survival mode that turns into a real battle of the bulge! First, the body calls on its hunger troops to maintain the status quo, thinking that it is fighting for survival. When the hunger continues, the body thinks it has to struggle against starvation. Its next tactic is to decrease its metabolic rate to conserve energy in the form of calories. At this point, the dieter has a simple choice: either cut down even more on calories or increase the body's metabolic rate by exercise. The latter choice is certainly preferable.

Here is how exercise can change the energy balance in the dieter's favour. By decreasing your food intake by 500 calories a day, you would lose one pound a week. By increasing the energy you expend by exercising regularly, you could add another 500 calories to your daily expenditure. Exercise not only burns calories but also gives you a feeling of well-being, firms up your muscles, and is a terrific way to combat stress (again, see Chapter 9)—whether you're dieting or not!

Calories Aren't All That Count

Many people believe that all there is to losing weight is adding up the number of calories they consume in a day and then cutting down. In fact, the energy equation is more complex than this. Energy taken in can affect energy burned in several ways, and considerable research is being done on this relationship of food intake to the metabolic rate.

Food has a heating, or thermal, effect on the body. When you eat, you increase your metabolism to some extent. Thus, if you ate six small meals a day, your metabolic rate would be faster than if you ate larger amounts two or three times a day. In fact, the very act of eating breakfast revs up your body's engine and increases your metabolic rate. This effect lasts for a short while, and then it's time to eat again. As with everything, though, don't take this idea too far and consume too many calories in a futile effort to make your body's metabolic rate go over the top.

The ideal energy intake should be spread over three meals a day plus a couple of snacks. By eating more often, you can sneak in a little more food and still lose weight. The kinds of food you eat can also affect the metabolic rate. One study found that a meal that was high in carbohydrate raised the metabolic rates of overweight people higher than a meal containing a comparable number of calories, but made up mostly of fats.

All this points to the pitfalls of counting calories as the sole way of controlling weight.

Someone who only counts calories might save up his or her calorie quota for one meal and thus miss out on the thermal effect of eating often. By rating foods just according to calories, foods high in fat can be consumed instead of carbohydrates with the same calorie count, causing the dieter to lose out on an increase in metabolic rate. What is more, counting calories with no thought to nutrients, particularly carbohydrate, protein, and fat, can lead to a severe drop in energy.

This plummeting energy level can result in cravings— often for all the wrong foods, like the sugary Danish that is the breakfast skipper's answer to hunger pangs. Eating nutrient-dense foods at frequent intervals is a better way to diet than relying on calorie counts alone. Remember also that eating correctly early in the day becomes preventive eating when it controls the intake later in the day (there's more on breakfast in Chapter 8).

Eating a large evening meal is another pitfall of the dieter who relies on counting calories. Instead, eating a big meal in the morning and tapering off consumption toward day's end is a much better method. By eating a smaller evening meal and forgoing those midnight snacks, your body will begin to be hungrier in the morning, which is what you want.

Another minefield for calorie counters is the "I'll be

good today" or "I'll be really good tomorrow" school of thought. People who are wracked by guilt if they eat a chocolate bar or piece of cake are likely to give up their weight-loss program completely and are headed down the perpetual dieters' path to failure. This is why rigid diets that promote self-denial and guilt are self-defeating.

Yet another weakness of calorie counting as a way of losing weight is that it keeps you out of touch with that most important of mechanisms—regulation of appetite. A meal pattern that paces your food intake regularly throughout the day with built-in calorie controls, however, will help your body relearn the animal ability to recognize hunger and satiety. This means eating small quantities of food every three to four hours and cutting down, if necessary, at the evening meal when your body needs food least.

Mind over Matter
No matter how sound your weight-loss program is, however, it will not work if you do not have motivation.

Trying to lose weight without being motivated can be more detrimental than not trying at all. When hunger strikes the unmotivated dieter—a good sign that weight is being lost—he or she tends to eat more. Failure to stick to the diet leads to frustration and a tendency to simply give up. There goes the diet, and up goes the weight! Such a person would do well to figure out why he or she is not motivated and, if possible, reverse the situation.

For many people, motivation is difficult when they are faced with a task that seems so overwhelming and a goal that seems so far away. One solution is to make short-term goals. Try planning for a two-week stint, which could mean losing four pounds, and then renegotiating for two weeks more.

Some people lose motivation after they have lost a substantial amount of weight because they cannot face the hunger that would be caused by losing more. They should stop dieting at this point, concentrate on trying to maintain their weight loss, and then find a way to get motivated if they need to lose more. If losing more weight is critical for health reasons, their best recourse is to seek the help of a qualified professional.

Today's obsession with thinness can cause another problem—dieting by people who have no reason to and whose goals are unrealistic. These efforts are doomed to failure and can be risky to people's health, especially that of teenage girls. Those with normal weight who diet in fear of gaining are equally misguided and should learn the art of healthy eating.

For the Record
The best way to start losing weight is to write down everything you eat *before* you eat it so you can assess exactly what aspects of your eating habits need to be changed. This can be an extremely helpful, if sometimes painful, revelation of where your eating problems lie and what habits should be changed. It is also a good idea to keep this food record during the period you are trying to lose weight. By analyzing it once a week, you will gain many insights into what foods you missed as well as what foods you could have done without. Keep it in a handy spot, and put it on a convenient size of paper so you can carry it with you easily.

In particular, this record will pinpoint "danger" foods that you consume in excess—much to your body's dismay. These could be salty items like potato chips, which seem to have an addictive quality that has you eating the whole package when you intended only to munch a couple. Realizing which foods cause such snack attacks will help you plan your strategy, which might be to avoid salty munchies altogether or to grab a few and to start eating them only once the package is safe and sound inside a cupboard!

What you learn from your food record can also help you understand why certain eating habits die hard. An adult who returns home to the family nest where overeating is a way of life can easily slip back into the old routine. Stress can also cause old habits to reappear. Once life is back to normal or the person is back home, however, it takes special concentration to get back into that healthy way of eating.

A food record can also reveal how moods or physical condition influence the way you eat. Feeling tired, for example, is the cue for many people to open the fridge. Try taking a cat nap or doing a little exercise instead. If holidays are your time to sample different foods, this might not be the time to lose weight, but rather to maintain it. Finding other ways to fill your holiday time is also a good idea.

Above all, use your food record to make positive changes in your eating habits. Once you have noted how problems or habits influence what you eat, don't be neg-

DAILY FOOD RECORD

Time	Food*	Amount	Place	Am I Hungry? (Yes/No)

* Include type of preparation, for example, fried, baked, or broiled.

ative about your ability to change. Work at one area at a time in order to make permanent changes. One good way is to go meal by meal, perhaps working on breakfast first, then moving on to lunch, and so on. Soon you will have a whole new set of eating habits that, like the pieces of a jigsaw puzzle, fall happily into place.

Guilt and Other Diet Demons
One unfortunate sign of our times is the way nutrition has become for many people a moral issue with all the evangelical trappings of a new religion. So fanatical are its adherents that eating a whole chocolate bar or devouring

several scoops of ice cream are labelled major transgressions for which one must surely pay!

This attitude has no place in the down-to-earth matter of healthy eating. Anyone who tries to unlearn certain eating habits and replace them with new ones is bound to make mistakes. There is absolutely no place here for perfectionism, criticism, blame, or guilt.

Changing many small aspects of your behaviour and weathering the setbacks are all part of the weight-loss learning process. Alter one aspect at a time, and you will end up with a new, improved set.

One nifty trick for overcoming dieter's guilt is to approach a delicious-looking food that you know is not nutritious with the following game plan. Take one bite and rate it from one to ten. Finish eating it only if it scores a top-notch ten out of ten. You will be surprised how many chocolate cakes do not live up to their gorgeous looks! You will also discover a discriminating palate you may not have known you had.

A positive attitude is the key to making any change, whether the problem is food or anything else. A negative attitude ensures failure.

An example of this is the person who eats the wrong kinds of food at parties with the rationalization, "I've always overeaten at parties and it's a bad habit, but there's nothing I can do about it." A positive approach would be to try some new strategies such as eating regularly on the day of the party and having a snack before leaving home so as not to arrive starving. Another trick is not to eat while you are engaged in stimulating conversation. If you do, you won't fully appreciate the food's taste and probably won't notice if it is laden with fat.

Learn from each experience. Discover which ways of eating work for you and which do not. The good experiences will encourage you to make more changes.

Anatomy of a Diet
If you need the structure of a reducing diet to lose weight, you must assess its safety, reliability, and prognosis for helping you make long-term changes.

This is not an easy task because fad diets that feed on the public's desire for slimness are an ever-growing breed. Beware of diets promising miracles, claiming that you will shed pounds effortlessly either by eating food in intricate combinations, by avoiding milk, or by consuming only fruit for breakfast. If a diet makes claims that are too good to be true, then its claims are exactly that!

Diets that give day-to-day menus are not a good idea either. The most efficient, lasting way to lose weight is learning to make choices and gaining control of your eating pattern, not giving it up. In the end, it is the freedom to decide what foods to eat when *you* decide to eat them, not when someone else's menu plan decides you should.

Joining a weight-loss group is helpful to some people for the benefits of peer pressure. Before you join, assess the group's common sense and let good nutrition principles be your guide. Again, beware of get-thin-quick fads and scams.

Fed up with Fads
Here are some pointers to help you avoid fad diets. Watch out for these danger signs in a diet if:

- It advocates unusual eating patterns in an enthusiastic, often messianic fashion.

- It promotes a particular food or combination of foods as having special virtues. Such foods take on an aura of "super" or "wonder" foods.

- It eliminates certain nutritious foods from the diet, claiming that they are harmful.

- It relies on the testimony of individuals rather than on scientific study and makes false claims that are often difficult to spot because they are couched in scientific terminology.

- It is endorsed by pseudo-professionals and takes on a cult-like quality.

The results of diets that fill this bill are plain and simple: losing weight temporarily and regaining weight rapidly.

How to Be a Happy Loser
Here are some guidelines for choosing a good weight-loss program. Once you have made sure the program complies with these guidelines, embark on it only once you have discussed your choice with your physician.

- It follows the principles of the four food groups and

meets the body's needs for nutrients rather than relying on supplements. It also advocates a sensible balance of protein to fat to carbohydrate.

- It advocates an adequate intake of calories. A diet of less than 1,000 calories a day should be followed only under a doctor or dietitian's supervision and only in rare instances.

- It assesses individual eating habits and nutrient requirements and takes the dieter's likes, dislikes, and lifestyle into consideration.

- There are few if any forbidden foods.

- It allows healthy snacks and emphasizes controlling portions.

- Its weight-loss claims are reasonable, that is, an average of two pounds a week.

- It attempts to change undesirable eating habits in order to initiate and then maintain weight loss on a long-term basis.

- It recommends exercise.

- It does not advocate special foods or treatments like hormone injections.

Maintaining the Slim Status Quo
Once you have lost the amount of weight you wanted, maintaining your new body weight can be tricky. So here are some tips to help you:

- Beware of keeping a constant vigil over everything you eat. This is likely to result in a routine whereby you find yourself dieting from Monday to Friday and eating non-stop from Friday evening to Sunday night. This pattern is doomed to failure.

- Find a meal pattern that allows you to relax your vigil without causing you to gain weight. The best way to do this is to increase your intake by small amounts throughout the day and monitor your resulting hunger. If you find that dinner is your hungry time, eat a little extra at lunch and add an afternoon snack. This will help you establish an eating pattern in tune with your body's appetite that maintains a good weight.

- Keep tabs on your weight by weighing yourself once a week. If your weight inches up a pound or two, cut back on unnecessary treats. If your weight goes up four or five pounds, then you need to follow a more stringent plan for several weeks. Plan meals that keep fat at a minimum, and keep tabs on your hunger as a good sign of weight loss. The importance of preventing your weight from climbing more than five pounds above the ideal level cannot be overemphasized.

On the Eatin' Track

The best way to keep your weight where you want it is to eat right.

Eating right allows your body to regulate your weight so you won't be dieting for the rest of your life. You may have to lose a few pounds from time to time, but you won't be an obsessive dieter watching every mouthful. Once eating right becomes second nature, you and your body will become a harmonious team, choosing nutritious foods in the right amounts.

Follow the principles outlined in this book, and battling the bulge will be a struggle that is just plain history!

13 Food Facts and Fallacies

How easy things would be if there were a wonder food that could meet all our nutritional needs in one fell swoop. However, this kind of wishful thinking belongs in the wonderful world of fantasy, along with the princess and the pea and Love Potion No. 9!

The search for miracle foods that would relieve us of the often mundane responsibility of seeking out the right things to eat is understandable, but misguided. Here are some common fallacies and their accompanying facts.

Fallacy   Honey is a better choice of sweetening agent than white sugar because it is nutritionally superior.

Fact   Both honey and white sugar are simple sugars, of which the average North American eats too much. Honey does contain some vitamins and minerals, but in negligible amounts. A person would have to eat 50 tablespoons of honey, for example, to get the same amount of calcium as he or she would get from one ounce of cheddar or two-thirds of a cup of milk!

There are also some hazards associated with honey. It should not be fed to infants under one year of age because of the slight risk of botulism poisoning. Although extremely rare, such poisoning can occur if honey is a carrier of clostridium botulinum spores. These spores are not dangerous to adults but can cause constipation, progressive weakness, and ultimately respiratory arrest in infants. Corn syrup, which can also be a carrier of these spores, is not recommended to infants under one year for the same reasons. Research is currently being directed at a possible connection between Sudden Infant Death Syndrome and botulism poisoning in infants.

Honey's one nutritional advantage over sugar is that it is slightly sweeter and can thus be used in recipes in smaller amounts and for fewer calories.

Fallacy   Lecithin is a wonder product that can retard senility, aid in weight loss, and lower blood cholesterol.

Fact   Lecithin is a compound produced by the body and is therefore not an essential nutrient. It is found in many of the foods we eat, for example, eggs, meat, wheat, and legumes, and is used by the body to maintain cell structure.

Lecithin is useful in therapeutic doses to treat certain neurological disorders such as Huntingdon's disease and the senile dementia that occurs with Alzheimer's disease, where the body is deficient in *acetylcholine*, a substance the body manufactures from lecithin. This does not mean, however, that taking lecithin is beneficial to people without an acetylcholine deficiency.

Research has not yet proved that lecithin helps lower blood cholesterol substantially, whereas it has been shown that cholesterol is lowered by consumption of polyunsaturated fats and soluble fibres like oat bran.

Taking lecithin supplements as part of a weight-loss diet has only a placebo effect. They are ineffectual in a physical sense, but could give the dieter the incentive to stick to a low-calorie eating plan and lose weight. As with all placebos, however, lecithin is no substitute for will-power and common sense.

Fallacy   Bee pollen can act as an appetite suppressant to aid weight loss, promote weight gain, prevent premature aging, aid in mental retardation, remedy bowel problems, increase energy levels, and help treat allergies.

Fact   The list of wonders attributed to bee pollen—the tiny seeds carried by bees from the flower to the hive—is as long as it is mind-boggling! However, the preceding and other purported merits of bee pollen have not been documented in scientific literature. What have been documented are cases of people who have had an allergic reaction to the bee pollen they took as a treatment for allergies!

Fallacy   Hair analysis can diagnose everything from heavy metal toxicity to nutritional deficiencies, headaches, and sallow skin.

Fact   Hair analysis may be a valuable diagnostic tool in the future because of the ease of obtaining and storing samples. The problem to date, however, has been that methods of analysis and interpretation have not been standardized. In addition, there are many factors that can affect the results of hair analysis. Trace minerals found in hair are affected by hair treatments (shampoo, colouring, conditioners, etc.) as well as environmental factors like air pollution and chlorinated water from a swimming pool.

Until the results and interpretations of hair analysis have been standardized to reflect excesses or deficiencies, be wary of anyone who uses it as a test on you!

Fallacy High-colonic enemas are helpful in ridding the body of toxins.

Fact High-colonic enemas are the irrigation of the bowel with large amounts (more than 15 gallons) of water mixed with various herbs and enzymes. They are administered by some chiropractors, naturopaths, and self-styled "nutrition professionals," who claim that they wash toxins out of the body. The healthy way to maintain regular bowel movements and to rid one's body of waste products most efficiently is to eat a balanced diet that is high in fibre and water. High-colonic enemas are a risky procedure that could cause electrolyte and fluid imbalance as well as infection or even perforation of the bowel.

Fallacy Herbs are a safe, natural way to treat ailments and are superior to pharmaceutical drugs.

Fact Medication prescribed by a doctor, unlike a herbal remedy, is carefully tested for dosage and long-term effects before it is allowed on the market. Herbs, however, are readily available in unrestricted amounts and have not been reliably tested for dosage or long-term effects.

With all the concern these days about the caffeine contained in tea and coffee, many people are switching to herbal teas without being aware of their hazards. Allergic reactions to herbal teas are quite common; for example, drinking camomile tea, a member of the ragweed family, could adversely affect a person who suffers from hay fever.

Some herbal teas have even stranger properties. Coca leaf tea, for example, is a herbal tea packaged in Peru. Its ingredients are listed as "decocainized coca leaves," but random sampling in the United States has shown that these leaves do indeed contain some cocaine. In fact, most of the cocaine is released by simple infusion when the leaves are made into tea. Although two cups of coca leaf tea a day contain less cocaine than one intra-nasal dose and do not cause any serious side effects, cocaine ingested this way shows up in a urine test. It also causes mild stimulation, mood elevation, and increased heart rate.

In general, when drinking herbal teas as an alternative beverage, treat them the same way you would any others that contain caffeine—drink them in moderation and alternate them with other liquids.

Other herbs are taken as laxatives. Aloe vera, which causes intestinal cramping, could be dangerous to pregnant women because of its action on the abdominal muscles. Like other herbs that are purported to cure constipation, aloe vera is no substitute for a healthy diet in promoting regular bowel movements. If a laxative is absolutely necessary to cure constipation, then a pharmaceutical version that acts as a stimulant to the bowel is a wiser choice than a herbal one that does exactly the same thing, simply because the pharmaceutical version has been more thoroughly tested.

"Diet" teas—herbal products sold as aids for weight loss—simply act as laxatives, frequently causing cramps and diarrhea. They carry the added risk of water loss and dehydration. Drinking them is hardly a desirable way to lose weight and no different than the unhealthy practice of using an over-the-counter laxative to slim down!

When you cook with herbs, there is no danger as long as you use them in moderation. However, a Health and Welfare Canada committee researching the effects of all manner of herbs, from oregano to saffron, warns that some herbs eaten in large amounts can have toxic effects. Some herbs simply should not be consumed. For example, the *British Medical Journal* has told the story of a man who had been diagnosed as having digoxin toxicity, with the symptoms of headache, nausea, loss of appetite, and heart block. It was discovered that for many years, he had been concocting and drinking a special herbal tea containing foxglove. Equally dangerous are white poppy seeds and castor beans. Herbs that may be harmful to a fetus when consumed in abnormal amounts during pregnancy include parsley oil and oregano.

Fallacy   We all need a certain amount of refined sugar in our diets.

Fact	The body cannot differentiate between the simple sugars contained in fruit, vegetables, and milk and the sugars contained in refined products such as table sugar. It seems obvious then that we should opt for foods like fruits and vegetables that combine sugar with vitamins and minerals rather than choosing the refined sugar in a chocolate bar that consists almost entirely of empty calories. Remember that to identify the amount of sugar in a product, check the label for sucrose, fructose, glucose, dextrose, and maltose. Ingredients are listed in descending order of amount, so the closer a sugar is to the beginning of the list, the greater the amount.
Fallacy	Certain pills or aids such as amphetamines, thyroid extracts, bulk producers, diuretics, and injections of substances like human chorionic gonadotropin (HCG) are helpful in weight reduction.
Fact	Amphetamines act as stimulants and thereby cause a decrease in appetite. Their unfavourable side effects include nervousness, irritability, insomnia, and possible addiction. Thyroid extracts increase the metabolic rate and thus cause people to burn more calories—but not without negative side effects such as heart palpitations and hyperactivity. Bulk producers do reduce appetite by causing a "full" sensation. What they don't do is help a person learn new, healthier eating habits. If they are high in insoluble fibres and the person's diet is already low in certain trace minerals, they can lower the absorption of certain nutrients. Diuretics cause water loss, not fat loss. It is only temporary and can have side effects such as depletion of certain minerals, in particular potassium. Injections of human chorionic gonadotropin, a sex hormone, are of no proven benefit when it comes to weight loss. It is rather the accompanying low-calorie diet, along with the psychological effects of daily visits to the therapist for injections, that cause any weight reduction. The exorbitant fees usually charged are added reason for the patient to believe that this diet really works! The hazards of these injections are the use of accompanying diuretics and a low-calorie diet lacking in nutrients.
Fallacy	Eating a little mouldy food won't hurt you. After all, penicillin comes from mouldy cheese.

Fact   Moulds are fungi that grow on a variety of vegetable and animal matter, especially under warm, moist conditions.

Recent research has shown that mouldy food can be extremely dangerous because of the toxins—called *myco-toxins*—that some moulds produce. Mycotoxins have been found to cause cancer in animal tests. They seep in and around the mould and cannot therefore simply be scraped off along with it. Some mycotoxins can survive in food for a long time, and some are not even destroyed by heat during cooking.

Here are some tips on avoiding the risk of mycotoxins on mouldy food. Don't buy foods with a musty odour or produce with bruises on the skin or signs of rot around the stems. Avoid nuts that are discoloured, and store nuts in a cool, dry place.

Avoid exposing cheese to air unnecessarily after use. It can become contaminated, and mould can grow days later, even in the fridge. If hard cheese develops a patch of mould, you can salvage the cheese by cutting the mould away to a depth of 1 inch (2.5 cm). Discard liquid or semi-solid foods like jam or maple syrup if you find mould on them. Discard wrappings that have been in contact with mouldy foods to prevent cross-contamination. The rule of thumb is: When in doubt, throw it out!

Fallacy   Sulphites used to preserve food are harmless.

Fact   Sulphites are chemicals used to preserve packaged foods and to retain the crisp texture and prevent the browning of fresh produce. They are used extensively to keep salad bars looking bright and perky and preserve potatoes prepared for commercial use. Sulphites are also used in the production of wine and beer.

Most people, it seems, are not sensitive to the effects of sulphites. There is a small segment of the population, however, that has such an adverse physical reaction to them that their use must be examined. Reactions include hives, stomach upset, shortness of breath, severe wheezing, and in extreme cases, even death. People at risk are frequently asthmatic.

Sulphites are listed among ingredients on packaged foods and are contained in the following additives: potassium bisulphite, potassium metabisulphite, sodium bisulphite, sodium metabisulphite, sodium sulphite, sodium dithionite, and sulphurous acid.

Because sulphites are often used in bulk foods for

which there is no ingredient list, here is a list of foods in which they are often used: fresh and dried fruits and vegetables; alcoholic and fruit beverages; pastries and baked goods; jams, jellies, pickles, and relishes; mustards; molasses; frozen fish; and processed tomato products such as spaghetti sauce and tomato paste.

If you suspect that you are sensitive to sulphites, start looking for sources in your diet. Ask whether foods in a restaurant have been treated with sulphites, although you may or may not get an answer—it is often the suppliers who use them, a fact the management may not be aware of. It is a good idea, however, to let the restaurant know why you are avoiding a food that might contain sulphites in order to help increase awareness of the problem. Avoiding sulphite-containing processed foods will also help deter food companies from using them. And reporting any adverse reaction to foods containing sulphites to the appropriate government agency will also speed up efforts to determine the extent of public sensitivity.

Fallacy "Natural" foods are better for you.

Fact The word *natural* has become a catch-all and is often used by food companies eager to jump on the nutritional bandwagon. These companies are well aware of the increasing concern among consumers about the meaning of ingredient lists on the foods they buy. Worried about chemical additives as well as the nutritional content of packaged foods, the food-buying public is understandably drawn to foods that are as close to their natural states as possible.

But here's the hitch. There are no rules governing the use of the word *natural*, nothing that says that it must mean "unadulterated" or "minus food additives." As a result, it can mean almost anything. *Natural* can be just an adjective describing the noun it precedes. For example, "natural apple flavour" can be one of the ingredients in a dessert that is chock-full of additives. One thing the word *natural* does usually mean is a few cents added to the price of the food it's in. This is another case of "Food buyer beware!"

In general, it is best to opt for the fresh product whenever possible. However, all of us must eat processed foods in certain instances to attain a balanced diet, so we should choose nutritious foods that additives increase our use of. For example, the lecithin added to whole-milk powder helps it dissolve in water, and the sequestering agent used in canned lima beans helps to retain their colour. On the other hand, it's not essential to buy a salad dressing to which emulsifiers have been added so you won't have to shake it before use—a little elbow grease is a better solution than unnecessary additives. If you have a choice, for example, of canned cherries with or without added colouring, go for the unadulterated version. Exercise your power as a consumer. The more demand there is for processed foods free of additives, the more such foods will be produced.

Let's not forget that dismissing processed foods altogether is another case of throwing the baby out with the bath water. Processing adds to the variety of foods available to us—and variety and its cohort, moderation, are keys to healthy eating.

Fallacy   "Natural" or "natural source" vitamins are better for you than synthetic ones.

Fact   Your body does not know the difference between "natural" and synthetic vitamins. The chemical formulas derived from them are identical. Because the synthetic version is often cheaper, it can be a wiser choice.

Fallacy   It is better to choose foods that have been grown "organically."

Fact   The use of the word *organic* is not regulated by government, so it can mean a multitude of things. It often refers to foods grown with the aid of natural rather than chemical fertilizers. But a plant cannot recognize the difference between the two; plants grown with the help of natural and chemical fertilizers produce identical minerals.

Pesticide residues have been found in both "organic" crops and crops that have been grown by conventional methods. This is because pesticides exist in the environment and are absorbed by the soil. Although pesticides increase crop yield and thus help keep down the price of some foods, we should be vigilant about the amounts and varieties used and support environmental groups that monitor their use. Legislation that would limit the use of any questionable pesticides and thereby encourage pesticide-free, "organic" farming is also desirable for health reasons.

Fallacy   Eating plenty of grapefruit helps you lose weight.

Fact   Contrary to popular belief, grapefruit does not burn or melt fat! Even unsweetened grapefruit contains a fair amount of calories because of its sugar content. Its main virtue is a good dose of vitamins and minerals. Grapefruit, like the hot water and lemon juice recommended on some diets, has no magical powers to cause weight loss and must be included in a total calorie count like any other food.

Fallacy   All barbecued food is bad for you.

Fact   How food is barbecued may affect the apparent carcinogenic effects of this cooking method. When fat drips onto a wood or charcoal fire, benzopyrene forms. This is a carcinogen that can get into the food through the smoke or flames. Smoked foods, such as meat and fish, can also contain benzopyrene. To minimize the risk of benzopyrene getting into your food when you are barbecuing, cook food slowly over a raised grill or wrap it in foil before cooking.

Fallacy   "Light" foods are lower in calories and a better nutritional choice.

Fact   Legislation governing the use of the word *light* is so vague that it can mean almost anything. Foods described this way can be legitimately fat-reduced, like certain salad dressings, or can actually be high in fat and sugar, like some "light" muffins that are actually cupcakes! A "light" pudding can be low in sugar and fat but is certainly not once it has been baked into a pastry crust. This is another case of reading the label and "Food buyer beware": "light" may be describing the taste, colour, or texture of the food product, not the number of calories.

Fallacy   Stress tablets (vitamin B complex with C) are necessary for long periods of mental stress.

Fact   The kind of stress that increases the body's need for these nutrients is physical, not mental, stress. Surgery, burns, and illness all produce physical stress. Although a long day at work may be stressful and tiring, it does not deplete the body of these nutrients.

Fallacy   Natural calcium supplements like bone meal and dolomite are superior to food sources of calcium because they contain the right magnesium-calcium balance for maximum calcium absorption.

Fact   First, valid scientific research has not shown that a specific magnesium-calcium balance affects calcium absorption. Second, bone meal and dolomite contain, along with calcium, toxic metals such as arsenic, cadmium, mercury, and lead. These substances could be dangerous to small children and pregnant women, who absorb them more readily, or to anyone who consumes them in excess.

    The best way to consume adequate calcium is in food, but if you need a supplement, look for the amount of elemental calcium on the label. The amount of calcium in a supplement depends on the type of calcium. Calcium carbonate, for example, is 40 percent calcium, whereas calcium gluconate is only 9 percent.

Fallacy   Foods labelled "Contains no cholesterol" are a good choice for people who are careful not to eat much cholesterol.

Fact   Foods such as non-dairy creamers with "Contains no cholesterol" on the label are free of cholesterol, but they may be high in saturated fats. These fats tend to raise cholesterol levels and should not be eaten if at all possible.

Fallacy   Hypoglycemia is a very common condition.

Fact   Hypoglycemia is not a common medical condition, but some of the symptoms experienced by hypoglycemics may be common.

    Hypoglycemia is a disease in which too much insulin is released into the bloodstream. This causes low blood sugar. Low blood sugar can also occur after an absence of food in the body or when too much sugar is eaten alone. As the blood sugar drops to low levels, symptoms such as headache, irritability, and nausea can progress to blackouts. The less severe symptoms can be experienced by people with poor eating habits, who could be mistakenly diagnosed as hypoglycemic. Going for hours on end without eating can cause many of the symptoms of hypoglycemia without the disease.

If you think you are hypoglycemic, see a physician. An improvement in eating habits can help alleviate symptoms for people who have the disease and for those who have not been eating properly.

In a Nutshell

Much as we might like to have total control over our bodies, this is not possible. Many diseases are the result of complex variables, which cannot be connected with what we eat or any other aspect of daily life that is within our control.

There are, on the other hand, many things we do to our bodies that clearly affect our health. Here are some of the ways we can adapt our lifestyles to our bodies' advantage:

- Maintain a good body weight.

- Decrease the amount of fat in our diets.

- Increase our intake of dietary fibre.

- Moderate our intake of sugar, caffeine, alcohol, and salt.

- Increase our exercise or activity levels.

- Eat small, balanced meals more often.

Simple as these guidelines are, however, there are many complexities in the whole matter of nutrition that we must keep in mind. With the continual barrage of scientific information that comes our way about the latest finding on this or that nutrient, it is easy to become confused. This is why we must be aware of the crucial ingredients in the recipe for a healthy diet—namely, moderation and balance.

The more we fool around with nutrients, the more we can disturb their balance. A nutrient may not be toxic by itself, but too much of it could disturb the balance of certain others. An example is the iron-zinc-copper balancing act. If you take too much iron in supplement form, you could upset your body's zinc status. Overdo the amount of zinc you ingest, as some food faddists recommend, and you could set the amount of copper in your body off kilter. The same applies to vitamin C.

And so the list continues.

What is the solution? Given that eating certain foods can contribute to better health and even help prevent disease, what is the ideal eating plan?

The answer is sweet and simple. Vary your diet, while incorporating the nutrition guidelines listed above. We trust that this book will also help demystify what sometimes seems like a mind-boggling task.

Make changes gradually. The more changes you need to make, the longer the process will take. Plan to overhaul your eating habits meal by meal, habit by habit. One good method is to start at the beginning of the day with breakfast. Move on to lunch through the morning snack, then to the afternoon snack. Finally, work on that evening meal.

And if you need outside help, a dietitian can give terrific insights—not to mention moral support. Above all, learn to be in harmony with your body. Once you and it are a team, you'll have it made!

Appendixes

Food	Measure	Weight (g)	Water (%)	Energy (kcal)	Protein (g)	Carbohydrate (g)	Fat (g)	SFA (g)
Alfalfa seeds, sprouted with seed, raw	100 mL	14	91	29	4	4	tr	tr
Almonds, shelled, whole	100 mL	60	4	589	20	20	52	5
Anchovies	3 fillets	12	59	176	19	tr	10	4
Apple juice, canned or bottled, + vitamin C	100 mL	105	88	47	tr	12	tr	tr
Apple sauce, canned, sweetened	100 mL	108	80	76	tr	20	tr	tr
Apple sauce, canned, unsweetened	100 mL	103	88	43	tr	11	tr	tr
Apples, raw, with skin	1 medium	138	84	59	tr	15	tr	tr
Apricot nectar, canned, + vitamin C	100 mL	106	85	56	tr	14	tr	tr
Apricots, canned, whole, heavy syrup, no skins	100 mL	109	78	83	tr	21	tr	tr
Apricots, dried, uncooked	100 mL	55	31	238	4	62	tr	tr
Apricots, raw	1 whole	36	86	48	1	11	tr	tr
Asparagus, boiled, drained, pieces	100 mL	76	92	25	3	4	tr	tr
Asparagus, canned, drained, pieces	100 mL	102	94	19	2	2	tr	tr
Avocados, California (winter), raw	1 whole	173	73	177	2	7	17	3
Avocados, Florida (summer/autumn), raw	1 whole	230	80	112	2	9	9	2
Bacon, back, sliced, grilled	100 mL	62	62	185	24	1	8	3
Bacon, side, pan-fried, crisp	2 slices	13	13	576	30	tr	49	17
Bagels	1 medium	68	29	294	10	56	3	tr
Bamboo shoots, canned, drained, solids	100 mL	55	94	19	2	3	tr	tr

PUFA (g)	Cholesterol (mg)	Calcium (mg)	Iron (mg)	Sodium (mg)	Potassium (mg)	Vitamin A (RE)	Thiamin (mg)	Riboflavin (mg)	Niacin (NE)	Folate (mcg)	Vitamin C (mg)	Dietary Fibre (g)
tr	0	32	1.0	6	79	16	.08	.13	1.2	36	8	2.2
11	0	266	3.7	11	732	0	.21	.78	9.3	59	tr	7.2
3	55	168	2.9	823	590	66	.03	.20	8.9	13	0	—
tr	0	7	.4	3	119	0	.02	.02	.1	tr	33	.3
tr	0	4	.4	3	61	1	.01	.03	.2	tr	2	1.4
tr	0	3	.1	2	75	3	.01	.03	.2	tr	1	1.4
tr	0	7	.2	0	115	5	.02	.01	.1	3	6	2.5
tr	0	7	.4	3	114	132	tr	.01	.3	1	33	.3
tr	0	9	.4	11	134	124	.02	.02	.6	2	3	—
tr	0	45	4.7	10	1378	724	tr	.15	4.1	10	2	8.1
tr	0	14	.5	1	296	261	.03	.04	.9	9	10	1.7
tr	0	24	.7	4	310	83	.10	.12	1.5	98	27	1.5
tr	0	16	1.8	390	172	53	.06	.10	1.3	96	18	1.5
2	0	11	1.2	12	634	61	.11	.12	2.3	66	8	—
1	0	11	.5	5	488	61	.11	.12	2.2	53	8	—
tr	58	10	.8	1546	390	0	.82	.20	10.9	4	22	—
6	85	12	1.6	1596	486	0	.69	.29	12.2	5	34	—
1	0	43	2.6	360	74	0	.38	.29	5.4	—	0	1.1
tr	0	8	.3	7	80	1	.03	.03	.4	3	1	2.6

Food	Measure	Weight (g)	Water (%)	Energy (kcal)	Protein (g)	Carbohydrate (g)	Fat (g)	SFA (g)
Bananas, raw	1 medium	114	74	92	1	23	tr	tr
Barbecue sauce	100 mL	106	81	75	2	13	2	tr
Barley, pearled, light, uncooked	100 mL	84	11	349	8	79	1	tr
Bean sprouts, mung, boiled, drained	100 mL	52	93	21	2	4	tr	tr
Beans, common white, cooked, drained	100 mL	80	69	118	8	21	tr	tr
Beans, lima, dry, cooked, drained	100 mL	80	64	138	8	26	tr	tr
Beans, red kidney, cooked, drained	100 mL	78	69	118	8	21	tr	tr
Beans, snap, green/yellow/Italian, boiled, drained	100 mL	53	89	35	2	8	tr	tr
Beans, snap, green/yellow/Italian, canned, drained	100 mL	57	93	20	1	5	tr	tr
Beans and wieners, canned	100 mL	108	71	144	8	13	7	3
Beans with tomato sauce and pork, canned	100 mL	108	71	122	6	19	3	tr
Beef, corned, brisket, cooked	100 g raw	70	60	251	18	tr	19	6
Beef, corned, canned	1 slice	21	58	250	27	0	15	6
Beef, corned, hash with potatoes	100 mL	93	67	181	9	11	11	5
Beef, ground, lean, broiled	100 g raw	74	59	241	26	0	14	6
Beef, ground, regular, broiled	100 g raw	67	54	289	24	0	21	8
Beef, ground, regular, pan-fried	100 g raw	68	52	306	24	0	23	9
Beef, roast, blade, lean and fat, braised	100 g raw	45	49	325	29	0	23	9
Beef, roast, blade, lean only, braised	100 g raw	38	55	260	32	0	14	6
Beef, roast, rib, lean only, roasted	100 g raw	48	59	191	29	0	8	3
Beef, roast, rump, lean only, roasted	100 g raw	61	60	222	30	0	10	4

PUFA (g)	Cholesterol (mg)	Calcium (mg)	Iron (mg)	Sodium (mg)	Potassium (mg)	Vitamin A (RE)	Thiamin (mg)	Riboflavin (mg)	Niacin (NE)	Folate (mcg)	Vitamin C (mg)	Dietary Fibre (g)
tr	0	6	.3	1	396	8	.05	.10	.7	19	9	2.1
tr	0	19	.9	815	174	87	.03	.02	1.2	4	7	—
tr	0	16	2.0	3	160	0	.12	.05	4.6	20	0	—
tr	0	12	.7	10	101	1	.05	.10	1.3	29	11	1.1
tr	0	50	2.7	7	416	0	.14	.07	2.1	46	0	6.3
tr	0	29	3.1	2	612	0	.13	.06	2.2	45	0	5.4
tr	0	38	2.4	3	340	tr	.11	.06	2.1	47	0	7.9
tr	0	46	1.3	3	299	67	.07	.10	.9	33	10	2.6
tr	0	26	.9	251	109	35	.02	.06	.4	32	5	2.6
3	13	37	1.9	539	262	13	.07	.06	2.7	24	0	—
tr	4	54	1.8	463	210	13	.08	.03	1.7	24	2	7.3
tr	98	8	1.9	1134	145	—	.03	.17	5.8	—	0	—
tr	86	—	2.1	1006	136	0	.02	.15	6.5	—	2	—
tr	33	13	2.0	540	200	0	.01	.09	3.7	13	0	—
tr	84	7	2.4	70	313	—	.06	.27	10.3	9	0	—
tr	90	11	2.4	83	292	—	.03	.19	10.7	9	0	—
tr	89	11	2.5	84	300	—	.03	.20	10.7	9	0	—
tr	103	15	2.9	49	273	—	.07	.23	7.2	5	0	—
tr	106	18	3.5	58	326	—	.08	.28	8.5	6	0	—
tr	81	10	2.3	71	376	—	.08	.21	9.5	8	0	—
tr	82	6	2.4	67	404	—	.10	.23	9.8	10	0	—

Food	Measure	Weight (g)	Water (%)	Energy (kcal)	Protein (g)	Carbohydrate (g)	Fat (g)	SFA (g)
Beef, steak, inside (top) round, lean only, broiled	100 g raw	66	63	203	30	0	8	3
Beef, steak, sirloin, lean only, broiled	100 g raw	55	62	210	29	0	9	4
Beef, stewing, lean only, simmered	100 mL	59	58	227	33	0	9	4
Beef and vegetable stew, canned	100 mL	103	83	79	6	7	3	2
Beef pot pie, baked	$\frac{1}{3}$ pie	210	55	246	10	19	15	4
Beer	100 mL	101	92	42	tr	4	0	0
Beet greens, boiled, drained	100 mL	61	89	27	3	5	tr	tr
Beets, canned, sliced, drained	100 mL	72	91	31	tr	7	tr	tr
Beets, diced or sliced, boiled, drained	250 mL	72	91	31	1	7	tr	tr
Biscuits, baking powder	1 medium	28	27	369	7	46	17	4
Blackberries, raw	100 mL	61	86	52	tr	13	tr	0
Blueberries, raw	100 mL	61	85	56	tr	14	tr	0
Bluefish, baked or broiled	1 piece, medium	92	68	159	26	0	5	1
Bologna, beef and pork	1 slice	22	54	316	12	3	28	11
Bouillon cubes	1	6	3	170	17	16	4	2
Brazil nuts, raw	100 mL	59	3	656	14	13	66	16
Bread, cracked-wheat	1 slice	25	35	263	9	52	2	tr
Bread, French/Vienna	1 slice	20	31	290	9	55	3	tr
Bread, Melba toast	1 piece	4	—	405	13	73	6	—
Bread, mixed-grain	1 slice	25	37	260	8	48	4	tr
Bread, oatmeal	1 slice	25	37	260	8	48	4	tr

PUFA (g)	Cholesterol (mg)	Calcium (mg)	Iron (mg)	Sodium (mg)	Potassium (mg)	Vitamin A (RE)	Thiamin (mg)	Riboflavin (mg)	Niacin (NE)	Folate (mcg)	Vitamin C (mg)	Dietary Fibre (g)
tr	84	5	2.8	51	400	—	.12	.27	11.7	12	0	—
tr	89	17	3.1	57	383	—	.13	.30	9.8	10	0	—
tr	101	8	3.2	47	345	—	.08	.29	10.0	11	0	—
tr	14	12	.9	411	174	291	.03	.05	2.1	13	3	—
3	21	14	1.8	284	159	246	.14	.14	4.2	8	3	—
0	0	5	.0	7	25	0	.00	.03	.7	6	0	—
tr	0	114	1.9	241	909	510	.12	.29	1.2	14	25	—
tr	0	15	1.8	274	148	1	.01	.04	.3	30	4	—
tr	0	11	.6	49	312	1	.03	.01	.5	53	6	—
4	1	121	2.4	626	117	0	.30	.29	4.0	11	tr	—
0	0	32	.6	0	196	16	.03	.04	.5	34	21	4.5
0	0	6	.2	6	89	10	.05	.05	.4	6	13	2.7
1	70	29	.7	104	420	15	.11	.10	6.7	13	0	—
2	55	12	1.5	1019	180	0	.17	.14	4.3	5	21	—
tr	4	60	2.2	4000	403	15	.20	.24	6.5	32	0	—
24	0	176	3.4	2	600	0	1.00	.12	6.0	4	tr	—
tr	2	88	2.8	529	134	0	.34	.25	4.8	42	0	4.1
tr	3	43	2.8	580	90	0	.40	.24	5.0	36	0	2.0
—	—	122	3.6	736	152	0	.22	.30	3.5	36	0	—
1	0	108	3.2	424	224	tr	.40	.40	5.9	—	tr	3.7
2	0	60	2.8	496	156	0	.48	.28	5.1	—	0	2.2

Food	Measure	Weight (g)	Water (%)	Energy (kcal)	Protein (g)	Carbohydrate (g)	Fat (g)	SFA (g)
Bread, pita	1 medium	60	31	275	10	55	2	tr
Bread, raisin	1 slice	25	35	262	7	54	3	tr
Bread, rye, dark, pumpernickel	1 slice	32	34	246	9	53	1	tr
Bread, rye, light	1 slice	25	36	243	9	52	1	tr
Bread, white	1 slice	28	36	270	9	51	3	tr
Bread, whole-wheat (100%)	1 slice	25	36	243	11	48	3	tr
Bread, whole-wheat (60%)	1 slice	25	36	250	10	48	4	tr
Breadcrumbs, white bread, dry	100 mL	42	7	392	13	73	5	1
Broccoli, raw	1 spear	151	91	28	3	5	tr	tr
Broccoli spears, 1-cm pieces, boiled, drained	250 mL	65	90	29	3	6	tr	tr
Brussels sprouts, boiled, drained	100 mL	66	87	39	3	9	tr	tr
Bulgur	100 mL	74	10	354	11	76	2	tr
Buns, hamburger or hot dog	1	55	31	298	8	53	6	1
Butter	100 mL	96	16	717	tr	tr	81	50
Cabbage, red, shredded, raw	100 mL	30	92	27	1	6	tr	tr
Cabbage, shredded, boiled, drained	100 mL	63	94	21	tr	5	tr	tr
Cabbage, shredded, raw	100 mL	30	93	24	1	5	tr	tr
Cake from mix, angelfood	1 piece, medium	76	34	259	6	59	tr	0
Cake from mix, cupcakes	1 medium	33	26	350	5	56	12	3
Cake from mix, coffee cake	1 piece, medium	72	30	322	6	52	10	3
Cake from mix, devil's food + icing	1 piece, medium	69	24	339	4	58	12	5

PUFA (g)	Cholesterol (mg)	Calcium (mg)	Iron (mg)	Sodium (mg)	Potassium (mg)	Vitamin A (RE)	Thiamin (mg)	Riboflavin (mg)	Niacin (NE)	Folate (mcg)	Vitamin C (mg)	Dietary Fibre (g)
tr	0	82	2.3	565	118	0	.45	.20	5.5	—	0	.9
tr	3	71	2.9	365	233	0	.38	.24	3.6	36	0	2.2
tr	1	84	2.9	569	454	0	.29	.21	3.6	23	0	3.2
tr	1	75	2.7	557	145	0	.30	.22	4.5	23	0	—
tr	3	84	2.8	507	105	0	.40	.24	4.9	36	0	1.6
tr	3	99	3.0	527	273	0	.26	.12	4.7	54	0	5.7
tr	4	93	3.0	530	275	0	.28	.18	4.4	49	0	—
1	5	122	4.1	736	152	0	.35	.35	7.1	36	0	—
tr	0	48	.9	27	325	154	.07	.12	1.1	71	93	2.8
tr	0	114	1.2	11	163	141	.08	.21	1.3	68	63	2.8
tr	0	36	1.2	21	317	72	.11	.08	1.1	60	62	3.0
tr	0	29	3.7	4	229	0	.28	.14	6.6	42	0	—
1	6	74	2.8	506	95	0	.40	.24	4.8	36	0	—
3	219	24	.2	827	26	754	tr	.03	.2	3	0	—
tr	0	51	.5	11	206	4	.05	.03	.5	21	57	2.0
tr	0	33	.4	19	205	9	.06	.06	.4	20	24	2.0
tr	0	47	.6	18	246	13	.05	.03	.5	57	47	2.0
0	0	95	.6	146	60	0	.06	.15	1.6	7	0	—
2	60	161	1.8	453	84	45	.19	.20	2.5	9	tr	—
2	65	61	1.7	431	109	45	.19	.21	2.9	—	tr	—
1	48	59	2.0	262	130	45	.10	.15	1.7	7	tr	—

Food	Measure	Weight (g)	Water (%)	Energy (kcal)	Protein (g)	Carbohydrate (g)	Fat (g)	SFA (g)
Cake, home recipe, Boston cream pie	1 piece, medium	69	35	302	5	50	9	3
Cake, home recipe, carrot, + cream cheese icing	1 piece, medium	60	23	402	4	50	22	4
Cake, home recipe, fruitcake, dark	1 slice, medium	60	18	379	5	60	15	3
Cake, home recipe, pound cake	1 slice, medium	30	17	473	6	47	30	8
Cake, home recipe, white, plain	1 piece, medium	86	25	364	5	56	14	4
Cake, home recipe, yellow layer + chocolate icing	1 piece, medium	75	21	365	4	60	13	5
Cake, home recipe, yellow layer, no icing	1 piece, medium	54	24	363	5	58	13	4
Candy, caramels, plain or chocolate	3	30	8	399	4	77	10	6
Candy, chocolate coated peanuts	100 mL	72	1	561	16	39	41	11
Candy, chocolate fudge	100 mL	128	8	400	3	75	12	4
Candy, gum drops	5	30	12	347	tr	87	tr	0
Candy, hard	6	30	1	386	0	97	1	0
Candy, jelly beans	100 mL	93	6	367	0	93	tr	0
Candy, licorice	100 mL	93	7	315	4	74	2	0
Candy, marshmallows	4	28	17	319	2	80	0	0
Candy, mints or fondant	100 mL	84	8	364	tr	90	2	tr
Cantaloupe, raw	$\frac{1}{2}$	267	90	35	tr	8	tr	0
Carrots, boiled, drained	100 mL	66	87	45	1	10	tr	tr
Carrots, canned, drained	100 mL	62	93	23	tr	6	tr	tr
Carrots, raw	1 medium	72	88	43	1	10	tr	tr
Cashew nuts, roasted	100 mL	55	4	576	16	29	48	10

PUFA (g)	Cholesterol (mg)	Calcium (mg)	Iron (mg)	Sodium (mg)	Potassium (mg)	Vitamin A (RE)	Thiamin (mg)	Riboflavin (mg)	Niacin (NE)	Folate (mcg)	Vitamin C (mg)	Dietary Fibre (g)
2	86	67	1.3	186	89	63	.13	.15	2.1	9	tr	—
7	77	46	1.4	291	112	16	.12	.13	1.7	—	1	—
3	45	72	2.8	158	496	36	.16	.16	2.0	12	tr	—
7	147	21	1.8	110	60	84	.16	.18	2.3	11	0	—
3	65	64	1.5	300	79	51	.16	.18	2.1	8	tr	—
2	44	68	1.5	208	108	48	.13	.17	2.0	7	tr	—
2	54	71	1.6	258	78	45	.17	.19	2.3	9	tr	—
tr	2	148	1.4	226	192	3	.03	.17	.9	—	0	—
7	1	116	1.5	60	504	0	.37	.18	10.4	56	0	—
2	1	77	1.0	190	147	0	.02	.09	.7	—	0	—
0	0	6	.5	35	5	0	.00	.00	.0	0	0	—
0	0	21	1.9	32	4	0	.00	.00	.0	0	0	—
0	0	12	1.1	12	1	0	.00	.00	.0	0	0	—
0	0	63	8.0	75	216	0	.00	.00	.7	0	0	—
0	1	18	1.6	39	6	0	.00	.00	.0	0	0	—
tr	0	14	1.1	212	5	0	.00	.00	.0	—	0	—
0	0	11	.2	9	309	322	.04	.02	.7	17	42	1.0
tr	0	31	.6	66	227	2455	.03	.06	.7	14	2	3.0
tr	0	25	.6	241	179	1377	.02	.03	.7	9	3	3.0
tr	0	27	.5	35	323	2813	.10	.06	1.1	14	9	3.0
8	0	41	4.1	17	530	0	.42	.18	6.0	68	0	—

Food	Measure	Weight (g)	Water (%)	Energy (kcal)	Protein (g)	Carbohydrate (g)	Fat (g)	SFA (g)
Cauliflower, boiled, drained	100 mL	52	93	24	2	5	tr	tr
Cauliflower, raw	100 mL	42	92	24	2	5	tr	tr
Celery, diced, raw	100 mL	51	95	16	tr	4	tr	tr
Cereal, bran (All Bran)	100 mL	36	4	252	12	75	2	—
Cereal, bran (100%)	100 mL	28	3	257	11	83	2	tr
Cereal, bran flakes with raisins	100 mL	21	10	317	8	77	1	—
Cereal, corn bran	100 mL	15	2	392	7	86	4	—
Cereal, corn flakes, plain	100 mL	10	4	369	7	86	tr	—
Cereal, corn flakes, sugar coated (Frosted Flakes)	100 mL	15	3	379	5	90	tr	—
Cereal, corn + oats (Cap'n Crunch)	100 mL	16	2	395	4	81	6	4
Cereal, corn + wheat + oats (Fruit Loops)	100 mL	12	3	389	6	88	2	—
Cereal, granola, homemade	100 mL	52	3	487	12	55	27	5
Cereal, oatmeal, regular/quick-cooking, cooked	100 mL	99	85	62	3	11	1	tr
Cereal, oatmeal, regular/quick-cooking, dry	100 mL	34	9	384	16	67	6	1
Cereal, oats +, + marshmallows (Lucky Charms)	100 mL	13	3	395	7	86	3	tr
Cereal, oats +, puffed (Cheerios)	100 mL	10	7	385	13	71	7	1
Cereal, oats +, puffed, presweetened (Alpha-Bits)	100 mL	12	2	393	7	87	3	—
Cereal, Red River, cooked	100 mL	100	—	66	3	13	tr	—
Cereal, rice, puffed	100 mL	6	2	390	6	90	tr	—
Cereal, rice (Rice Krispies)	100 mL	12	4	372	7	85	tr	—
Cereal, rice + wheat (Special K)	100 mL	9	4	373	20	72	tr	—

PUFA (g)	Cholesterol (mg)	Calcium (mg)	Iron (mg)	Sodium (mg)	Potassium (mg)	Vitamin A (RE)	Thiamin (mg)	Riboflavin (mg)	Niacin (NE)	Folate (mcg)	Vitamin C (mg)	Dietary Fibre (g)
tr	0	27	.4	6	323	1	.06	.05	1.0	51	55	1.7
tr	0	29	.6	15	355	2	.08	.06	1.1	66	72	1.7
tr	0	36	.5	88	284	13	.03	.03	.5	9	6	1.5
—	0	85	13.3	910	1055	0	2.00	.20	17.2	96	0	29.3
tr	0	77	13.3	—	1248	0	2.00	.36	25.4	71	0	28.4
—	0	44	13.3	676	527	0	2.00	.00	7.4	60	0	8.8
—	0	75	13.3	863	220	0	2.00	.03	6.1	60	0	20.3
—	0	3	13.3	973	108	0	2.00	.03	6.1	60	0	.4
—	0	3	13.3	570	75	0	2.00	.03	5.7	60	0	.4
tr	0	14	13.3	740	100	0	2.00	.03	5.4	60	0	1.4
—	0	10	13.3	410	115	0	2.00	.03	5.8	60	0	1.1
14	0	62	4.0	10	502	4	.60	.25	4.2	81	1	—
tr	0	8	.7	1	56	2	.11	.02	.7	4	0	.9
3	0	52	4.2	4	350	10	.73	.14	4.4	32	0	6.0
1	0	0	13.3	480	180	0	—	.10	6.4	60	0	1.8
3	0	117	13.3	890	360	0	.07	.10	7.8	60	0	3.2
—	0	3	13.3	40	157	5	2.00	.17	6.3	60	0	1.8
—	0	—	.3	6	—	0	.03	tr	.9	10	0	1.9
—	0	8	.6	8	115	0	.04	.07	3.3	9	0	.3
—	0	14	13.3	1040	122	0	2.00	.03	6.2	60	0	.4
—	tr	42	13.3	864	160	0	2.00	—	8.5	60	0	.7

Food	Measure	Weight (g)	Water (%)	Energy (kcal)	Protein (g)	Carbohydrate (g)	Fat (g)	SFA (g)
Cereal, wheat, flakes (Grape-Nuts)	100 mL	14	6	360	10	80	1	—
Cereal, wheat, flakes (Wheaties)	100 mL	12	5	360	11	82	2	tr
Cereal, wheat, puffed	100 mL	5	2	385	15	79	1	—
Cereal, wheat, puffed, presweetened (Sugar-Crisp)	100 mL	14	4	377	8	87	1	—
Cereal, wheat, whole (Shredded Wheat)	1	25	6	379	11	82	1	—
Cereal, wheat, whole (Shreddies)	100 mL	22	5	384	10	85	tr	—
Chard, Swiss, boiled, drained	100 mL	74	93	20	2	4	tr	0
Cheese, blue	100 mL	105	42	353	21	2	29	19
Cheese, brick	100 mL	105	41	371	23	3	30	19
Cheese, Camembert	100 mL	104	52	300	20	tr	24	15
Cheese, cheddar	100 mL	105	37	403	25	1	33	21
Cheese, cottage, creamed, 4.5% B.F.	100 mL	95	79	103	12	3	5	3
Cheese, cottage, 2% B.F.	100 mL	95	79	90	14	4	2	1
Cheese, cream	100 mL	98	54	349	8	3	35	22
Cheese, feta	100 mL	104	53	272	15	4	22	15
Cheese, Gouda	100 mL	104	41	364	25	2	28	18
Cheese, mozzarella	100 mL	107	52	293	20	2	22	14
Cheese, mozzarella, made with partly skimmed milk	100 mL	45	52	263	25	3	16	10
Cheese, Parmesan, grated	100 mL	34	18	456	42	4	30	19
Cheese, processed, cheddar	100 mL	105	39	375	22	2	31	20
Cheese, processed, cheddar, made with skim milk	100 mL	105	—	191	24	10	6	—

PUFA (g)	Cholesterol (mg)	Calcium (mg)	Iron (mg)	Sodium (mg)	Potassium (mg)	Vitamin A (RE)	Thiamin (mg)	Riboflavin (mg)	Niacin (NE)	Folate (mcg)	Vitamin C (mg)	Dietary Fibre (g)
—	0	3	13.3	473	313	5	2.00	.07	7.9	60	0	6.4
tr	0	0	13.3	780	405	0	2.00	.00	8.2	60	0	7.1
—	0	27	3.5	6	355	0	.11	.19	9.3	25	0	4.3
—	0	3	2.3	113	187	2	2.00	.17	6.9	60	0	2.1
—	0	41	3.2	8	340	0	.28	.28	7.9	40	0	9.6
—	0	36	13.3	—	—	0	2.00	.17	6.5	60	0	7.3
0	0	58	2.3	179	549	314	.03	.09	.7	9	18	—
tr	75	528	.3	1395	256	228	.03	.38	6.2	36	0	—
tr	94	674	.4	560	136	302	.01	.35	5.5	20	0	—
tr	72	388	.3	842	187	252	.03	.49	5.7	62	0	—
tr	105	721	.7	621	98	303	.03	.38	5.4	18	0	—
tr	15	60	.1	405	84	48	.02	.16	2.4	12	0	—
tr	8	69	.2	406	96	20	.02	.19	2.7	13	0	—
1	110	80	1.2	296	119	437	.02	.20	1.2	13	0	—
tr	92	509	.7	1154	64	132	.16	.87	4.5	33	0	—
tr	116	714	.2	836	123	178	.03	.34	6.1	21	0	—
tr	82	538	.2	388	70	251	.02	.25	4.8	7	0	—
tr	60	678	.2	482	87	183	.02	.31	6.0	9	0	—
tr	79	376	1.0	1862	107	173	.05	.39	9.6	8	0	—
tr	94	616	.4	1430	162	290	.03	.35	5.5	8	0	—
—	—	562	.3	1540	295	105	.05	.43	2.7	—	0	—

Food	Measure	Weight (g)	Water (%)	Energy (kcal)	Protein (g)	Carbohydrate (g)	Fat (g)	SFA (g)
Cheese, processed spread, cheddar	100 mL	103	48	290	16	9	21	13
Cheese, processed spread, made with skim milk	100 mL	105	—	192	24	11	6	tr
Cheese, Provolone	100 mL	104	41	351	26	2	27	17
Cheese, ricotta, made with whole milk	100 mL	104	72	174	11	3	13	8
Cheese, Swiss	100 mL	91	37	376	28	3	27	18
Cheeseburger, 4-oz. patty	1	194	46	271	15	21	16	8
Cheesecake	1 piece, medium	92	46	302	5	29	19	11
Cherries, sour, red, canned, water pack	100 mL	103	90	36	tr	9	tr	tr
Cherries, sweet, raw	100 mL	61	81	72	1	17	tr	tr
Chicken à la king, home recipe	100 mL	103	68	191	11	5	14	5
Chicken pot pie, baked	$\frac{1}{3}$ pie	232	57	235	10	18	14	5
Chicken, broiler/fryer, breast, meat only, roasted	$\frac{1}{2}$	86	65	165	31	0	4	1
Chicken, broiler/fryer, breast, meat + skin, roasted	$\frac{1}{2}$	98	62	197	30	0	8	2
Chicken, broiler/fryer, breast, meat + skin + batter, fried	$\frac{1}{2}$	140	52	260	25	9	13	4
Chicken, canned, boned, with broth	100 mL	87	69	165	22	0	8	2
Chicken, roasting, flesh only, roasted	4 slices	92	67	167	25	0	7	2
Chickpeas (garbanzos), boiled, drained	100 mL	69	60	166	9	28	2	tr
Chili con carne with beans, canned	100 mL	108	72	133	8	12	6	3
Chili con carne without beans, canned	100 mL	108	67	200	10	6	15	7
Chocolate bars, "Caravan/Caramilk" type		30	8	416	4	78	14	4
Chocolate bars, "Oh Henry" type with nuts		30	7	459	9	59	23	6

PUFA (g)	Cholesterol (mg)	Calcium (mg)	Iron (mg)	Sodium (mg)	Potassium (mg)	Vitamin A (RE)	Thiamin (mg)	Riboflavin (mg)	Niacin (NE)	Folate (mcg)	Vitamin C (mg)	Dietary Fibre (g)
tr	55	562	.3	1625	242	189	.05	.43	4.1	7	0	—
tr	—	—	—	1973	408	—	—	—	5.7	—	0	—
tr	69	756	.5	876	138	264	.02	.32	5.9	10	0	—
tr	51	207	.4	84	105	134	.01	.20	2.2	12	0	—
tr	92	961	.2	260	111	253	.02	.37	6.8	6	0	—
1	54	122	2.3	631	210	66	.17	.25	6.6	—	2	—
—	185	56	.5	222	98	75	.03	.13	1.5	—	5	—
tr	0	11	1.4	7	98	75	.02	.04	.3	8	2	—
tr	0	15	.4	0	224	21	.05	.06	.6	4	7	1.2
1	76	52	1.0	310	165	138	.04	.17	4.3	9	5	—
2	31	30	1.3	256	148	399	.14	.14	3.9	9	2	—
tr	85	15	1.0	74	256	6	.07	.11	19.7	4	0	—
2	84	14	1.1	71	245	27	.07	.12	18.4	4	0	—
3	85	20	1.3	275	201	20	.12	.15	15.3	6	0	—
2	62	14	1.6	503	138	34	.02	.13	10.4	4	2	—
2	75	12	1.2	75	229	12	.06	.15	12.7	5	0	—
1	0	49	3.0	7	291	tr	.11	.06	2.2	—	0	—
tr	17	32	1.7	531	233	6	.03	.07	2.7	36	0	—
0	26	38	1.4	531	233	15	.02	.12	4.1	8	0	—
tr	5	127	1.6	173	211	12	.06	.17	.9	7	0	—
4	2	127	1.1	128	222	0	.26	.15	5.4	32	0	—

Food	Measure	Weight (g)	Water (%)	Energy (kcal)	Protein (g)	Carbohydrate (g)	Fat (g)	SFA (g)
Chocolate bars, milk, plain		30	tr	520	8	57	32	18
Chocolate-flavoured powder + skim milk, made with water	100 mL	108	86	49	1	11	tr	tr
Chocolate-flavoured powder, no milk, made with whole milk	100 mL	106	81	85	3	11	3	2
Chocolate syrup, fudge type	100 mL	127	25	330	5	54	14	8
Chocolate syrup, thin type	100 mL	127	32	245	2	63	2	1
Chocolate, baking, bitter	1 square	28	2	505	11	29	53	30
Chocolate, baking, sweet	1 square	28	tr	528	4	58	35	19
Clams, canned, drained, solids	100 mL	68	77	98	16	2	3	tr
Coconut, dried, sweetened, shredded	100 mL	39	13	501	3	48	35	31
Cod, fresh, broiled	1 piece, medium	88	65	170	29	0	5	1
Coffee	100 mL	101	99	2	tr	tr	0	0
Coffee whitener (non-dairy), liquid, frozen	100 mL	101	77	136	1	11	10	9
Coffee whitener (non-dairy), powdered	100 mL	40	2	546	5	55	35	33
Coleslaw (cabbage salad)	100 mL	51	82	69	1	12	3	tr
Cone, ice cream	1	4	9	377	10	78	2	1
Cookies, brownies with nuts, home recipe	1	20	10	485	7	51	31	7
Cookies, chocolate chip, commercial	2	22	3	471	5	70	21	6
Cookies, chocolate chip, home recipe	2	20	3	516	5	60	30	8
Cookies, chocolate marshmallow (Mallows)	1	17	10	409	4	72	13	8
Cookies, fig bars	2	28	14	358	4	75	6	2
Cookies, oatmeal with raisins	2	26	3	451	6	74	15	4

PUFA (g)	Cholesterol (mg)	Calcium (mg)	Iron (mg)	Sodium (mg)	Potassium (mg)	Vitamin A (RE)	Thiamin (mg)	Riboflavin (mg)	Niacin (NE)	Folate (mcg)	Vitamin C (mg)	Dietary Fibre (g)
tr	20	228	1.1	94	384	81	.06	.34	1.7	7	0	—
tr	tr	44	.1	67	108	tr	.02	.08	.4	—	tr	—
tr	12	112	.3	66	192	29	.04	.16	.7	—	1	—
tr	0	127	1.3	89	284	45	.04	.22	1.3	—	0	—
tr	0	17	1.6	52	282	0	.02	.07	.8	—	0	—
1	0	78	6.7	4	830	18	.05	.24	3.5	12	0	—
tr	1	94	1.4	33	269	3	.02	.14	1.1	12	0	—
tr	63	55	4.1	120	140	30	.01	.11	3.9	13	0	—
tr	0	15	1.9	262	337	0	.03	.02	1.0	8	tr	—
1	81	31	1.0	110	407	54	.08	.11	8.2	19	0	—
0	0	2	.4	2	54	0	.00	.00	.2	tr	0	—
tr	0	9	tr	79	191	9	.00	.00	.2	0	0	—
tr	0	22	1.2	181	812	20	.00	.17	1.1	0	0	—
1	8	45	.6	23	181	82	.07	.06	.6	27	33	—
0	0	156	.4	232	244	0	.05	.21	2.3	—	0	—
5	83	41	2.0	251	190	60	.22	.14	2.1	11	0	—
5	39	39	2.8	401	134	36	.17	.16	2.5	9	0	—
7	49	34	2.4	348	117	33	.15	.14	2.3	12	0	—
1	76	21	1.6	209	91	78	.12	.13	1.8	10	tr	—
1	39	78	2.2	252	198	33	.18	.17	2.3	10	0	—
4	39	21	3.2	162	370	15	.28	.20	3.0	20	tr	—

Food	Measure	Weight (g)	Water (%)	Energy (kcal)	Protein (g)	Carbohydrate (g)	Fat (g)	SFA (g)
Cookies, peanut butter, home recipe	2	24	3	510	8	58	29	8
Cookies, sandwich, chocolate/vanilla, commercial	2	20	2	495	5	69	23	6
Cookies, shortbread, commercial	2	28	3	498	7	65	23	6
Cookies (Social Tea or Arrowroot)	2	13	6	442	8	71	14	3
Cookies, sugar, from refrigerated dough	2	24	4	490	4	65	25	5
Cookies (Vanilla Wafers)	5	20	4	463	5	73	18	5
Corn, sweet, boiled, kernels, drained	100 mL	69	70	108	3	25	1	tr
Corn, sweet, canned, kernels, drained	100 mL	69	77	81	3	19	1	tr
Corn, sweet, canned, cream style	100 mL	108	79	72	2	18	tr	tr
Cornmeal, degermed, dry	100 mL	58	12	364	8	78	1	tr
Corn oil	100 mL	92	0	884	0	0	100	13
Cornstarch	100 mL	54	12	362	tr	88	0	0
Crab, canned, solids only	100 mL	57	77	101	17	1	3	tr
Crackers, cheese	4	14	4	479	11	60	21	8
Crackers, graham	4	28	6	384	8	73	9	2
Crackers, soda (Saltines)	4	11	4	433	9	72	12	3
Crackers, wheat (Wheat Thins)	4	8	3	438	13	63	13	6
Cranberries, whole, raw	100 mL	40	87	49	tr	13	tr	0
Cranberry juice, cocktail, bottled	100 mL	107	85	58	tr	15	tr	0
Cranberry sauce, canned, sweetened	100 mL	117	61	151	tr	39	tr	—
Cream, cereal (half & half), 12% B.F.	100 mL	102	80	135	3	4	12	7

PUFA (g)	Cholesterol (mg)	Calcium (mg)	Iron (mg)	Sodium (mg)	Potassium (mg)	Vitamin A (RE)	Thiamin (mg)	Riboflavin (mg)	Niacin (NE)	Folate (mcg)	Vitamin C (mg)	Dietary Fibre (g)
6	46	44	2.3	296	229	10	.15	.15	5.5	—	0	—
5	39	26	2.0	483	38	0	.23	.17	3.0	6	0	—
5	39	70	3.0	60	66	24	.45	.27	4.4	9	0	—
tr	1	32	3.0	370	156	0	.50	.43	5.7	10	6	—
8	60	104	1.9	544	69	23	.19	.13	3.1	—	0	—
5	63	40	2.0	375	125	35	.18	.25	3.4	—	0	—
tr	0	2	.6	17	249	22	.22	.07	2.0	46	6	2.8
tr	0	5	.9	323	195	16	.03	.08	1.5	49	9	2.8
tr	0	3	.4	285	134	10	.03	.05	1.2	45	5	2.8
tr	0	6	1.1	1	120	132	.14	.05	2.4	22	0	—
59	0	0	.0	0	0	0	.00	.00	.0	0	0	—
0	0	0	.0	0	0	0	.00	.00	.0	—	0	—
1	101	45	.8	1000	110	327	.08	.08	5.1	20	0	—
3	32	336	3.5	1039	109	108	.39	.35	5.8	16	0	—
2	0	40	3.5	670	384	0	.12	.61	4.5	16	0	—
3	0	21	4.8	1100	120	0	.45	.35	6.1	16	0	—
5	0	38	3.8	863	213	0	.50	.38	7.3	—	0	—
—	0	7	.2	1	71	5	.03	.02	.2	2	14	—
—	0	3	.2	4	24	0	tr	.02	tr	tr	22	—
—	0	4	.2	29	26	2	.02	.02	.1	—	2	—
tr	39	104	tr	41	129	112	.03	.15	.8	2	tr	—

Food	Measure	Weight (g)	Water (%)	Energy (kcal)	Protein (g)	Carbohydrate (g)	Fat (g)	SFA (g)
Cream, sour, 14% B.F.	100 mL	99	74	188	3	4	18	11
Cream, table (coffee), 18% B.F.	100 mL	102	75	185	3	4	18	11
Cream, whipped topping, pressurized	100 mL	25	61	257	3	12	22	14
Cream, whipping, 35% B.F.	100 mL	100	60	328	2	3	35	22
Croissants	1	57	22	412	9	47	21	6
Cucumber, raw	100 mL	44	96	13	tr	3	tr	tr
Danish pastry, plain, round	1 medium	65	22	422	7	46	24	7
Date squares	1	90	—	251	2	50	6	—
Dates, pitted, chopped	100 mL	75	23	275	2	74	tr	0
Dessert topping (non-dairy), semisolid (frozen)	100 mL	32	50	318	1	23	25	22
Dessert topping (non-dairy), whipped, pressurized	100 mL	30	60	264	tr	16	22	19
Doughnuts, yeast-leavened	1	42	28	414	6	38	27	7
Eggnog, commercial	100 mL	107	74	135	4	14	7	4
Eggplant, cubed, boiled, drained	100 mL	41	92	28	tr	7	tr	tr
Egg substitute, frozen (yolk replaced)	100 mL	101	73	160	11	3	11	2
Eggs, large, fried in butter	1	46	72	180	12	1	14	5
Eggs, large, raw/cooked in shell, without shell	1	50	75	158	12	1	11	3
Eggs, large, scrambled, + milk + butter	1	64	76	148	9	2	11	4
Eggs, white, large, raw/cooked in shell	100 mL	103	88	49	10	1	tr	0
Eggs, yolk, large, raw/cooked in shell	1	17	49	369	16	tr	33	10
English muffins, with egg, cheese, and bacon	1	138	49	261	13	22	13	6

PUFA (g)	Cholesterol (mg)	Calcium (mg)	Iron (mg)	Sodium (mg)	Potassium (mg)	Vitamin A (RE)	Thiamin (mg)	Riboflavin (mg)	Niacin (NE)	Folate (mcg)	Vitamin C (mg)	Dietary Fibre (g)
tr	42	112	tr	49	139	168	.04	.15	.8	11	tr	—
tr	61	98	tr	40	123	169	.03	.15	.7	2	tr	—
tr	76	101	tr	130	147	207	.04	.07	.8	3	0	—
1	128	66	tr	36	82	380	.02	.11	.5	4	tr	—
2	23	35	3.7	793	119	23	.30	.23	3.9	—	0	—
tr	0	14	.3	2	149	5	.03	.02	.4	14	5	.8
4	64	50	1.9	366	112	93	.28	.30	3.9	36	0	—
—	—	27	1.4	150	300	3	.08	.06	.1	16	—	—
0	0	32	1.2	3	652	5	.09	.10	3.0	13	0	7.6
tr	0	6	.1	25	18	86	.00	.00	.3	0	0	—
tr	0	5	tr	62	19	47	.00	.00	.2	0	0	—
6	25	38	2.1	234	80	18	.23	.22	3.1	22	0	—
tr	59	130	.2	54	165	80	.03	.19	1.0	tr	2	—
tr	0	6	.4	3	248	6	.08	.02	.7	14	1	—
6	2	73	2.0	199	213	135	.12	.39	2.9	16	tr	—
2	534	56	2.0	313	126	180	.07	.28	3.2	47	0	—
1	548	56	2.1	138	130	156	.09	.30	3.3	65	0	—
1	388	74	1.5	243	133	139	.06	.24	2.5	35	tr	—
0	0	11	tr	152	137	0	tr	.29	2.7	16	0	—
4	602	152	5.6	49	90	552	.25	.44	4.1	152	0	—
tr	154	143	2.2	603	146	116	.33	.36	5.1	—	tr	—

Food	Measure	Weight (g)	Water (%)	Energy (kcal)	Protein (g)	Carbohydrate (g)	Fat (g)	SFA (g)
English muffins, plain	1	57	42	246	9	47	2	tr
Figs, dried, uncooked	100 mL	84	28	255	3	65	1	tr
Fish cakes, fried	1 medium	60	66	172	15	9	8	3
Fish sandwich, large, no cheese, fast food	1	170	48	276	11	24	16	4
Fish sticks, breaded, frozen, cooked	3	90	66	176	17	7	9	3
Fruit cocktail, canned, heavy syrup	100 mL	108	80	73	tr	19	tr	tr
Fruit cocktail, canned, water pack	100 mL	103	91	32	tr	9	tr	tr
Fruit-flavoured drinks, canned/ bottled, + vitamin C	100 mL	105	87	49	tr	13	0	0
Fruit-flavoured drinks, crystals, + water + vitamin C	100 mL	114	88	41	0	11	0	0
Fruit salad, tropical, canned	100 mL	109	77	86	tr	22	tr	—
Gelatin, dry powder	1 envelope	7	13	335	86	0	tr	0
Gelatin dessert, dietetic	100 mL	101	99	8	2	tr	tr	0
Gelatin dessert, prepared with water ("Jello")	100 mL	101	84	59	2	14	0	0
Grapefruit juice, canned, sweetened	100 mL	106	87	46	tr	11	tr	tr
Grapefruit juice, canned, unsweetened	100 mL	104	90	38	tr	9	tr	tr
Grapefruit juice, fresh	100 mL	104	90	39	tr	9	tr	tr
Grapefruit juice, frozen, unsweetened, diluted	100 mL	104	89	41	tr	10	tr	tr
Grapefruit, canned, syrup pack	100 mL	107	84	60	tr	15	tr	tr
Grapefruit, pink and red, raw	$\frac{1}{2}$	123	91	30	tr	8	tr	tr
Grapefruit, white, raw	$\frac{1}{2}$	118	90	33	tr	8	tr	tr
Grape juice, canned or bottled	100 mL	107	84	61	tr	15	tr	tr

PUFA (g)	Cholesterol (mg)	Calcium (mg)	Iron (mg)	Sodium (mg)	Potassium (mg)	Vitamin A (RE)	Thiamin (mg)	Riboflavin (mg)	Niacin (NE)	Folate (mcg)	Vitamin C (mg)	Dietary Fibre (g)
tr	0	168	3.0	663	581	0	.46	.33	5.5	—	0	—
tr	0	144	2.2	11	712	13	.07	.09	1.1	8	tr	—
2	42	11	.4	177	348	0	.04	.07	4.3	12	0	—
6	54	36	1.3	365	221	9	.21	.14	4.0	—	tr	—
2	47	11	.4	177	348	0	.04	.07	4.6	13	0	—
tr	0	6	.3	6	88	20	.02	.02	.4	3	2	.6
tr	0	5	.3	4	94	25	.02	.01	.4	3	2	.6
0	0	5	.2	9	27	1	.02	.02	.3	tr	25	.1
0	0	28	tr	7	tr	0	.00	.00	.0	0	21	.0
—	0	13	.5	2	131	13	.05	.05	.6	—	18	—
0	0	11	.0	90	22	0	.00	.00	.1	0	0	—
tr	0	0	.0	7	37	0	.00	.00	.0	0	0	—
0	0	0	.0	51	2	0	.00	.00	.0	0	0	—
tr	0	8	.4	2	162	0	.04	.02	.4	10	27	.4
tr	0	7	.2	1	153	1	.04	.02	.3	10	29	.4
tr	0	9	.2	1	162	1	.04	.02	.3	10	38	—
tr	0	8	.1	1	136	1	.04	.02	.3	4	34	—
tr	0	14	.4	2	129	0	.04	.02	.3	9	21	—
tr	0	11	.1	0	129	26	.03	.02	.2	12	38	1.3
tr	0	12	tr	0	148	1	.04	.02	.3	10	33	1.3
tr	0	9	.2	3	132	1	.03	.04	.4	3	tr	.5

Food	Measure	Weight (g)	Water (%)	Energy (kcal)	Protein (g)	Carbohydrate (g)	Fat (g)	SFA (g)
Grape juice, frozen, sweetened, diluted, + vitamin C	100 mL	106	87	51	tr	13	tr	tr
Grapes, Canadian type (slip skin), raw	100 mL	39	81	63	tr	17	tr	tr
Grapes, European type (adherent skin), raw	100 mL	68	81	71	tr	18	tr	tr
Gravy, brown, canned	100 mL	98	87	53	4	5	2	1
Gum, chewing	1 stick	4	4	317	0	95	0	0
Haddock, coated with breadcrumbs, milk and egg, fried	1 fillet	110	66	165	20	6	6	2
Halibut, broiled with butter or margarine	1 piece, medium	92	67	171	25	0	7	4
Ham, luncheon meat, sliced, packaged	1 slice, medium	27	65	182	18	3	11	3
Ham, roasted, lean only	100 mL	59	68	147	22	tr	6	2
Ham, roasted, lean and fat	100 mL	59	58	243	22	0	17	6
Hamburger, 4-oz. patty	1	174	50	256	14	22	12	4
Honey, strained, liquid	100 mL	143	17	304	tr	82	0	0
Honeydew melon, raw	100 mL	72	90	35	tr	9	tr	0
Ice cream, vanilla, 16% B.F.	100 mL	62	59	236	3	22	16	10
Ice cream, vanilla, 10% B.F.	100 mL	56	61	202	4	24	11	7
Ice milk, vanilla, soft serve	100 mL	74	69	140	4	22	4	3
Icing, chocolate, made with milk and fat	100 mL	116	14	376	3	67	14	8
Icing, white, boiled	100 mL	40	18	316	1	80	0	0
Jams and preserves	100 mL	135	29	272	tr	70	tr	0
Jellies	100 mL	127	29	273	tr	71	tr	0
Ketchup	100 mL	115	69	106	2	25	tr	0

PUFA (g)	Cholesterol (mg)	Calcium (mg)	Iron (mg)	Sodium (mg)	Potassium (mg)	Vitamin A (RE)	Thiamin (mg)	Riboflavin (mg)	Niacin (NE)	Folate (mcg)	Vitamin C (mg)	Dietary Fibre (g)
tr	0	4	.1	2	21	1	.02	.03	.2	1	15	tr
tr	0	14	.3	2	191	10	.09	.06	.4	4	4	1.3
tr	0	11	.3	2	185	7	.09	.06	.4	4	11	1.3
tr	3	6	.7	50	81	0	.03	.04	.7	2	0	—
0	0	0	.0	0	0	0	.00	.00	.0	0	0	—
2	64	40	1.2	177	348	—	.04	.07	6.8	13	2	—
tr	60	16	.8	134	525	204	.05	.07	12.9	12	0	—
1	57	7	1.0	1317	332	0	.86	.25	8.8	3	28	—
tr	52	7	.8	1516	371	0	.93	.23	9.7	4	0	—
2	62	7	.9	1187	286	0	.60	.22	8.5	3	0	—
tr	41	43	2.8	439	232	16	.22	.22	7.1	—	tr	—
0	0	5	.5	5	51	0	tr	.04	.4	2	1	—
—	0	6	tr	10	271	4	.08	.02	.7	31	25	—
tr	59	102	tr	73	149	148	.03	.19	.7	2	tr	—
tr	45	132	tr	87	193	100	.04	.25	1.0	2	tr	—
tr	14	134	.1	80	202	40	.06	.27	1.0	2	tr	—
tr	16	60	1.2	61	195	63	.02	.10	.8	3	tr	—
0	0	2	.0	143	18	0	.00	.03	.0	tr	0	—
0	0	20	1.0	12	88	3	.01	.03	.3	8	2	—
0	0	21	1.5	17	75	3	.01	.03	.2	—	4	—
0	0	22	.8	1042	363	140	.09	.07	2.0	15	15	—

Food	Measure	Weight (g)	Water (%)	Energy (kcal)	Protein (g)	Carbohydrate (g)	Fat (g)	SFA (g)
Kidney, beef, simmered	100 g raw	43	69	144	25	tr	3	1
Kiwi fruit, raw	1 large	91	83	61	tr	15	tr	—
Lamb, leg, roasted, lean and fat	2 slices, medium	87	54	279	25	0	19	11
Lamb, leg, roasted, lean only	2 slices, medium	87	62	186	29	0	7	4
Lamb, loin chop, broiled, lean only	198 g raw	87	62	188	28	0	8	4
Lamb, shoulder, roasted, lean only	3 slices, medium	83	61	205	27	0	10	6
Lard	100 mL	87	0	902	0	0	100	41
Lemon juice, canned or bottled, unsweetened	100 mL	103	92	21	tr	6	tr	tr
Lemon juice, fresh	100 mL	103	91	25	tr	9	0	0
Lemon, raw, without peel	1 medium	84	89	29	1	9	tr	tr
Lemonade, frozen concentrate, diluted	100 mL	105	89	44	tr	11	0	0
Lentils, cooked, drained	100 mL	84	72	106	8	19	tr	tr
Lettuce, iceberg, raw	1 leaf	20	96	13	1	2	tr	tr
Lime juice, canned or bottled, unsweetened	100 mL	104	93	21	tr	7	tr	tr
Lime juice, fresh	100 mL	104	90	27	tr	9	tr	tr
Liquor, gin, rum, vodka, whisky	100 mL	95	67	231	0	0	0	0
Liver, beef, pan-fried	100 g raw	65	56	217	27	8	8	3
Liver, calf's, fried	3 slices, medium	95	51	261	30	4	13	3
Liver, chicken, simmered	100 mL	59	68	157	24	tr	5	2
Liver, pork, braised	100 g raw	78	64	165	26	4	4	1
Liverwurst	15 mL	15	52	326	14	2	29	11

PUFA (g)	Cholesterol (mg)	Calcium (mg)	Iron (mg)	Sodium (mg)	Potassium (mg)	Vitamin A (RE)	Thiamin (mg)	Riboflavin (mg)	Niacin (NE)	Folate (mcg)	Vitamin C (mg)	Dietary Fibre (g)
tr	387	17	7.3	134	179	373	.19	4.06	11.8	98	tr	—
—	0	26	.4	5	332	18	.02	.05	.7	—	75	—
tr	98	11	1.7	62	283	0	.15	.27	10.1	2	0	—
tr	100	13	2.2	70	321	0	.16	.30	11.5	2	0	—
tr	100	12	2.0	69	316	0	.15	.28	11.3	2	0	—
tr	100	12	1.9	66	300	0	.15	.28	10.6	7	0	—
11	95	tr	.0	tr	tr	0	.00	.00	.0	0	0	—
tr	0	11	.1	21	102	2	.04	tr	.3	10	25	—
—	0	7	tr	1	124	2	.03	.01	.2	13	46	—
tr	0	26	.6	2	138	3	.04	.02	.3	11	53	—
—	0	1	.0	0	16	—	tr	tr	tr	5	7	—
tr	0	25	2.1	13	249	2	.07	.06	2.0	34	0	3.7
tr	0	19	.5	9	158	33	.05	.03	.3	56	4	1.5
tr	0	12	.2	16	75	2	.03	tr	.2	8	6	—
tr	0	9	tr	1	109	1	.02	.01	.2	8	29	—
0	0	0	.0	1	2	0	.00	.00	.0	—	0	—
2	482	11	6.3	106	364	11	.21	4.14	20.9	220	23	—
1	438	13	14.2	118	453	9810	.24	4.17	21.9	200	37	—
tr	631	14	8.5	51	140	4913	.15	1.75	10.2	770	16	—
1	355	10	17.9	49	150	5399	.26	2.20	14.5	163	24	—
3	158	26	6.4	860	170	8300	.27	1.03	6.9	30	0	—

Food	Measure	Weight (g)	Water (%)	Energy (kcal)	Protein (g)	Carbohydrate (g)	Fat (g)	SFA (g)
Lobster, canned	100 mL	61	77	95	19	tr	2	0
Luncheon meat, canned	1 slice, medium	45	52	334	12	2	30	11
Macaroni, enriched, cooked	100 mL	59	72	111	3	23	tr	tr
Macaroni and cheese, home recipe	100 mL	84	58	215	8	20	11	6
Mackerel, canned, solids and liquid	100 mL	63	66	183	19	0	11	3
Mangoes, raw, peeled	1	176	82	65	tr	17	tr	tr
Maple syrup	100 mL	133	33	252	0	65	0	0
Margarine, tub, vegetable oils, polyunsaturates declared	100 mL	96	16	716	tr	tr	80	15
Margarine, tub, vegetable oils, polyunsaturates not declared	100 mL	96	16	716	tr	tr	80	13
Mayonnaise, over 65% oil	100 mL	91	16	732	1	1	80	8
Meat loaf, homemade	1 slice, medium	73	64	160	17	5	8	—
Milk, buttermilk	100 mL	103	90	40	3	5	tr	tr
Milk, chocolate, partly skimmed, 2% B.F.	250 mL	106	84	72	3	10	2	1
Milk, condensed, sweetened, canned	100 mL	129	27	321	8	54	9	5
Milk, dry, skim, powder, instantized	100 mL	29	91	358	35	52	tr	tr
Milk, dry, whole	100 mL	54	2	496	26	38	27	17
Milk, evaporated, whole, 7.6% B.F., undiluted	100 mL	106	74	134	7	10	8	5
Milk, evaporated, 2% B.F., undiluted	100 mL	107	78	92	7	11	2	1
Milk, hot cocoa, made with whole milk	100 mL	106	82	87	4	10	4	2
Milk, human, whole, mature	100 mL	104	88	70	1	7	4	2
Milk, partly skimmed, 2% B.F.	100 mL	103	89	50	3	5	2	1

PUFA (g)	Cholesterol (mg)	Calcium (mg)	Iron (mg)	Sodium (mg)	Potassium (mg)	Vitamin A (RE)	Thiamin (mg)	Riboflavin (mg)	Niacin (NE)	Folate (mcg)	Vitamin C (mg)	Dietary Fibre (g)
0	85	65	.8	210	180	0	.10	.07	4.9	17	0	—
4	62	6	.7	1289	215	0	.37	.19	5.2	6	1	—
tr	0	8	1.5	1	61	0	.14	.26	1.7	3	0	.8
tr	34	181	.9	543	120	129	.10	.20	2.4	8	tr	—
—	94	185	2.1	74	420	129	.06	.21	9.3	13	0	—
tr	0	10	.1	2	156	389	.06	.06	.7	—	28	1.1
0	0	104	1.2	10	176	0	.13	.06	.0	—	0	—
34	0	27	.0	1079	38	1059	tr	.03	.2	1	tr	—
15	0	27	.0	1079	38	1059	tr	.03	.2	1	tr	—
27	59	10	.2	519	12	25	.01	.03	.3	tr	1	—
—	92	38	2.3	653	374	—	.07	.19	11.1	—	2	—
tr	4	116	tr	105	151	8	.03	.15	.7	5	tr	—
tr	7	114	.2	60	169	57	.04	.16	.9	5	tr	—
tr	34	284	.2	127	371	81	.09	.42	2.1	11	3	—
tr	18	231	.3	549	1705	710	.41	1.74	9.1	50	6	—
tr	97	912	.5	371	1330	280	.28	1.21	6.8	37	9	—
tr	29	261	.2	106	303	54	.05	.32	1.8	8	17	—
tr	8	276	.2	111	318	117	.05	.31	1.9	9	16	—
tr	13	119	.3	49	192	34	.04	.17	1.0	5	tr	—
tr	14	32	tr	17	51	64	.01	.04	.5	5	5	—
tr	8	122	tr	50	154	57	.04	.17	.9	5	tr	—

Food	Measure	Weight (g)	Water (%)	Energy (kcal)	Protein (g)	Carbohydrate (g)	Fat (g)
Milk shake, chocolate, thick, commercial	100 mL	84	72	119	3	21	3	2
Milk, skim	100 mL	103	91	35	3	5	tr	tr
Milk, soy fluid	100 mL	103	92	33	3	2	2	0
Milk, whole, 3.3% B.F.	100 mL	103	88	61	3	5	3	2
Molasses, blackstrap or cooking	100 mL	139	24	213	0	55	0	0
Muffins, blueberry, home recipe	1 medium	40	39	281	7	42	9	3
Muffins, bran, home recipe	1 medium	40	35	261	8	43	10	3
Muffins, corn, made from mix + milk + eggs	1 medium	40	30	324	7	50	11	3
Mushrooms, canned, pieces, drained	100 mL	66	91	24	2	5	tr	tr
Mushrooms, pieces, raw	100 mL	30	92	25	2	5	tr	tr
Mustard, prepared, yellow	100 mL	106	80	75	5	6	4	tr
Nectarines, raw, peeled	1 medium	136	86	49	tr	12	tr	0
Noodles, egg, enriched, cooked	100 mL	68	70	125	4	23	1	tr
Nuts, mixed, dry-roasted, with peanuts	100 mL	58	2	594	17	25	51	7
Nuts, mixed, oil-roasted, with peanuts, salt added	100 mL	60	2	617	17	21	56	9
Olive oil	100 mL	91	0	884	0	0	100	14
Olives, black	1 large	4	80	129	1	3	14	2
Olives, green	1 medium	4	78	116	1	1	13	1
Onion rings (breaded), frozen, heated in oven	5	50	29	407	5	38	27	9
Onions, chopped, raw	100 mL	68	91	34	1	7	tr	tr
Onions, spring, chopped, raw	15 mL	42	92	25	2	6	tr	tr

PUFA (g)	Cholesterol (mg)	Calcium (mg)	Iron (mg)	Sodium (mg)	Potassium (mg)	Vitamin A (RE)	Thiamin (mg)	Riboflavin (mg)	Niacin (NE)	Folate (mcg)	Vitamin C (mg)	Dietary Fibre (g)
tr	11	132	.3	111	224	21	.05	.22	.8	5	0	—
tr	2	123	tr	52	166	61	.04	.14	.9	5	tr	—
0	0	21	.8	0	196	4	.08	.03	.8	3	0	—
tr	14	119	tr	49	152	31	.04	.16	.9	5	tr	—
0	0	684	16.1	96	2927	0	.11	.19	2.0	—	0	—
2	83	84	2.1	632	115	66	.22	.25	3.2	10	1	—
2	103	142	3.9	448	431	69	.17	.26	5.7	7	tr	—
2	58	241	1.9	479	110	72	.21	.22	3.1	7	tr	—
tr	0	11	.8	425	129	0	.09	.02	2.3	12	0	2.5
tr	0	5	1.2	4	370	0	.10	.45	4.9	21	4	2.5
tr	0	84	2.0	1252	130	0	.00	.00	.0	—	0	—
—	0	5	.2	0	212	74	.02	.04	1.2	4	5	—
tr	31	10	1.5	2	44	21	.14	.26	2.0	4	0	—
11	0	70	3.7	12	597	1	.20	.20	9.1	50	tr	—
13	0	108	3.2	652	581	2	.50	.22	9.2	83	tr	—
8	0	tr	.4	tr	0	0	.00	.00	.0	0	0	—
tr	0	84	1.6	813	34	6	.00	.00	.0	—	0	—
tr	0	61	1.6	2400	55	30	.00	.00	.0	—	0	—
5	0	31	1.7	375	129	23	.28	.14	4.8	13	1	—
tr	0	25	.4	2	155	0	.06	.01	.4	20	8	1.3
tr	0	60	1.9	4	257	500	.07	.14	.5	14	45	—

Food	Measure	Weight (g)	Water (%)	Energy (kcal)	Protein (g)	Carbohydrate (g)	Fat (g)	SFA (g)
Orange juice, canned	100 mL	105	89	42	tr	10	tr	tr
Orange juice, fresh	100 mL	105	88	45	tr	10	tr	tr
Orange juice, frozen concentrate, diluted	100 mL	105	88	45	tr	11	tr	tr
Oranges, raw, peeled	1 medium	131	87	47	tr	12	tr	tr
Oysters, raw, meat only	100 mL	101	85	66	8	3	2	tr
Pancakes, plain, made from mix + eggs + milk	1 medium	27	51	225	7	32	7	3
Papayas, raw, peeled	1 medium	311	89	39	tr	10	tr	tr
Parsley, chopped, raw	100 mL	25	88	33	2	7	tr	0
Parsnips, boiled, drained, slices	100 mL	66	78	81	1	20	tr	tr
Peaches, canned halves/slices, heavy syrup	100 mL	108	79	74	tr	20	tr	tr
Peaches, canned halves/slices, water pack	100 mL	103	93	24	tr	6	tr	tr
Peaches, dried halves, cooked, no added sugar	100 mL	109	78	77	1	20	tr	tr
Peaches, dried halves, uncooked	100 mL	68	32	239	4	61	tr	tr
Peaches, frozen, sliced, sweetened	100 mL	106	75	94	tr	24	tr	tr
Peaches, raw, pared, sliced	100 mL	72	88	43	tr	11	tr	tr
Peanut butter	100 mL	109	1	591	28	16	51	9
Peanut butter, salt added	100 mL	109	1	591	28	16	51	9
Peanut oil	100 mL	91	0	884	0	0	100	17
Peanuts, oil-roasted	100 mL	61	2	580	27	18	49	7
Peanuts, oil-roasted, salt added	100 mL	62	2	580	27	18	49	7
Pears, canned halves/slices, heavy syrup	100 mL	108	80	74	tr	19	tr	tr

PUFA (g)	Cholesterol (mg)	Calcium (mg)	Iron (mg)	Sodium (mg)	Potassium (mg)	Vitamin A (RE)	Thiamin (mg)	Riboflavin (mg)	Niacin (NE)	Folate (mcg)	Vitamin C (mg)	Dietary Fibre (g)
tr	0	8	.4	2	175	18	.06	.03	.3	18	34	.4
tr	0	11	.2	1	200	20	.09	.03	.4	30	50	.4
tr	0	9	.1	1	190	8	.08	.02	.2	44	39	—
tr	0	40	.1	0	181	21	.09	.04	.4	30	53	2.0
tr	50	94	5.5	73	121	93	.14	.18	4.0	—	30	—
1	74	215	1.2	564	154	75	.15	.24	2.1	11	tr	—
tr	0	24	.1	3	257	201	.03	.03	.5	—	62	.9
0	0	130	6.2	39	536	520	.08	.11	1.3	183	90	—
tr	0	37	.6	10	367	0	.08	.05	1.0	58	13	3.5
tr	0	3	.3	6	92	33	.01	.02	.6	3	3	.5
tr	0	2	.3	3	99	53	tr	.02	.5	3	3	.5
tr	0	9	1.3	2	320	20	tr	.02	1.6	tr	4	—
tr	0	28	4.1	7	996	216	tr	.21	4.5	tr	5	—
tr	0	3	.4	6	130	28	.01	.04	.7	3	94	1.4
tr	0	5	.1	0	197	54	.02	.04	1.0	3	7	1.4
15	0	33	1.8	17	685	0	.15	.11	19.2	82	0	—
15	0	33	1.8	469	685	0	.15	.11	19.2	82	0	—
32	0	tr	tr	tr	tr	0	.00	.00	.0	0	0	—
16	0	86	1.9	15	703	0	.29	.10	20.2	106	0	8.1
16	0	86	1.9	432	703	0	.29	.10	20.2	106	0	8.1
tr	0	5	.2	5	65	0	.01	.02	.3	1	1	1.8

Food	Measure	Weight (g)	Water (%)	Energy (kcal)	Protein (g)	Carbohydrate (g)	Fat (g)	SFA (g)
Pears, canned halves, juice pack	100 mL	105	86	50	tr	13	tr	tr
Pears, raw, with skin	1 medium	169	84	59	tr	15	tr	tr
Peas, edible-podded (snow peas), boiled, drained	100 mL	68	89	42	3	7	tr	tr
Peas, green, boiled, drained	100 mL	68	78	84	5	16	tr	tr
Peas, green, canned, drained	100 mL	72	82	69	4	13	tr	tr
Peas, split, cooked	100 mL	84	70	115	8	21	tr	tr
Pecans, halves	100 mL	46	5	667	8	18	68	5
Peppers, sweet, green, raw	100 mL	42	93	25	tr	5	tr	tr
Perch, ocean, frozen, breaded, fried, reheated	1 piece, medium	93	43	319	19	17	19	5
Pickle relish, sweet	100 mL	59	63	138	tr	34	tr	0
Pickles, assorted, sweet	100 mL	103	69	116	2	27	tr	0
Pickles, dill	100 mL	65	93	11	tr	2	tr	0
Pie, apple, 2 crusts	1 piece, medium	158	48	256	2	38	11	3
Pie, lemon meringue, 1 crust	1 piece, medium	140	47	255	4	38	10	3
Pie, mincemeat, 2 crusts	1 piece, medium	158	43	271	3	41	12	3
Pie, pumpkin, 1 crust	1 piece, medium	152	59	211	4	25	11	4
Piecrust, baked shell	1 medium	180	15	500	6	44	33	8
Pies, fried, fast food, cherry	1 pie	85	42	294	2	38	16	7
Pineapple, canned, crushed, heavy syrup	100 mL	108	79	78	tr	20	tr	tr
Pineapple, canned, cubes, water pack	100 mL	104	91	32	tr	8	tr	tr
Pineapple, raw, diced	100 mL	65	87	49	tr	12	tr	tr

PUFA (g)	Cholesterol (mg)	Calcium (mg)	Iron (mg)	Sodium (mg)	Potassium (mg)	Vitamin A (RE)	Thiamin (mg)	Riboflavin (mg)	Niacin (NE)	Folate (mcg)	Vitamin C (mg)	Dietary Fibre (g)
tr	0	9	.3	4	96	1	.01	.01	.3	1	2	1.8
tr	0	11	.3	0	125	2	.02	.04	.2	7	4	2.8
tr	0	42	2.0	4	240	13	.13	.08	1.1	29	48	1.6
tr	0	27	1.5	3	271	60	.26	.15	2.6	63	14	4.5
tr	0	20	1.0	219	173	77	.12	.08	1.2	44	10	4.5
tr	0	11	1.7	13	296	4	.15	.09	2.4	11	0	4.7
17	0	36	2.1	1	392	13	.85	.13	4.2	39	2	—
tr	0	6	1.3	3	195	53	.09	.05	.7	17	128	1.3
6	58	33	1.3	153	284	0	.10	.11	5.3	9	0	—
—	0	20	.8	712	200	10	.00	.02	.0	—	6	—
—	0	23	1.5	527	200	9	.00	.02	.0	—	6	—
—	0	26	1.0	1428	200	10	.00	.02	.0	—	6	—
2	0	8	1.0	301	80	3	.11	.08	1.4	6	1	—
2	93	14	1.0	282	50	51	.07	.10	1.3	6	3	—
2	1	28	1.7	448	178	tr	.10	.09	1.5	5	1	—
2	61	51	.9	214	160	247	.09	.14	1.5	9	0	—
7	0	14	2.5	611	50	0	.30	.22	3.9	12	0	—
tr	15	13	.8	436	72	22	.07	.07	1.1	—	1	—
tr	0	14	.4	1	104	1	.09	.03	.4	5	7	—
tr	0	15	.4	1	127	2	.09	.03	.4	5	8	—
tr	0	7	.4	1	113	2	.09	.04	.5	11	15	1.4

Food	Measure	Weight (g)	Water (%)	Energy (kcal)	Protein (g)	Carbohydrate (g)	Fat (g)	SFA (g)
Pineapple juice, canned, + vitamin C	100 mL	106	86	56	tr	14	tr	tr
Pistachio nuts, dry-roasted, salt added	100 mL	54	2	606	.15	28	53	7
Pizza, cheese	1 piece, medium	65	48	236	12	28	8	3
Pizza, sausage	1 piece, medium	65	43	282	13	27	13	3
Plums, purple, canned, heavy syrup	100 mL	109	76	89	tr	23	tr	tr
Plums, raw	1 medium	66	85	55	tr	13	tr	tr
Popcorn, air-popped, plain	100 mL	3	4	386	13	77	5	tr
Popcorn, popped with oil and salt	100 mL	5	3	456	10	59	22	16
Popsicle	1	85	80	71	0	18	0	0
Pork, loin, centre-cut chop, lean and fat, broiled	100 g raw	59	50	316	27	0	22	8
Pork, loin, centre-cut chop, lean only, broiled	100 g raw	47	57	231	32	0	10	4
Pork, shoulder, whole, roasted, lean only	100 g raw	48	59	244	25	0	15	5
Pork, spareribs, braised, lean + fat	100 g raw	39	40	397	29	0	30	12
Postum, made with water	100 mL	101	—	7	tr	2	0	0
Potato chips	10	20	3	523	6	52	35	9
Potato flour	100 mL	15	8	351	8	80	tr	tr
Potato salad	100 mL	106	76	143	3	11	8	1
Potatoes, baked in skin, flesh and skin	1 medium	206	71	109	2	25	tr	tr
Potatoes, baked in skin, flesh only	100 mL	52	75	93	2	22	tr	tr
Potatoes, dehydrated flakes, prepared	100 mL	89	76	113	2	15	6	3
Potatoes, french-fried, cooked in deep fat	100 mL	48	38	315	4	40	17	7

PUFA (g)	Cholesterol (mg)	Calcium (mg)	Iron (mg)	Sodium (mg)	Potassium (mg)	Vitamin A (RE)	Thiamin (mg)	Riboflavin (mg)	Niacin (NE)	Folate (mcg)	Vitamin C (mg)	Dietary Fibre (g)
tr	0	17	.3	1	134	0	.06	.02	.3	23	33	—
8	0	70	3.2	780	970	24	.42	.25	4.8	59	7	—
tr	18	221	2.2	702	130	189	.22	.31	4.5	16	8	—
1	29	188	1.4	668	196	168	.08	.18	3.8	16	9	—
tr	0	9	.8	19	91	26	.02	.04	.4	3	tr	—
tr	0	4	.1	0	172	32	.04	.10	.6	2	10	1.7
3	0	11	2.7	3	256	0	.37	.12	4.5	—	0	—
2	0	8	2.1	1940	256	0	.37	.09	3.5	—	0	—
0	0	0	tr	10	4	0	.00	.00	.0	0	0	—
2	97	4	.8	70	359	3	1.00	.27	10.9	5	tr	—
1	98	5	.9	78	420	2	1.15	.31	12.7	6	tr	—
2	97	8	1.5	76	352	2	.58	.36	10.0	5	tr	—
4	121	47	1.9	93	320	3	.41	.38	12.0	4	0	—
0	0	3	.3	3	52	—	.02	.00	—	—	0	—
18	0	24	1.2	469	1298	0	.15	.02	5.4	45	42	—
tr	0	33	17.2	34	1588	0	.42	.14	5.6	51	19	—
4	68	19	.7	529	254	33	.08	.06	1.6	7	10	—
tr	0	10	1.4	8	418	0	.11	.03	2.2	11	13	1.7
tr	0	5	.4	5	391	0	.11	.02	1.9	9	13	1.0
tr	14	49	.2	332	233	21	.11	.05	1.0	7	10	—
1	13	19	.8	216	732	0	.18	.03	4.2	29	10	—

Food	Measure	Weight (g)	Water (%)	Energy (kcal)	Protein (g)	Carbohydrate (g)	Fat (g)	SFA (g)
Potatoes, french-fried, frozen, heated	10	50	53	222	3	34	9	4
Potatoes, hash brown, home-prepared	100 mL	66	75	153	2	7	14	5
Potatoes, mashed, milk and butter added	100 mL	89	76	106	2	17	4	1
Potatoes, peeled before boiling	100 mL	66	77	86	2	20	tr	tr
Potatoes, peeled after boiling	100 mL	66	77	87	2	20	tr	tr
Pretzels	5	15	5	390	10	76	5	tr
Prune juice, canned or bottled	100 mL	108	81	71	tr	17	tr	tr
Prunes, dried, uncooked	100 mL	68	32	239	3	63	tr	tr
Prunes, dried, cooked, without added sugar	100 mL	90	70	107	1	28	tr	tr
Pudding, canned, chocolate	100 mL	106	68	144	2	21	8	7
Pudding, cornstarch, cooked	100 mL	110	70	124	3	23	3	2
Pudding, custard, baked	100 mL	112	77	115	5	11	6	3
Pudding, rice with raisins	100 mL	112	66	146	4	27	3	2
Pudding, tapioca (Minute)	100 mL	70	72	134	5	17	5	2
Pudding mix, low-calorie, prepared with skim milk	100 mL	110	78	100	3	20	2	tr
Pumpkin, canned	250 mL	259	90	34	1	8	tr	tr
Pumpkin and squash, seed kernels, dry	100 mL	58	7	541	25	18	46	9
Quiche Lorraine	1 slice, medium	176	47	341	7	16	27	13
Radishes, raw, without tops	100 mL	49	95	17	tr	4	tr	tr
Raisins, seedless	100 mL	66	15	300	3	79	tr	tr
Raspberries, frozen, sweetened	100 mL	106	73	103	tr	26	tr	tr

PUFA (g)	Cholesterol (mg)	Calcium (mg)	Iron (mg)	Sodium (mg)	Potassium (mg)	Vitamin A (RE)	Thiamin (mg)	Riboflavin (mg)	Niacin (NE)	Folate (mcg)	Vitamin C (mg)	Dietary Fibre (g)
tr	0	9	1.3	31	457	0	.12	.03	3.1	17	11	1.0
2	0	8	.8	24	321	0	.07	.02	2.6	8	6	1.0
1	2	26	.3	295	289	20	.08	.04	1.6	8	6	1.0
tr	0	8	.3	5	328	0	.10	.02	1.8	9	7	1.0
tr	0	5	.3	4	379	0	.11	.02	1.9	10	13	1.0
1	0	22	1.5	1680	130	0	.02	.03	2.5	—	0	—
tr	0	12	1.2	4	276	0	.02	.07	.9	tr	4	—
tr	0	51	2.5	4	745	199	.08	.16	2.4	4	3	11.9
tr	0	23	1.1	2	334	31	.02	.10	.9	tr	3	—
tr	tr	52	.8	201	179	22	.03	.12	.8	—	tr	—
tr	12	102	.3	129	136	39	.02	.15	.7	3	tr	—
tr	105	112	.4	79	146	105	.04	.19	1.1	7	tr	—
tr	11	98	.4	71	177	33	.03	.14	.9	5	0	—
tr	97	105	.4	156	135	87	.04	.18	1.0	6	1	—
tr	1	144	.5	139	141	15	.03	.15	.1	6	tr	—
tr	0	26	1.4	5	206	2206	.02	.05	.6	12	4	—
21	0	43	15.0	18	807	38	.21	.32	8.9	58	2	—
2	162	120	.6	371	161	258	.06	.18	1.4	—	0	—
tr	0	21	.3	24	232	1	tr	.05	.4	27	23	—
tr	0	49	2.1	12	751	1	.16	.09	1.4	3	3	8.7
tr	0	15	.7	1	114	6	.02	.05	.4	26	17	5.1

Food	Measure	Weight (g)	Water (%)	Energy (kcal)	Protein (g)	Carbohydrate (g)	Fat (g)	SFA (g)
Raspberries, raw	100 mL	52	87	49	tr	12	tr	tr
Rhubarb, frozen, cooked with added sugar	250 mL	254	68	116	tr	31	tr	0
Rhubarb, raw, diced	100 mL	52	94	21	tr	5	tr	0
Rice, brown, cooked	100 mL	72	70	119	3	26	tr	tr
Rice, white, enriched, long-grain, parboiled, cooked	100 mL	68	73	106	2	23	tr	tr
Rice, white, unenriched, short-grain, cooked	100 mL	74	73	109	2	24	tr	tr
Rolls, commercial, hard	1 round	50	25	312	10	60	3	tr
Rutabagas, boiled, drained, cubed	100 mL	72	90	34	1	8	tr	tr
Rutabagas, raw, cubed	100 mL	59	90	36	1	8	tr	tr
Rye flour, light	100 mL	40	11	357	9	78	1	tr
Salad dressing, mayonnaise type, over 35% oil	100 mL	99	40	390	tr	24	33	12
Salad dressing, Thousand Island, commercial	100 mL	106	46	399	1	17	35	2
Salad dressing, French, calorie-reduced, commercial	100 mL	110	69	149	tr	15	10	tr
Salad dressing, French, regular, commercial	100 mL	106	38	402	tr	14	40	3
Salad dressing, home-cooked, boiled	100 mL	108	69	157	4	15	10	3
Salami, cooked, beef and pork	1 slice, medium	22	60	250	14	2	20	8
Salami, dry type	1 slice, medium	6	35	418	23	3	34	12
Salmon, canned, solids and liquid	100 mL	63	64	203	22	0	12	2
Salmon, fresh, broiled or baked with butter or margarine	1 piece, medium	92	63	182	27	0	7	2
Salt, table	100 mL	123	tr	0	0	0	0	0
Sardines, canned in oil, solids only	7 medium	84	62	203	24	0	11	2

PUFA (g)	Cholesterol (mg)	Calcium (mg)	Iron (mg)	Sodium (mg)	Potassium (mg)	Vitamin A (RE)	Thiamin (mg)	Riboflavin (mg)	Niacin (NE)	Folate (mcg)	Vitamin C (mg)	Dietary Fibre (g)
tr	0	22	.6	0	152	13	.03	.09	1.1	26	25	5.1
0	0	145	.2	1	96	7	.02	.02	.3	5	3	1.0
0	0	86	.2	4	288	10	.02	.03	.5	7	8	—
tr	0	12	.5	282	70	0	.09	.02	1.9	10	0	1.2
tr	0	19	.8	358	43	0	.11	.01	1.6	8	0	.3
tr	0	10	.2	374	28	0	.02	.01	.8	9	0	.3
tr	3	47	2.8	625	97	0	.40	.24	5.1	36	0	—
tr	0	42	.5	18	287	0	.07	.04	.8	16	22	2.2
tr	0	47	.5	20	337	0	.09	.04	.9	21	25	2.2
tr	0	22	1.1	1	156	0	.15	.07	2.3	78	0	4.5
16	26	14	.2	711	9	84	.01	.02	.2	6	0	—
12	26	11	.6	698	108	96	.01	.02	.2	6	0	—
3	6	11	.4	1938	36	0	.00	.00	tr	0	0	—
13	58	11	.4	1595	4	20	tr	.02	.2	4	0	—
2	57	84	.5	734	121	123	.06	.15	2.9	0	tr	—
2	65	13	2.7	1065	198	0	.24	.38	5.5	2	12	—
3	79	8	1.5	1860	378	0	.60	.29	8.4	2	26	—
5	37	154	.9	74	420	70	.03	.16	11.4	26	0	—
2	47	127	1.2	116	443	48	.16	.06	14.8	26	0	—
0	0	253	.1	8758	4	0	.00	.00	.0	0	0	—
2	140	437	2.9	823	590	66	.03	.20	9.8	16	0	—

Food	Measure	Weight (g)	Water (%)	Energy (kcal)	Protein (g)	Carbohydrate (g)	Fat (g)	SFA (g)
Sauerkraut, canned, solids and liquid	100 mL	100	93	19	tr	4	tr	tr
Sausages, beef & pork, cooked	1 regular	15	45	396	14	3	36	13
Sausages, pork, cooked	1 regular	15	45	369	20	1	31	11
Scallops, steamed	100 mL	57	73	112	23	3	1	0
Sesame butter (tahini), from unroasted kernels	100 mL	95	3	607	18	18	56	8
Sesame seeds, dry	100 mL	63	5	588	26	9	55	8
Shake and Bake, dry	100 mL	39	5	406	9	62	15	8
Sherbet, orange	100 mL	82	66	140	1	30	2	1
Shortening, vegetable oils	100 mL	87	0	900	0	0	100	31
Shrimp, canned solids	100 mL	54	70	116	24	tr	1	tr
Shrimp, fried, batter-dipped	100 mL	57	57	225	20	10	11	3
Soft drinks, soda water	100 mL	100	0	0	0	0	0	0
Soft drinks, cola type	100 mL	104	89	41	0	10	0	0
Soft drinks, cola type, with aspartame	100 mL	100	0	34	0	9	0	0
Soft drinks, tonic water	100 mL	103	91	34	0	9	0	0
Sole, baked with lemon juice, with butter	1 fillet	90	73	141	19	tr	7	4
Sole, baked with lemon juice, without added fat	1 fillet	90	78	94	20	tr	1	tr
Soup, bean with bacon, canned, + water	100 mL	107	84	68	3	9	2	tr
Soup, beef noodle, canned, + water	100 mL	103	92	34	2	4	1	tr
Soup, chicken noodle, dehydrated, + water	100 mL	107	94	21	1	3	tr	tr
Soup, clam chowder, without tomato, + whole milk	100 mL	105	85	66	4	7	3	1

PUFA (g)	Cholesterol (mg)	Calcium (mg)	Iron (mg)	Sodium (mg)	Potassium (mg)	Vitamin A (RE)	Thiamin (mg)	Riboflavin (mg)	Niacin (NE)	Folate (mcg)	Vitamin C (mg)	Dietary Fibre (g)
tr	0	30	1.5	661	170	2	.02	.02	.3	24	15	—
4	71	10	1.1	805	189	0	.36	.15	5.6	2	0	—
4	83	32	1.3	1294	361	0	.74	.25	7.1	2	2	—
0	53	115	3.0	265	476	30	.10	.06	5.6	16	0	—
25	—	141	6.4	1	459	7	1.59	.12	12.2	98	0	—
24	0	131	7.8	40	407	7	.72	.09	12.6	96	0	—
tr	0	65	2.5	3500	200	0	.20	tr	3.6	36	0	—
tr	7	54	.2	46	103	20	.02	.05	.3	7	2	—
—	0	0	.0	tr	tr	0	.00	.00	.0	—	0	—
tr	150	115	3.1	140	122	18	.01	.03	6.2	20	0	—
3	150	72	2.0	186	229	0	.04	.08	6.4	20	0	—
0	0	5	.0	21	2	0	.00	.00	.0	0	0	—
0	0	3	.0	4	1	0	.00	.00	.0	0	0	—
0	0	3	.2	7	1	0	.00	.00	.0	0	0	—
0	0	1	.0	4	0	0	.00	.00	.0	0	0	—
tr	80	15	.4	171	320	64	.06	.09	5.3	—	1	—
tr	69	15	.4	119	336	12	.06	.09	5.7	—	1	—
tr	1	32	.8	376	159	35	.04	.01	.8	13	tr	—
tr	2	6	.5	390	41	26	.03	.02	.8	2	tr	—
tr	1	13	.2	509	12	2	.03	.02	.2	tr	tr	—
tr	9	75	.6	400	121	16	.03	.10	1.2	4	1	—

Food	Measure	Weight (g)	Water (%)	Energy (kcal)	Protein (g)	Carbohydrate (g)	Fat (g)	SFA (g)
Soup, cream of mushroom, canned, + water	100 mL	103	90	53	tr	4	4	1
Soup, cream of mushroom, canned, + whole milk	100 mL	105	85	82	2	6	5	2
Soup, cream of chicken, canned, + water	100 mL	103	91	48	1	4	3	tr
Soup, minestrone, canned, + water	100 mL	102	91	34	2	5	1	tr
Soup, onion, dehydrated, + water	100 mL	104	96	11	tr	2	tr	tr
Soup, split pea with ham, canned, + water	100 mL	107	82	75	4	11	2	tr
Soup, tomato, canned, + water	100 mL	103	90	35	tr	7	tr	tr
Soup, vegetable, canned, + water	100 mL	102	92	30	tr	5	tr	tr
Soybean flour, defatted	100 mL	42	8	326	47	38	tr	0
Soybean oil	100 mL	92	0	884	0	0	100	14
Soybeans, mature seeds, cooked, drained	100 mL	76	71	130	11	11	6	tr
Spaghetti, enriched, cooked	100 mL	59	73	111	3	23	tr	tr
Spaghetti, with meat balls and tomato sauce, homemade	100 mL	105	70	134	8	16	5	1
Spaghetti, with tomato sauce and cheese, canned	100 mL	106	80	76	2	15	tr	tr
Spinach, boiled, drained	100 mL	76	91	23	3	4	tr	tr
Spinach, chopped, raw	100 mL	24	92	22	3	4	tr	tr
Squash, summer (zucchini), boiled, drained	100 mL	89	95	16	tr	4	tr	tr
Squash, winter (hubbard), boiled, mashed	100 mL	100	91	30	1	6	tr	tr
Squash, winter, baked, cubes	100 mL	87	89	39	tr	9	tr	tr
Strawberries, frozen, sweetened, whole	100 mL	108	78	78	tr	21	tr	tr
Strawberries, frozen, unsweetened	100 mL	63	90	35	tr	9	tr	tr

PUFA (g)	Cholesterol (mg)	Calcium (mg)	Iron (mg)	Sodium (mg)	Potassium (mg)	Vitamin A (RE)	Thiamin (mg)	Riboflavin (mg)	Niacin (NE)	Folate (mcg)	Vitamin C (mg)	Dietary Fibre (g)
2	1	19	.2	423	41	0	.02	.04	.5	2	tr	—
2	8	72	.2	434	109	15	.03	.11	.9	4	tr	—
tr	4	14	.3	404	36	23	.01	.03	.6	tr	tr	—
tr	1	14	.4	378	130	97	.02	.02	.6	7	tr	—
tr	0	5	tr	345	26	0	.01	.02	.2	tr	tr	—
tr	3	9	.9	398	158	18	.06	.03	1.2	1	tr	—
tr	0	5	.7	357	108	28	.04	.02	.7	6	27	—
tr	0	9	.5	341	87	125	.02	.02	.5	4	tr	—
0	0	265	11.1	1	1820	4	1.09	.34	11.2	380	0	—
58	0	tr	tr	0	0	0	.00	.00	.0	0	0	—
3	0	73	2.7	2	540	3	.21	.09	2.6	62	0	—
tr	0	8	1.5	1	61	0	.14	.26	1.7	4	0	.8
tr	30	50	1.5	407	268	192	.10	.12	3.0	8	9	—
tr	3	16	1.1	382	121	111	.14	.11	2.2	5	4	—
tr	0	136	3.6	70	466	819	.10	.24	1.2	146	10	2.3
tr	0	99	2.7	79	558	672	.08	.19	1.4	194	28	4.0
tr	0	13	.4	3	253	24	.04	.04	.5	17	5	2.0
tr	0	10	.3	5	214	401	.04	.03	.7	10	7	—
tr	0	14	.3	1	437	356	.09	.02	.9	28	10	1.2
tr	0	11	.5	1	98	3	.02	.08	.4	4	40	2.0
tr	0	16	.8	2	148	4	.02	.04	.5	17	41	2.0

Food	Measure	Weight (g)	Water (%)	Energy (kcal)	Protein (g)	Carbohydrate (g)	Fat (g)	SFA (g)
Strawberries, raw, hulled	100 mL	63	92	30	tr	7	tr	tr
Sugar, brown	100 mL, packed	93	2	373	0	96	0	0
Sugar, white, granulated	100 mL	84	tr	385	0	100	0	0
Sunflower oil	100 mL	92	0	884	0	0	100	10
Sunflower seed kernels, dry	100 mL	61	5	570	23	19	.50	5
Sweet potatoes, baked, peeled after baking	100 mL	84	73	103	2	24	tr	tr
Sweet potatoes, candied	1 piece, medium	112	67	137	tr	28	3	1
Sweet potatoes, canned, vacuum pack, mashed	100 mL	108	76	91	2	21	tr	tr
Table syrup (blends)	100 mL	139	24	290	0	75	0	0
Taco, fast food	1	81	55	241	11	19	14	5
Tangerines (mandarins), raw	1 medium	84	88	44	tr	11	tr	tr
Tangerines (mandarins), canned, light syrup	100 mL	106	83	61	tr	16	tr	tr
Tea	100 mL	101	0	1	0	tr	0	0
Tofu	100 mL	107	85	71	8	3	4	tr
Tomato juice, canned or bottled	100 mL	103	94	17	tr	4	tr	tr
Tomato purée, canned	100 mL	106	87	41	2	10	tr	tr
Tomato sauce, canned	100 mL	103	89	30	1	7	tr	tr
Tomatoes, canned, stewed	100 mL	108	91	26	tr	6	tr	tr
Tomatoes, raw	1 medium	123	94	19	tr	4	tr	tr
Tongue, beef, simmered	100 g raw	57	56	283	22	tr	21	9
Trout, lake, broiled or baked	1 piece, medium	93	71	216	23	tr	14	6

PUFA (g)	Cholesterol (mg)	Calcium (mg)	Iron (mg)	Sodium (mg)	Potassium (mg)	Vitamin A (RE)	Thiamin (mg)	Riboflavin (mg)	Niacin (NE)	Folate (mcg)	Vitamin C (mg)	Dietary Fibre (g)
tr	0	14	.4	1	166	3	.02	.07	.3	18	57	2.0
0	0	85	3.4	30	344	0	.01	.03	.2	—	0	—
0	0	0	.1	1	3	0	.00	.00	.0	—	0	—
66	0	0	.0	0	0	0	.00	.00	.0	0	0	—
33	0	116	6.8	3	689	5	2.29	.25	10.3	227	1	—
tr	0	28	.5	10	348	2182	.07	.13	1.0	23	25	2.4
tr	8	26	1.1	70	189	419	.02	.04	.6	11	7	2.4
tr	0	22	.9	53	312	798	.04	.06	1.1	17	26	2.4
0	0	46	4.1	68	4	0	.00	.00	.0	—	0	—
tr	26	135	1.5	563	325	70	.11	.09	3.8	—	1	—
tr	0	14	.1	1	157	92	.11	.02	.3	20	31	—
tr	0	7	.4	6	78	84	.05	.04	.5	5	20	—
0	0	0	tr	3	37	0	.00	.01	.0	5	0	—
2	0	90	1.9	7	42	0	.06	.03	1.5	—	0	—
tr	0	9	.6	361	220	56	.05	.03	.8	20	18	—
tr	0	15	.9	20	420	136	.07	.05	1.9	11	35	—
tr	0	14	.8	605	371	98	.07	.06	1.3	9	13	—
tr	0	33	.7	254	239	55	.05	.04	.8	5	13	1.5
tr	0	7	.5	8	207	113	.06	.05	.7	9	18	1.5
tr	107	7	3.4	60	180	—	.03	.35	5.0	5	tr	—
—	63	50	5.0	91	292	96	.12	.27	5.8	13	3	—

Food	Measure	Weight (g)	Water (%)	Energy (kcal)	Protein (g)	Carbohydrate (g)	Fat (g)	SFA (g)
Tuna, canned in oil, drained, solids	100 mL	68	61	197	29	0	8	2
Tuna, canned in water, drained, solids	100 mL	68	63	159	35	0	1	tr
Tuna salad	100 mL	87	63	183	16	9	9	2
Turkey, all classes, dark meat only, roasted	2 slices	86	63	187	29	0	7	2
Turkey, all classes, light meat only, roasted	2 slices	86	66	157	30	0	3	1
Turkey roll, light and dark meat	2 slices	57	70	149	18	2	7	2
Turnips, boiled, drained, mashed	100 mL	97	94	18	tr	5	tr	tr
Turnips, raw, cubed	100 mL	55	92	27	tr	6	tr	tr
Veal, loin, cutlet or chop, broiled	1 piece, medium	92	59	234	26	0	13	6
Veal, round with rump, broiled	2 slices, medium	87	60	216	27	0	11	5
Vegetable juice cocktail, canned	100 mL	102	94	19	tr	5	tr	tr
Vegetables, mixed, canned, drained	100 mL	69	87	47	3	9	tr	tr
Vegetables, mixed, frozen, boiled, drained	100 mL	69	83	59	3	13	tr	tr
Vinegar, white	100 mL	101	95	12	0	5	0	0
Waffles, made from mix + eggs + milk	1	75	42	275	9	36	11	4
Walnuts, English, halves	100 mL	42	4	642	14	18	62	6
Watermelon, raw	1 slice, medium	368	92	32	tr	7	tr	0
Wheat bran	100 mL	20	12	213	16	62	5	tr
Wheat flour, all-purpose	100 mL	53	12	364	11	76	1	tr
Wheat flour, whole	100 mL	51	12	333	13	71	2	tr
Wheat germ	100 mL	47	12	363	27	47	11	2

PUFA (g)	Cholesterol (mg)	Calcium (mg)	Iron (mg)	Sodium (mg)	Potassium (mg)	Vitamin A (RE)	Thiamin (mg)	Riboflavin (mg)	Niacin (NE)	Folate (mcg)	Vitamin C (mg)	Dietary Fibre (g)
2	65	8	1.9	800	301	24	.05	.12	17.2	15	0	—
tr	56	20	.7	551	300	38	.04	.12	19.9	—	0	—
—	39	15	1.2	428	259	26	.03	.07	9.4	—	3	—
2	85	32	2.3	79	290	0	.06	.25	9.1	9	0	—
tr	69	19	1.4	64	305	0	.06	.13	12.5	6	0	—
2	55	32	1.4	586	270	0	.09	.28	8.1	5	0	—
tr	0	22	.2	50	135	0	.03	.02	.4	9	12	2.2
tr	0	30	.3	67	191	0	.04	.03	.6	15	21	2.2
tr	101	11	3.2	65	296	0	.07	.25	10.2	5	0	—
tr	101	11	3.2	66	304	0	.07	.25	10.4	5	0	—
tr	0	11	.4	365	193	117	.04	.03	.8	21	28	—
tr	0	27	1.1	149	291	1165	.05	.05	1.0	24	5	2.4
tr	0	25	.8	35	169	428	.07	.12	1.3	19	3	2.3
0	0	0	.0	1	15	0	.00	.00	.0	0	0	—
2	60	239	1.6	686	195	69	.19	.30	2.8	12	tr	—
39	0	94	2.4	10	502	12	.38	.15	4.2	66	3	—
0	0	8	.2	2	116	37	.08	.02	.3	2	10	.3
2	0	119	14.9	9	1121	0	.72	.35	23.9	143	0	41.2
tr	0	16	2.9	2	95	0	.64	.40	7.2	21	0	2.9
tr	0	41	3.3	3	370	0	.55	.12	6.7	43	0	8.9
5	0	72	9.4	3	827	0	2.01	.68	9.1	210	0	—

Food	Measure	Weight (g)	Water (%)	Energy (kcal)	Protein (g)	Carbohydrate (g)	Fat (g)	SFA (g)
Whitefish, baked, stuffed	1 piece, medium	92	63	215	15	6	14	4
Wieners, beef and pork	1 regular	37	54	320	11	3	29	11
Wieners, turkey	1 regular	37	63	226	14	1	18	6
Wine, dessert	100 mL	100	77	137	tr	8	0	0
Wine, red table	100 mL	98	88	74	0	3	0	0
Wine, white table	100 mL	98	87	78	0	3	0	0
Yeast, baker's, dry, granulated	100 mL	47	5	282	37	39	2	0
Yogurt, frozen, fruit, 6.3% B.F.	100 mL	103	—	118	3	18	4	—
Yogurt, fruit flavour, 1.4% B.F.	100 mL	103	74	105	5	19	1	tr
Yogurt, plain, 1.5% B.F.	100 mL	103	85	63	5	7	2	1

Source: Adapted from Department of National Health and Welfare, Health Protection Branch, "Nutrients in Canadian Foods," rev. ed. (Ottawa, 1986).

PUFA (g)	Cholesterol (mg)	Calcium (mg)	Iron (mg)	Sodium (mg)	Potassium (mg)	Vitamin A (RE)	Thiamin (mg)	Riboflavin (mg)	Niacin (NE)	Folate (mcg)	Vitamin C (mg)	Dietary Fibre (g)
—	44	36	.5	195	291	600	.11	.11	5.1	13	0	—
3	50	11	1.2	1120	167	0	.20	.12	4.0	4	26	—
5	107	106	1.8	1426	179	0	.04	.18	6.0	8	0	—
0	0	8	.0	4	75	0	.01	.02	.2	—	0	—
0	0	8	.4	5	111	—	.00	.03	tr	—	0	—
0	0	9	.3	5	81	—	.00	.01	tr	—	0	—
0	0	44	16.1	52	1998	0	2.33	5.41	43.5	—	0	—
—	—	116	—	50	159	—	.02	.21	.1	—	3	—
tr	6	169	tr	65	216	15	.04	.20	.6	10	tr	—
tr	6	183	tr	70	234	16	.04	.21	.6	11	tr	—

SUMMARY EXAMPLES OF RECOMMENDED NUTRIENT INTAKES

Age	Sex	Weight (kg)	Protein (g/day)[c]	Fat-Soluble Vitamins			Water-Soluble Vitamins		
				Vitamin A (RE/day)[d]	Vitamin D (μg/day)[e]	Vitamin E (mg/day)[f]	Vitamin C (mg/day)	Folacin (μg/day)[c,g]	Vitamin B_{12} (μg/day)
Months									
0–2	Both	4.5	11[h]	400	10	3	20	50	0.3
3–5	Both	7.0	14[h]	400	10	3	20	50	0.3
6–8	Both	8.5	17[h]	400	10	3	20	50	0.3
9–11	Both	9.5	18	400	10	3	20	55	0.3
Years									
1	Both	11	19	400	10	3	20	65	0.3
2–3	Both	14	22	400	5	4	20	80	0.4
4–6	Both	18	26	500	5	5	25	90	0.5
7–9	M	25	30	700	2.5	7	35	125	0.8
	F	25	30	700	2.5	6	30	125	0.8
10–12	M	34	38	800	2.5	8	40	170	1.0
	F	36	40	800	2.5	7	40	180	1.0
13–15	M	50	50	900	2.5	9	50	150	1.5
	F	48	42	800	2.5	7	45	145	1.5
16–18	M	62	55	1000	2.5	10	55	185	1.9
	F	53	43	800	2.5	7	45	160	1.9
19–24	M	71	58	1000	2.5	10	60	210	2.0
	F	58	43	800	2.5	7	45	175	2.0
25–49	M	74	61	1000	2.5	9	60	220	2.0
	F	59	44	800	2.5	6	45	175	2.0
50–74	M	73	60	1000	2.5	7	60	220	2.0
	F	63	47	800	2.5	6	45	190	2.0
75+	M	69	57	1000	2.5	6	60	205	2.0
	F	64	47	800	2.5	5	45	190	2.0
Pregnancy (additional)									
1st Trimester			15	100	2.5	2	0	305	1.0
2nd Trimester			20	100	2.5	2	20	305	1.0
3rd Trimester			25	100	2.5	2	20	305	1.0
Lactation (additional)			20	400	2.5	3	30	120	0.5

| Minerals | | | | |
Calcium (mg/day)	Magnesium (mg/day)[c]	Iron (mg/day)	Iodine (µg/day)	Zinc (mg/day)
350	30	0.4[i]	25	2[j]
350	40	5	35	3
400	50	7	40	3
400	50	7	45	3
500	55	6	55	4
500	70	6	65	4
600	90	6	85	5
700	110	7	110	6
700	110	7	95	6
900	150	10	125	7
1000	160	10	110	7
1100	210	12	160	9
800	200	13	160	8
900	250	10	160	9
700	215	14	160	8
800	240	8	160	9
700	200	14	160	8
800	250	8	160	9
700	200	14[k]	160	8
800	250	8	160	9
800	210	7	160	8
800	230	8	160	9
800	220	7	160	8
500	15	6	25	0
500	20	6	25	1
500	25	6	25	2
500	80	0	50	6

[a] Recommended intakes of energy and of certain nutrients are not listed in this table because of the nature of the variables upon which they are based. The figures for energy are estimates of average requirements for expected patterns of activity. . . . For nutrients not shown, the following amounts are recommended: thiamin, 0.4 mg/1000 kcal (0.48 mg/5000 kJ); riboflavin, 0.5 mg/1000 kcal (0.6 mg/5000 kJ); niacin, 7.2 NE/1000 kcal (8.6 NE/5000 kJ); vitamin B_6, 15 µg, as pyridoxine, per gram of protein; phosphorus, same as calcium.

[b] Recommended intakes during periods of growth are taken as appropriate for individuals representative of the mid-point in each age group. All recommended intakes are designed to cover individual variations in essentially all of a healthy population subsisting upon a variety of common foods available in Canada.

[c] The primary units are expressed per kilogram of body weight. The figures shown here are only examples. . . .

[d] One retinol equivalent (RE) corresponds to the biological activity of 1 µg of retinol, 6 µg of β-carotene, or 12 µg of other carotenes.

[e] Expressed as cholecalciferol or ergocalciferol.

[f] Expressed as d-α-tocopherol equivalents, relative to which β- and γ-tocopherol and α-tocotrienol have activities of 0.5, 0.1, and 0.3 respectively.

[g] Expressed as total folate.

[h] Assumption that the protein is from breast milk or is of the same biological value as that of breast milk and that between 3 and 9 months, adjustment for the quality of the protein is made.

[i] It is assumed that breast milk is the source of iron up to 2 months of age.

[j] Based on the assumption that breast milk is the source of zinc for the first 2 months.

[k] After the menopause, the recommended intake is 7 mg/day.

Source: Department of National Health and Welfare, "Recommended Nutrient Intake for Canadians" (Ottawa, 1983), 179–81.

RECOMMENDED DAILY DIETARY ALLOWANCES,[a]

Designed for the Maintenance of Good Nutrition of Practically All Healthy People in the U.S.A.

	Age (years)	Weight (kg)	Weight (lbs)	Height (cm)	Height (in)	Protein (g)	Vitamin A (µg)[b]	Vitamin D (µg)[c]	Vitamin E (mg α)[d]	Vitamin C (mg)	Thiamin (mg)	Riboflavin (mg)	Niacin (mg NE)[e]	Vitamin B6 (mg)	Folacin[f] (µg)	Vitamin B12 (µg)
Infants	0.0–0.5	6	13	60	24	kg × 2.2	420	10	3	35	0.3	0.4	6	0.3	30	0.5[g]
	0.5–1.0	9	20	71	28	kg × 2.0	400	10	4	35	0.5	0.6	8	0.6	45	1.5
Children	1–3	13	29	90	35	23	400	10	5	45	0.7	0.8	9	0.9	100	2.0
	4–6	20	44	112	44	30	500	10	6	45	0.9	1.0	11	1.3	200	2.5
	7–10	28	62	132	52	34	700	10	7	45	1.2	1.4	16	1.6	300	3.0
Males	11–14	45	99	157	62	45	1000	10	8	50	1.4	1.6	18	1.8	400	3.0
	15–18	66	145	176	69	56	1000	10	10	60	1.4	1.7	18	2.0	400	3.0
	19–22	70	154	177	70	56	1000	7.5	10	60	1.5	1.7	19	2.2	400	3.0
	23–50	70	154	178	70	56	1000	5	10	60	1.4	1.6	18	2.2	400	3.0
	51+	70	154	178	70	56	1000	5	10	60	1.2	1.4	16	2.2	400	3.0
Females	11–14	46	101	157	62	46	800	10	8	50	1.1	1.3	15	1.8	400	3.0
	15–18	55	120	163	64	46	800	10	8	60	1.1	1.3	14	2.0	400	3.0
	19–22	55	120	163	64	44	800	7.5	8	60	1.1	1.3	14	2.0	400	3.0
	23–50	55	120	163	64	44	800	5	8	60	1.0	1.2	13	2.0	400	3.0
	51+	55	120	163	64	44	800	5	8	60	1.0	1.2	13	2.0	400	3.0
Pregnant						+30	+200	+5	+2	+20	+0.4	+0.3	+2	+0.6	+400	+1.0
Lactating						+20	+400	+5	+3	+40	+0.5	+0.5	+5	+0.5	+100	+1.0

Fat-Soluble Vitamins: Vitamin A, Vitamin D, Vitamin E
Water-Soluble Vitamins: Vitamin C, Thiamin, Riboflavin, Niacin, Vitamin B6, Folacin, Vitamin B12

Minerals

Calcium (mg)	Phosphorus (mg)	Magnesium (mg)	Iron (mg)	Zinc (mg)	Iodine (µg)
360	240	50	10	3	40
540	360	70	15	5	50
800	800	150	15	10	70
800	800	200	10	10	90
800	800	250	10	10	120
1200	1200	350	18	15	150
1200	1200	400	18	15	150
800	800	350	10	15	150
800	800	350	10	15	150
800	800	350	10	15	150
1200	1200	300	18	15	150
1200	1200	300	18	15	150
800	800	300	18	15	150
800	800	300	18	15	150
800	800	300	10	15	150
+400	+400	+150	h	+5	+25
+400	+400	+150	h	+10	+50

[a] The allowances are intended to provide for individual variations among most normal persons as they live in the United States under usual environmental stresses. Diets should be based on a variety of common foods in order to provide other nutrients for which human requirements have been less well defined.

[b] Retinol equivalents. 1 retinol equivalent = 1 µg retinol or 6 µg β-carotene.

[c] As cholecalciferol. 10 µg cholecalciferol = 400 IU vitamin D.

[d] α-tocopherol equivalents. 1 mg d-α-tocopherol = 1 α TE.

[e] 1 NE (niacin equivalent) is equal to 1 mg of niacin or 60 mg of dietary tryptophan.

[f] The folacin allowances refer to dietary sources as determined by *Lactobacillus casei* assay after treatment with enzymes (conjugases) to make polyglutamyl forms of the vitamin available to the test organism.

[g] The RDA for Vitamin B_{12} in infants is based on average concentration of the vitamin in human milk. The allowances after weaning are based on energy intake (as recommended by the American Academy of Pediatrics) and consideration of other factors such as intestinal absorption.

[h] The increased requirement during pregnancy cannot be met by the iron content of habitual American diets nor by the existing iron stores of many women; therefore, the use of 30–60 mg of supplemental iron is recommended. Iron needs during lactation are not substantially different from those of non-pregnant women, but continued supplementation of the mother for 2–3 months after parturition is advisable in order to replenish stores depleted by pregnancy.

Source: Reprinted, with permission, from "Recommended Dietary Allowances," 9th ed. (Washington, D.C.: National Academy Press, 1980).

Bibliography

American Heart Association. "Rationale of the Diet-Heart Statement of the American Heart Association." *Circulation* 65 (1982): 839A–854A.

Anderson, J., L. Story, et al. "Hypocholesterolemic Effects of Oat Bran or Bean Intake for Hypercholesterolemic Men." *American Journal of Clinical Nutrition* 40 (1984): 1146.

Bain, R. J. "Accidental Digitalis Poisoning due to Drinking Herbal Tea." *British Medical Journal* 290 (1985): 1624.

Beaudette, T. "Caffeine: Clinical Implications." *Seminars in Nutrition* 4 (1984): 1.

Burkitt, D., A. Walker, et al. "Dietary Fiber and Disease." *Journal of the American Medical Association* 229 (1974): 1068.

Canada. Department of Consumer and Corporate Affairs. "Guide for Food Manufacturers and Advertisers." Ottawa, 1984.

Canada. Department of National Health and Welfare. "Canada's Food Guide." Ottawa, 1983.

Canada. Department of National Health and Welfare. "Canada's Food Guide Handbook (Revised)." Ottawa, 1985.

Canada. Department of National Health and Welfare. "Feeding Babies." Ottawa, 1986.

Canada. Department of National Health and Welfare. "Nutrients in Canadian Foods." Rev. ed. Ottawa, 1986.

Canada. Department of National Health and Welfare. "Recommended Nutrient Intakes for Canadians." Ottawa, 1983.

Canada. Department of National Health and Welfare. "Report of the Expert Advisory Committee on Dietary Fibre." Ottawa, 1985.

Canada. Department of National Health and Welfare. "Report of the Expert Advisory Committee on Herbs and Botanical Preparations." Ottawa, 1986.

Canada. Department of National Health and Welfare. "Sorting out Sulphites." Ottawa, 1986.

Canadian Paediatric Society. Nutrition Committee. "Infant Feeding." *Canadian Journal of Public Health* 70 (1979): 376.

Consensus Development Conference. "Lowering Blood Cholesterol to Prevent Heart Disease." *Journal of the American Medical Association* 253 (1985): 2080–86.

Dalton, K. "Pyridoxine Overdose in Pre-Menstrual Syndrome." *Lancet* 1 (1985): 1168.

DeBakey, M. E., A. M. Gotto, et al. "Diet, Nutrition and Heart Disease." *Journal of the American Dietetic Association* 86 (1986): 729–31.

Eastwood, M. A., and R. Passmore. "Nutrition: The Changing Scene—Dietary Fibre." *Lancet* (July 1983): 202–206.

Franz, M. "Nutrition Update." *The Diabetes Educator* 11 (1986): 3.

Glomset, J. A. "Fish, Fatty Acids and Human Health." *New England Journal of Medicine* 319 (1985): 1253–54.

Kirkley, B. G. "Bulimia: Clinical Characteristics, Development and Etiology." *Journal of the American Dietetic Association* 86 (1986): 468–72.

Kromhout, D., E. B. Bosschieter, et al. "The Inverse Relation between Fish Consumption and 20-Year Mortality from Coronary Heart Disease." *New England Journal of Medicine* 312 (1985): 1205–1209.

Lanza, E., and R. R. Butrum. "A Critical Review of Food Fiber Analysis and Data." *Journal of the American Dietetic Association* 86 (1986): 732–40.

Lieber, C. S. "To Drink (Moderately) or Not to Drink?" *New England Journal of Medicine* 310 (1984): 846.

Lipid Research Clinics Program. "The Lipid Research Clinics Coronary Primary Prevention Trial Results, I: Reduction in Incidence of Coronary Heart Disease." *Journal of the American Medical Association* 251 (1984): 351–64.

_____. "The Lipid Research Clinics Coronary Primary Prevention Trial Results, II: The Relationship of Reduction in Incidence of Coronary Heart Disease to Cholesterol Lowering." *Journal of the American Medical Association* 251 (1984): 365–74.

Mirkin, G., and M. Shangold. "Sports Medicine." *Journal of the American Medical Association* 254 (1985): 2340.

North York. Department of Health. Nutrition Services. "Nutrition Matters." North York, Ont., 1982.

Ontario. Milk Marketing Board. "Calcium Absorption and Utilization from Food." *Spotlight on Nutrition Issues* (June 1986).

Ontario. Ministry of Health. "Healthy Beginnings—A Teacher's Kit." Toronto, 1983.

Ontario. Ministry of Health. "Infant Nutrition: A Guide for Professionals." Toronto, 1985.

Pennington, J. A., and H. N. Church. *Bowes and Church's Food Values of Portions Commonly Used.* J. B. Lippincott Company, 1985.

Phillipson, B. E., D. W. Rothrock, et al. "Reduction of Plasma Lipids, Lipoproteins, and Apoproteins by Dietary Fish Oils in Patients with Hypertriglyceridemia." *New England Journal of Medicine* 312 (1985): 1210–16.

Ross, J. K., C. English, et al. "Dietary Fiber Constituents of Selected Fruits and Vegetables." *Journal of the American Dietetic Association* 85 (1985): 1111–16.

Rossignal, A. M. "Caffeine-Containing Beverages and Pre-Menstrual Syndrome in Young Women." *American Journal of Public Health* 75 (1985): 1335.

Siegel, R. K., M. A. Eisohly, et al. "Cocaine in Herbal Tea." *Journal of the American Medical Association* 255 (1986): 40.

Simopoulos, A. P., and T. B. Van Itallie. "Body Weight, Health, and Longevity." *Annals of Internal Medicine* 100 (1984): 285–94.

Spencer, H. "Minerals and Mineral Interactions in Human Beings." *Journal of the American Medical Association* 86 (1986): 864–67.

Spencer, H., and L. Kramer. "NIH Consensus Conference: Osteoporosis: Factors Contributing to Osteoporosis." *Journal of Nutrition* 116 (1986): 316–19.

United States. Department of Agriculture and Department of Health, Education and Welfare. "Nutrition and Your Health: Dietary Guidelines for Americans." 2d ed. Washington, D.C., 1985.

United States. National Academy of Sciences—National Research Council. Food and Nutrition Board. "Diet, Nutrition and Cancer." Washington, D.C., 1985.

United States. National Academy of Sciences—National Research
Council. Food and Nutrition Board. "Recommended Dietary
Allowances." 9th rev. ed. Washington, D.C., 1980.

Van Horn, L. V., K. Liu, et al. "Serum Lipid Response to Oat Product Intake with a Fat-Modified Diet." *Journal of the American
Dietetic Association* 86 (1986): 759–64.

Watson, R. R., and T. K. Leonard. "Selenium and Vitamins A, E,
and C: Nutrients with Cancer Prevention Properties." *Journal
of the American Dietetic Association* 86 (1986): 505–510.

Wood, P. D. "The Science of Successful Weight Loss." *Medical and
Health Annual* (1984).

Recipe Index

Subject Index

vegetables, 114–16
Cornmeal, 80
Cream, 152
Creamers, non-dairy, 265

Diabetes, and exercise, 183
Diarrhea, 8
Dieting: *see* Energy requirements;
    Weight control
Diuretics, 161, 260
Diverticular disease, 28

Eggs
    nutrients in, 2, 6, 7, 8, 9
    nutrition concerns over, 45
    as source of iron, 36
Endorphins, 184
Enemas, high colonic, 258
Energy requirements, 245–47
Exercise
    and fluids, 187–88
    and metabolism, 183–84, 189
    and stress, 184
    timing of, 185–87
    tips on, 189–90

Fast foods, 195–202
Fat
    amounts of, 24, 25
    components of, 23
    and cooking, 26–28
    in food, 3–6
    mono-unsaturated, 25
    polyunsaturated, 9, 25
    saturated, 21, 25, 37, 265
    in vegetables, 116–17
Fibre
    and calories, 112–13
    and cancer, 28–29, 114
    sources of, 28–30
    and starch, 73–74
    tips on, 29–30
    types of, 29
Fish, 18, 38–40
Fluoride, 18
Folacin, 7, 36, 111
Folic acid: *see* Folacin
Food groups
    defined, 1–2
    lists of, 4–5
Fruit, 8, 18, 30, 111, 112–13, 260
Fruit juices, 111
Fruit peels, 112

Grains, 18, 29

Granola, 75
Grapes, 7

Hair analysis, 257–58
Healing process, 8
Heart disease, 20–21, 28
Heart rate, and exercise, 182–83
Hemoglobin, 7, 8
Herbal remedies, 258–59
Honey, 256
Hormones, 21
Human chorionic gonadotropin (HCG),
    260
Hummus, 74
Huntingdon's disease, 257
Hypertension, 17–18
Hypoglycemia, 265–66

Ice cream, 152, 153
Iodine, 18–19
Iron, 14, 36, 111

Kidney stones, 8, 13
Kidneys (food), 7, 8
Kidneys (function), 17

Lactose, 13, 149–50
Lamb, 6
Lecithin, 256–57
Legumes
    protein in, 40–43
    types of, 34
    vitamin B1 in, 6
Life cycle
    dietary changes during, 226–27
    and nutrients, 2
Light foods, 264
Lima beans, 7, 111
Lipoprotein, 23
Liver, 2, 6, 7, 8

Macronutrient minerals, 10
Magnesium, 18
Manganese, 18
Margarine, 26
Meat
    luncheon, 40
    nutrition in, 7, 8, 9, 18, 19
    red, 37–38
Medication, 228
Menadione, 10
Menopause, 190
Menstruation, 7, 14
Metabolic rate, 169, 189, 227, 247
Metabolism, 7, 248

Methylanxthines, 161
Micronutrient minerals, 10
Milk, 7, 8
   chloride in, 18
   fat in, 148–49
   intolerances to, 149–50
   lactose-hydrolyzed, 13
   magnesium in, 19
   nutrients in, 147
   raw, 150
   sugar in, 260
   Vitamin D in, 13
Milk products, 8
Mineral water, 160
Minerals
   defined, 6
   types of, 10
Mouldy food, 260–61
Muffins, 84

"Natural" foods, 75, 262–63
Nausea, 8, 214
Niacin, 7, 36
Nitrates and nitrites, 40
Nutrients
   energy-yielding, 2–3
   groups of, 1
   and life cycle, 2, 226–27
   recommended intake of, 1
   and variety, 2
Nuts, 6, 19, 30, 44

Oat bran, 29, 74
Oats, 81
Obesity, 28–29, 224
Oil content in fish, 39–40
Oral contraceptives, 7
Orange juice, 111
Oranges, 14, 18, 36
Organ meats, 7, 36
Organic foods, 263–64
Oxalic acid, 13
Oxygen, in blood, 14, 19

Pantothenic acid, 7, 74
Pasta, 82–83
Pastry dough, 84
Peanut butter, 35, 44
Peanuts, 7, 14
Peas, 43, 111
Peppers, 8
Phosphate, 14
Phosphorus, 9, 13, 14
Phytic acid, 13
Pinch test, 241

Popcorn, 80–81
Pork, 6
Potassium, 18
Potatoes, 2, 7
Poultry, 38
Pre-menstrual syndrome (PMS), 7
Pregnancy, 7, 10, 163, 214–16
Preservatives, 40, 74
Protein
   complementary, 35
   defined, 34
   in food, 3
   sources of, 35, 37–45
   timing consumption of, 36–37
Provitamin A, 14, 111
Pyrodoxine, 7

Quiche, 84

Rebound scurvy, 8
Recommended dietary allowances
   (RDA), 1
Recommended nutrient intake (RNI), 1
Red-blood cells, 7, 8
Rhodopsin, 8
Rhubarb, 13
Riboflavin, 6–7, 36
Rice, 81–82
Rye, 82

Salad dressing, 116–17
Salmon, 7, 9, 13
Salt tablets, 188
Sardines, 13
Seeds, 30, 44
Selenium, 19
7-dehydrocholesterol, 9
Shellfish, 19, 39
Shopping for food, 191, 228–29
Smoking, 13, 215
Snacking, 223
Sodium
   deficiencies in, 17
   exercise and, 187–88
   and hypertension, 17
   and potassium, 18
   uses for, 14
Soybeans, 34, 43
Spinach, 7, 13, 111
Starch, 73–74
Stir-fry, 202–4
Strawberries, 8
Stress, 184
Stress tablets, 264–65
Sugar, 2–3, 256, 259–60

Sulphites, as preservatives, 261–62
Teenagers
    iron deficiency in, 14
    nutriton for, 224–25
Teeth, nutrition for, 14, 18
Thiamin, 6, 36
Thyroid extracts, 260
Thyroid, enlargement of, 19
Tofu, 43–44
Tomatoes, 8
Toxic minerals, 10
Triglycerides, 23–24
Trihalomethanes, 160

Vegetable oil, 25
Vegetables
    cruciferous, 114
    fat in, 116
    for fibre, 30
    folacin in, 111
    green, 6
    leafy, 7, 8
    peels, 112
    phytic acid in, 13
    sugar in, 260
    see also Legumes
Vegetarians, 192–95
Vitamin A
    and carotene, 111
    destruction of, 9
    in foods, 8–9
    in high-protein foods, 36
    and iron, 14
    toxic amounts of, 39–40
Vitamin B
    and alcohol, 165
    destruction of, 114–16

Vitamin B1, 6
Vitamin B6, 7, 74
Vitamin B12, 8, 36, 114
Vitamin C
    destruction of, 9, 114–16
    in foods, 8
    and iron, 14
    and nitrates and nitrites, 40
Vitamin D
    and calcium absorption, 13
    in foods, 9, 114
    toxic amounts of, 39–40
Vitamin E, 9–10, 19
Vitamin K, 10
Vitamins
    defined, 6
    fat-soluble, 8–10
    importance of, 6
    water-soluble, 6–8

Water, 113, 158–61
Weight control
    and breakfast, 169–70, 248
    eating for, 243–45, 248
    and fat, 241–42
    motivation for, 249–50
    precautions for dieting for, 250–51
    techniques for, 250–51
Wheat, types of, 79–80
Wheat germ, 35
Whole grains, 18, 30, 35

Yogurt, 152–53

Zinc, 19